Prefaces to Inquiry

*A Study in the Origins and Relevance
of Modern Theories of Knowledge*

William Richard Gondin

KING'S CROWN PRESS
MORNINGSIDE HEIGHTS · NEW YORK
1941

King's Crown Press is a division of Columbia University Press organized for the purpose of making certain scholarly material available at minimum cost. Toward that end, the publishers have adopted every reasonable economy except such as would interfere with a legible format. The work is presented substantially as submitted by the author, without the usual editorial attention of Columbia University Press.

To BLANCHE and CAROL

FOREWORD

THIS BOOK BEGAN as an essay on a somewhat different theme than that about which it finally came to be centered. When I first undertook the studies which went into its immediate preparation, I was interested in exploring as near to the bottom as possible the basic difficulties which so persistently reappear to obstruct the efforts of men of sound mind and good faith to arrive at common understandings of their various ways of dealing with matters of common concern to them. It had long seemed to me that the cause of the most irreconcilable differences which divide such men, often with the most regrettable bitterness, does not lie so much in the *truth* or *falsity* of the many differing convictions at which they find themselves in all sincerity arriving, and for which they feel themselves bound in all honor to contend; but that it lies, rather, in the mutual unintelligibility of their differing modes of expression. The difficulty struck me as being primarily one of communication, and I proposed to examine it largely in terms appropriate to the analysis of communication.

This intention, however, was sidetracked very early. Although I recognized, as one inevitably must in these troubled days, that the issues of most immediate practical import which are thus affected are those of public policy, of social relationships, and, most generally, of the earnest pursuit of *the good life,* it seemed to me that the form, or structure, of the underlying difficulty is best exhibited in the relatively remote issues of metaphysical speculation where the attempt to state *first and last things* makes the kind of opposition in question most strikingly apparent. Metaphysics, I was inclined to believe, indeed, is essentially the attempt to define the ultimate appeals which may be made for the intelligibility of discourse; and I suspected that that is why the characteristic disagreements which arise from its pursuit so frequently end in seemingly absolute *impasses* with all participants protesting the utter senselessness of their opponents' very words.

But one does not so casually leave off the study of the intriguing literature of metaphysics as one may have taken it up. It was not long before I found myself forced to the conclusion that my original project required, not only more extensive consideration and more mature reflection than I was likely to be able to give it for some time to come, but also a certain amount of prior statement concerning particularly the *epistemological* part of metaphysics itself. The result is the present volume on *Prefaces to Inquiry* which, aside from this one remark, is otherwise announced by its own introductory chapter. Discussion of the earlier theme, although largely suppressed, is not completely missing from its pages; but fuller and more direct development is planned in a later work on *Language, Truth, and Meaning*.

For permission to quote from their publications as listed in the *Notes* at the back of this volume, I am indebted to The Columbia University Press, The John Day Company, Harcourt, Brace and Company, Henry Holt and Company, The Macmillan Company, W. W. Norton and Company, and Charles Scribner's Sons, all of New York City, and to The Cambridge University Press by permission of The Macmillan Company, New York.

I must express my appreciation here, too, to Dr. Neil Van Deusen, Prof. James Gutmann, Prof. Irwin Edman, Prof. Herbert W. Schneider, Prof. Horace L. Friess, Prof. Ernest Nagel, and Dr. Paul O. Kristeller, of Columbia University, and to Dean Richard McKeon of Chicago University, for their teaching and their many helpful suggestions; to Mr. Charles H. Mueller, of Columbia University Extension and the late Seth Low Junior College of Columbia University, for his practical assistance in making available much of the time which was necessary for this work; and to Mr. Henry M. Silver, 2nd, of King's Crown Press, for his very special interest in its publication.

And finally I must make special mention of my obligation to the late Prof. F. J. E. Woodbridge and to Prof. John H. Randall, Jr., of Columbia University, to Prof. G. F. Schulz of The College of the City of New York, and to my wife. It was largely my experience of the teaching of Prof. Woodbridge as "a living philosopher", and especially his personal use of the charge of "unintelligibility", that first suggested to me the original plan of this work. Prof. Randall has given its subsequent development the benefit of his broad knowledge of the history of thought and many excellent critical suggestions concerning the course of its argument. Prof. Schulz has painstakingly examined several drafts of its manuscripts, pointed out numberless possibilities for improvement in its style and form, and proof-read its galleys throughout. And my wife has prepared the many versions of its manuscript, and aided its entire project from beginning to end in ways which it were impossible to enumerate. The shortcomings of the final result have come only from my inability to put to better use the assistance and encouragement I have had.

College of the City of New York
September, 1941

CONTENTS

PART ONE

INTRODUCTION

INQUIRY CONCERNING INQUIRY

I: INQUIRY AS AN OBJECT OF INQUIRY

ATOMS, vegetables, triangles, stars, the flow of trade, the will of God, the fates of mice and men—such are the matters with which inquiry is usually concerned, and it is only natural that the literature of inquiry should, in the main, take the form of reports on what has been learned about them. But besides accounts of things investigated, the literature of inquiry also includes not a few works given over to critical reflection on the ways, the means, and the circumstances of investigation itself—to inquiry concerning inquiry, that is to say. Such books do not deal primarily with any of the ordinary objects of our probing. They deal instead with the probing of these things. They deal with *the fact of knowledge*, rather than with the *facts* of knowledge. And so, in broad non-technical senses of the terms, they may be said to treat of *epistemology* or the theory of knowledge.

Books with other themes may occasionally show critical awareness of what it is one does when one searches out the ways of things. Some may even give the matter the passing attention of commonsense suggestions. Nevertheless, they do not make it a central object of investigation in its own right. As is only natural, inquirers are usually too concerned with *what* they are seeking to pause and attend to the *fact* of their seeking. But the distinguishing feature of epistemological writings, as here broadly construed, is that they relate first and foremost to the activity of inquiring itself. They are books which apprehend the inquirer as he is busy at his usual tasks, and raise the question of what *he* is about.

Works of this latter kind, one need hardly insist, are to be encountered in all philosophically mature ages as quite inevitable products of inquiring minds with a reflective, self-critical turn.[1] The *Theatetus* of Plato shows unmistakably that in Hellenic culture there was interest in the theory, as contrasted to the direct quest, of knowledge at least as far back as the fifth century B.C.; many of the basic texts of mediaeval speculation reveal it to have been centered to a very large extent about the restatement and elaboration of classic thought along such lines[2]; the very titles of the principal treatises of modern philosophy indicate that from its inception it has been epistemological to the core; and as will be shown at some length in the concluding chapters below, there are not a few signs that the present age may well be recorded in later accounts of our intellectual life as a period of vigorous renaissance of epistemological interest.

Yet, notwithstanding the long, fairly continuous history of this tradition, and its particularly great relevance to contemporary intellectual developments, today it is quite ironically confused. On the one hand, its natural heirs, the philosophers, are of two very different minds about their legacy. Some of these men tend to confine their attention to the purely formal treatment of the technical difficulties in which they claim the epistemological literature of the last few centuries is involved, and to work toward ostensible solutions of these difficulties which have little or no bearing on the more general enterprise of learning which originally evoked the literature. Most of the others, meanwhile, are inclined to agree with the majority of lay critics that this endeavor has even less meaning than importance, and they tend to deny any obligation to consider such matters save only in so far as they regard it necessary to expose the alleged misconceptions which underlie the attempt to deal with them. Thus, whereas most philosophers who consider the epistemological problem of knowledge in earnest today tend to treat it as a kind of quaint academic puzzle to be solved by the dialectical manipulation of metaphysical terms, a very large proportion of the rest tend to protest that there is really no such problem and that epistemology so-called is at best an illusion, at worst a fraud. On the other hand, however, a very considerable number of research workers outside the philosophical tradition have recently had occasion to pause in their straightforward pursuit of their various special fields of inquiry to give more serious attention than hitherto to the general circumstances and commitments of such undertakings. These investigators have been driven by the actual course of their work to rediscover the general problem of knowledge at the bottom of their own special difficulties, and to consider it quite afresh in their own ways. The resulting situation, therefore, is that most scholars who are well prepared by their training to cultivate the theory of knowledge today are either nurturing a few of its more exotic off-shoots under highly artificial hothouse conditions or else letting it go altogether to seed for all they are concerned; and the task is left to the excellently motivated, but often amateurish, attention of those whose main business is with atoms, vegetables, triangles, and stars. . . . Vital epistemological interest has got separated from intimate familiarity with the epistemological tradition: and its current literature bears many marks of the resulting confusion.

One possible construction which can be placed on this situation, of course, is that it is indirect confirmation of the second of the attitudes just described. Perhaps the very idea of a theory of knowledge arises from basic misunderstanding, and perhaps this basic misunderstanding is the real underlying cause of the present state of affairs in the theory of knowledge. But it is difficult to believe that the age-old endeavor of such theorizing, enlisting as it has the best efforts of many of the greatest minds, does not have some important measure of soundness. If we consider the impulse behind the epistemological treatise, the sense and relevance of the undertaking it envisages would seem to be almost a corollary, or direct commonsense implication, of its very conception. Surely there can be no question of the matter with which it deals. As John Dewey remarks in his recent *Logic*: "In everyday living, men examine; they turn things over intellectually, they infer and judge as 'naturally' as they reap and sow, produce and exchange commodities. As a mode of conduct, inquiry is as accessible to objective study as are these other modes of behavior."[3] Inquiry concerning inquiry, then, would seem to be nothing other than intelligent consideration of the use of intelligence in ordinary matters. Presumably, if results testify to the effectiveness of intelligence in ordinary matters, we are not unreasonable in assuming that it may also be instructive when turned critically upon its own operations. If our investigations are as brilliantly successful as we commonly take for granted in the remoter and minuter parts of nature, it is not likely they could altogether fail us so near home.

Despite suspicions to the contrary, therefore, there is good reason to believe that the cause of present confusion in the theory of knowledge lies not so much in its inherent absurdity as in the kind of cultivation it has had in recent centuries. The state of affairs just described suggests that we should examine most critically the particular kind of epistemological literature which lies behind it.

II: MODERN "PROLEGOMENA" TO INQUIRY

Despite the common treatment of the outstanding epistemological essays of *the modern period*[4] as the most representative of their kind, the fact is that they tend to assume a unique form for such writings. Their prominence in the literature happens to be due more to their provocativeness on other scores than to their embodiment of its more typical features.

As has already been mentioned, contributions to the theory of knowledge are in general simply attempts to discover what can be learned about inquiry by directing its regular course back upon its own process. Ordinarily they are distinguished from other writings relating to inquiry only by reason of their peculiar reflexive twist. Consequently, they raise no claim to a special detachment such as would afford them a unique perspective inaccessible by the ordinary means of discovery which they themselves examine. But—and this is the matter which invites our attention here—the more typical modern essays in the theory of knowledge do tend to imply just such claims. Their procedures almost invariably leave them open to interpretation as attempts somehow to anticipate what inquiry essentially is, prior to its having actually been embarked upon, a feat which would require a circumvention of the conditions of its ordinary pursuit. Indeed, in the more striking instances of this peculiar implication of their development, the implied discontinuity between the regular course of inquiry and the procedures by which their epistemological conclusions are reached is emphasized by the fact that the latter tend to deny to the former the possibility of arriving at comparable conclusions about anything whatsoever. Illustrations of what inquiry actually is these works must in some sense be, since they are organized around specific explorable themes such as "method", "understanding", and "reason", if not about the usual sort of subject matters. But their propaedeutic pretensions tend to exclude anything of the kind as a project already under way, even with the reflexive twist of epistemologies in general. They demand acceptance as elucidations, or disciplines, preliminary to all such undertakings. Allegedly, they are *prolegomena to inquiry*.

In most cases, this trait of these writings derives largely from the implications of their total arguments; and consequently its adequate illustration requires a fairly complete exposition of a number of cases in point. But, leaving that to more detailed treatment in later chapters, we may find intimations of their propaedeutic claims even in some of their explicit statements taken partially out of context.

Consider, for example, what we encounter in the writings of René Descartes, who is commonly credited with beginning *modern philos-*

ophy and with laying down its epistemological foundations in doing so. Works like his *Geometry, Dioptrics, Meteors,* and *Books II, III,* and *IV* of his *Principles of Philosophy* are in the main examinations of subject matters continuous with the popular tradition of scientific research in the summaries of which their more valid conclusions figure. But at a crucial point of his *Discourse on Method* Descartes writes of his attempt to recommence all such investigations anew, and of his decision to hold them all temporarily in suspense until he " had *previously* spent sufficient time to plan the project of the work . . . , and to seek the true method of arriving at the knowledge of all things of which his mind was capable."[5] The force of the word "previously" should be noted here. Descartes does not limit its connotations to himself alone as the alleged pioneer explorer in such matters. Elsewhere[6] he insists that not until other inquirers have mastered his "true method" may they apply themselves to "true philosophy" which, by definition for him, comprehends the whole of genuine knowledge.[7] Indeed, he even insists that they should "exercise" in the use of this "logic which teaches the right conduct of the reason" until they have "acquired some skill in discovering the truth," before they actually go on to search for it, as he says, "in earnest"[8]. Remarks such as these invite interpretation of his "method" as an ostensible preliminary discipline in the technique of attaining knowledge, which must somehow be acquired before knowledge itself can be acquired. And in view of such an interpretation, the *Discourse* which expounds this "method" appears to be epistemological, not only in the broad general sense first mentioned above, but also in the characteristically modern narrow sense in question here.

Moreover, Descartes' works contain similar claims for a different form of epistemological writing. What he calls "metaphysics" comes after "method" in his order of exposition; and sometimes, as in the *Epistle* introducing the *Metaphysical Meditations,* it seems to be intended as the first application of the "method", presumably with "God" and "soul" taken as subject matter.[9] But in the *Preface* of his chief restatement of the *Meditations*[10] he writes of "metaphysics" as constituted by "the principles of knowledge"; and not only does he sharply distinguish these from "the principles of material things", as relating to knowing rather than to matters known, but he expounds them as necessary preliminaries to all the others. In the imagery of his famous simile in which he likens the various departments of knowledge to the various upper parts of the "tree of philosophy", he writes of this "metaphysics" as its

"roots"[11], thus implying the function of his epistemological precepts
to be to nourish the organism of knowledge without appearing themselves as fruitions of it. Supposedly they have a bearing on inquiry by
which—to change the figure—they enlighten and guide it; but, since
this bearing is alleged to be indispensable, they cannot also be discoveries arrived at in the regular course of inquiry as they define it.
They may be taken as attempts to anticipate, rather than to illustrate,
the workaday business of research. And so the treatises which expound
them may be interpreted as an ostensible second series of prolegomena
to the sort of scientific investigation reported in the rest of the Cartesian
opera.

As is quite natural, the epistemological writings of many of Descartes'
disciples illustrate the propaedeutic tendency in much the same manner
that his do; and this may well lead one to assume that we may find
quite the opposite tendency in those written by opponents of his general
philosophical position. But among the contributors to the genre must
be included most of the severest critics of Cartesianism, which fact calls
attention to an important point about the entire literature: Appeals
to propaedeutic understanding work so subtly in modern thought, and
especially in that which we fondly call *philosophic,* that they often
persist unchallenged beneath the surface of the very debates in which
the participants seem, and believe themselves to be, completely at odds
with each other. The dividing line between writers of prolegomena to
inquiry and less sophisticated essayists in the theory of knowledge does
not coincide with the common line of division in philosophical controversy. More often than not, the contenders who take part are merely
advocates for different kinds of preliminary understanding about inquiry.

John Locke, for instance, is usually introduced in the histories of
thought as one who began a way of thinking directly opposed to Descartes'; but a similar examination of his works reveals that his opposition does not run deep enough to challenge, as such, the propaedeutic
implications of Descartes' writings. That Locke too is an epistemologist
is clear from the fact that, whereas most of his works, such as those on
Government, Tolerance, Education, and *The Growth and Culture of
Vines and Olives,* etc., are attempts to arrive at understanding about
the sort of things that usually concern us, his great *Essay Concerning
Human Understanding* is introduced as an attempt to understand—
"understanding itself" which "like the eye, whilst it makes us see and

perceive all other things, takes no notice of itself; and requires art and pains to set it at a distance and make it its own object."[12] Moreover, it is also clear that Locke's *Essay* is conceived fully as much in what we may here call *the modern mode* as Descartes' epistemological writings. We learn from its *Epistle to the Reader* that the *Essay* was provoked by a conversation in which the point at issue became so confused "without coming any nearer a resolution", that Locke decided the disputants were taking "a wrong course", and that *"before* we set ourselves upon inquiries of that nature, it was necessary to examine our own abilities, and see what objects our understandings were, or were not, fitted to deal with."[13] Again note the force of the word "before". This passage may not insist on the priority of epistemological considerations in as absolute a manner as those quoted from Descartes. But we shall presently see that it introduces a total argument which is just as thoroughgoing in its claims of priority to inquiry proper.[14] Whatever Locke's differences from Descartes, they were not so great as to prevent him from contributing to the propaedeutic tradition in the theory of knowledge which Descartes had founded. It is not without reason that Descartes and Locke have figured in the histories of our intellectual development as founders of rival schools of conviction. Their differences are obvious and readily understandable in terms of the contrasting concerns, or interests, with which each pursued his own thinking. But it is important to note in the present connection that, although each objected to the other's particular kind of propaedeutic teaching, neither ever really contested the other's for what it essentially was. As was the case with practically all the controversalists who followed in their wake, neither referred the differences which developed between their respective kinds of position back to the fact that both derived from efforts to hold inquiry—"knowledge", "reason", "understanding", or what you will—in suspense until it should first have been construed in terms of a prior elucidation.

Immanual Kant's writings are singularly interesting on this score, since they illustrate with striking force how the attempt to anticipate inquiry through preliminary understanding tended in the modern period to persist even through the most careful critique of that very effort. Kant's education made it almost impossible for him to work out his own thinking as anything but a protest against what had become by his time the epistemological *schools* of *rationalism* and *empiricism*. He was their fated *critic*. Still, as the history of epistemological *criticism*

indirectly bears witness, in his own most constructive efforts he returned
to essentially the same kind of undertaking as gave rise to them. Like
Descartes and Locke, Kant was an inquiring spirit who early explored
such fields as anthropology and cosmology—the latter with enough competence, indeed, to make his *Universal Theory of the Heavens* famous
as containing remarkable anticipations of the nebular hypothesis of
Laplace. But later in life he became more concerned with "metaphysics", by which he meant nothing other than "knowledge lying beyond
experience", or a kind of "*a priori* knowledge, coming from pure Understanding and pure Reason" which he called "pure philosophical
cognition"[15]. This discipline, primary as his definition would imply it
to be, and bound up as it was with the dialectic of previous prolegomena to inquiry, appeared to Kant so thoroughly confused and perplexed in his day as in turn to require a very special kind of preliminary
clarification before anything of importance could be accomplished in
it.[16] The literature which he found devoted to the field seemed to him
to show more than anything else, that "it is a very common fate of
human reason first of all to finish its speculative edifice of thought as
soon as possible, and then only to inquire whether the foundation be
sure";[17] and he found it to result in so many irresolvable controversies
between dogmatists, "who taught nothing", and sceptics, "who did not
even promise anything", that his contemporaries were thoroughly weary
of the whole business.[18] This state of affairs, however, suggested to Kant
the idea of a prior examination of the faculties which he believed to
be involved in such inquiries. "It might seem natural that, after we have
left the solid ground of experience," he wrote, "we should not at once
proceed to erect an edifice with knowledge which we possess, without
knowing whence it came, and trust to principles the origin of which is
unknown, without having made sure of the foundations by means of
careful examinations."[19] So he found in the attitude of the "metaphysical *indifferentists*", not discouragement, but "a powerful appeal to
reason to undertake anew the most difficult of its duties, namely, self-
knowledge," which he in fact attempted in his great *Critique of Pure
Reason*.[20]

In thus shifting attention from "metaphysics" to "pure reason", Kant
exactly paralleled the procedure of Descartes and Locke in shifting attention from the usual concerns of "reason" and "understanding" to
these faculties themselves. If there was any important difference between
them, he was even more explicit than they in his claims for the essen-

tially prior relevance of his *Critique*. He did not even claim its findings to constitute an "organism of pure reason", but stated merely that "as at present it is still doubtful whether such an expansion of our knowledge is here possible, we may look on a mere criticism of pure reason, its sources and limits, as a kind of preparation *(Propadeutik)* for a complete system of pure reason."[21] His popular re-writing of his great *Critique*, therefore, was quite appropriately titled—*Prolegomena to Any Future Metaphysic*. Although Kant's final conclusions may have been prior to inquiry proper in a much more subtle sense than those emerging from the prolegomena of either Descartes or Locke, there could hardly be a more explicit proposal than the foregoing for theorizing concerning knowledge previous to actually acquiring it.

Comparable, if less striking, passages might be quoted from any number of related treatises of the modern period. In another chapter of this essay, where the same tendency is traced to its later expressions, very similar ones are quoted from such influential contemporary works as *The Meaning of Meaning* by Ogden and Richards, P. W. Bridgman's *Logic of Modern Physics,* and Sir Arthur Eddington's *Philosophy of Physical Science*. However, the passages already cited from the central, highly influential works of Descartes, Locke, and Kant serve sufficiently to illustrate the propaedeutic trend of modern epistemological literature, and to show how it differs from most inquiries concerning inquiry by assuming the particular form of prolegomena to inquiry. It is sufficiently clear from these that propaedeutic prolegomena to inquiry complicate any consideration of inquiry concerning inquiry today. As we shall now show at some length, moreover, it is their special turn which is largely responsible for contemporary misunderstanding of the general literature of the theory of knowledge, and for contemporary failure to realize its present possibilities.

III: GROUNDS FOR PAUSE

It appears that, whatever the claims of the grand attempts to anticipate inquiry, as actually worked out they have failed in a number of important ways. This fact does not warrant our lightly dismissing them. Much will be said on that in *section v* of this chapter and throughout the rest of the essay. But on the other hand, it does give us considerable grounds for pause in any critical attempt to understand the entire literature addressed to the clarification of inquiry.

For one thing, epistemological works of this sort seem subject to a peculiar kind of sidetracking which tends to deflect their characteristic turn at the very outset. The writers who have attempted propaedeutic prolegomena to inquiry have usually worked on the hunch that a special bit of information about such matters as "method", "understanding", "reason", "mind", "logic", or the like, associated with its pursuit, is a clue to what all knowledge, all inquiry, at bottom really is. And so, as is evidenced by the very titles of their works, they have centered their discourses about such matters. But of course, in view of the controlling propaedeutic purpose of the books in which they figure, these themes can actually be little more than expedient aids to exposition. It would not be overstatement to say that, in an important sense, *Method* is only incidental in Descartes' *Discourse on Method*, that *Understanding* is only incidental in Locke's *Essay Concerning Human Understanding*, and so on for the nominal topics of most similar treatises. The discussion of themes like these merely mediates the central undertaking, which allegedly is to illuminate all particular inquiries by a foresight of what inquiry itself is. Yet readers, influenced by recollections of what books usually undertake to do, tend to interpret the works in which they figure as addressed to the themes themselves. Like Leibniz, following up Locke's *Essay* with *New Essays*, they even enter the discussion to tell what they themselves think about "understanding", "method", "mind", "reason", and the like. And in this they assume that the attempted prolegomena to all inquiry differ from books like anthropologies and trigonometries, for example, only because their subject matters are quires an interlude in which all things like men and triangles are re-other than men and triangles. But the original project requires that in-quiry as we usually understand it be held somehow in suspense. It re-duced to a common denominator the examination of which tells nothing about them in their own right as particular objects of particu-lar researches. Its intention, therefore, is completely defeated by such *misunderstandings*, because as a result of them inquiry in the familiar sense reclaims the project for its own. For good or ill, the attempt to foretell what inquiry is tends to be sidetracked from the very outset by being accommodated back to inquiry proper.

Disconcerting as this fact may be, taken by itself it does not cast great suspicion on the project of the grand prolegomena. Alone it might simply indicate that modern epistemologists are always as scatterbrained as they are sometimes dull, and so cannot keep to a point. But it is not the only difficulty with which such writings are beset. Their working-out meets an even more ironical kind of defeat.

It may be observed that for the most part these essays are addressed to the fact that the ordinary course of inquiry is sometimes disturbed by confusing controversies. Descartes complained in his *Discourse*, for example, that in all his studies and travels he found no noteworthy truths free from question, wherefore he appealed to "method" and to "metaphysics" as grounds for unchallengeable assurance. For much the same reason, too, Spinoza sought in his *Improvement of the Understanding* for "foundations which must direct our thoughts" and "a path whereby the intellect . . . may attain to eternal things". And the complaints of Locke will readily be recalled on this point. Preliminary essayists of Locke's type may not be so rash as some others in their hopes of what certainty, what freedom from dispute, can be arrived at. But they are not, for that reason, less sure of so determining the limits of certainty as to dispose of the kind of contention and confusion from which they originally appeal. However narrow they find the limits of human understanding, they never question their own ability unmistakably to determine those limits and so keep speculation from the ranges of issues with respect to which contention is futile.

But in this attempt, too, prolegomena to inquiry have had a most disappointing outcome. Descartes may have been early upset by the fact that the most learned men disagree most sharply with one another. On announcing his epistemological discovery of how such disagreement can be disposed of, however, he found himself confronted with at least one man, Thomas Hobbes, who speaking for others as well, not only disagreed with him, but protested that he could not even "make sense" out of his "most certain of certainties". Descartes in turn found Hobbes' objections "incomprehensible". And controversy was thereupon renewed on a deeper level, to persist so to this day. Indeed, the attempts to dispose of controversy through such preliminary understandings have raised more issues than they have settled. So true is this that when men came to write histories of them, they found their materials most easily organized about the very controversies the attempts provoked. Ueberweg, for example, could find no better way to introduce the history of philosophical thinking after Descartes than by saying that it "is characterized by the coexistence, in developed form and *in relations of mutual antagonism*, of Empiricism and Dogmatism", etc., etc.[22] The great irony is that the historians have found both the form and continuity of

their accounts of these attempts finally to end debate in the very debates
to which these attempts themselves gave rise. It seems that whereas such
preliminary discourses are originally resorted to because the truths of
particular matters appear doubtful, what they reveal is that *truth itself*
can become even more doubtful as a consequence of the kind of treatment they give it. Whereas they take as their point of departure the
fact that men sometimes have difficulty in knowing this or that aright,
they raise the issue of the *validity* or *reality* of our knowing anything
at all, which is a much more disturbing matter. Whereas they are undertaken to remove the possibility of challenge when questions arise as to
the weight of this or that insistence, they end by challenging the very
meaningfulness of many statements which would have been questioned
before only as to their correctness, honesty, or sanity. Far from ending
the controversies to which they are addressed, therefore, they perpetuate new and more deep-seated ones.

Finally, still more disconcerting evidence that the grand prolegomena
have failed of successful working-out is to be found in the already mentioned fact that their characteristic turn is being repudiated today by
the dominant movements in philosophical thinking. Of course, there
has always been a tendency among a certain type of intellectual to shy
at weighty tomes in a philosophical vein. But most reactions of this sort
are based simply on a popular impression, just lately expressed again
by Lin Yutang, that "philosophy generally seems to be the science of
making simple things difficult to understand".[23] They are due partly
to a lack of popular sympathy for the philosopher's technical themes,
partly to sheer misunderstanding, and partly to the hard use of language
made by many who profess philosophy. The significant thing about the
writings here in question, however, is that their attempts have been
most severely criticized of late by those most competent to do so and
most likely to be in sympathy with them.

It is perhaps not surprising to find severe criticism of the propaedeutic
attempt coming from a "logical positivist" such as Rudolf Carnap, who
insists that the "logical syntax" of scientific language *"takes the place
of the inextricable tangle of problems which is known as philosophy."*[24]
One might accept almost as a corollary of his rejection of the bulk of
our entire philosophical tradition, his pronouncement that: "He who
wishes to investigate the questions of the logic of science must . . . re-
nounce the proud claims of a philosophy that sits enthroned above the
special sciences, and realize that he is working in exactly the same field

as the scientific specialist, only with a somewhat different emphasis." etc., etc.[25] But consider the attitude of Bertrand Russell, a contemporary thinker who has at times placed such great stress on epistemological considerations as practically to identify philosophy with them.[26] Although Russell begins his most summary statement of his own philosophical position with a proposal to examine "what 'knowing' is",[27] he is most cautious to explain that he does not propose this examination from the kind of perspective implied by ostensible prolegomena to inquiry. It appears that a certain amount of sophistication in the history of such attempts leads him to remark in the pivotal chapter of his volume on *Our Knowledge of the External World* that: "The philosophic scrutiny (of knowledge) . . . though sceptical in regard to every detail, is not sceptical as regards the whole. That is to say, its criticism of details will only be based upon their relation to other details, not upon some external criterion which can be applied to all the details equally."[28] Some argue, of course, that Russell's actual procedure in arriving at his epistemological "realism" and "neutral monism" is inconsistent with the point of such observations; but, however that may be, it is significant that he does his best to avoid the propaedeutic turn of epistemological prolegomena and that he tells his reader so in most emphatic terms. Moreover, it is also interesting that elsewhere, in his article on *Logical Atomism*,[29] Bertrand Russell writes that, although he persists in holding to the doctrines at which he arrives in such explorations, he does not really think it makes any difference what "metaphysics" of this kind a man holds.[30] According to this view, he could change his mind on such matters—change to "idealism", for example—without changing his thinking about other things in any important way. It is true that Russell writes on occasion very differently about his "logical atomism", and it is also true that there are grounds for suspecting that "logical atomism" is far from being incomparable to "realism" or "neutral monism". But the important point here is that, although he has been so interested in his epistemological doctrines as to labor long and hard on their formulation, he nevertheless has dismissed at least part of his contribution as not really mattering. One can imagine the consternation of Descartes, Spinoza, Locke, Kant, or any of their fellows, on hearing this. They could all have been much more easily persuaded that their preliminary writings were wrong in every detail, than that, right or wrong, they did not matter. To question the relevance of the great propaedeutic treatises is to question, not only their dignity, but the very sense of their being written at all. In the very nature of the case, they must be either all important or completely misguided. Presumably, then, these ventures of Mr. Russell's in the theory of knowledge have been of a very different character.

The current reaction against prolegomena to inquiry, however, goes much farther than a mere avoidance of their traditional associations, or a dismissal of their importance. It amounts to a thoroughgoing repudiation. In philosophy today dissatisfaction with the epistemology of the last few centuries runs deeper than the perennial impatience felt by each new generation of *moderns* concerning the incompleteness of the work of their predecessors. It is not so much an anxiousness to be up and doing as it is a demand for new beginnings along radically new lines. Of this the very currency of the theme of *Reconstruction in Philosophy* is symptomatic. And it is significant to note that John Dewey, the outstanding publicist of this movement, calls for the scrapping of the entire literature of grand prolegomena as an integral part of its program. In his appraisal, they have functioned, not to clarify inquiry as intended, but rather to reduce philosophy to a "show of elaborate terminology and a fictitious devotion to the mere external forms of comprehensive and minute demonstration", providing intellectualized grounds for the very traditional moral and social values he would have philosophers fundamentally reconsider.[31] Accordingly, in the very first chapter of his own chief epistemological[32] treatise, *Logic—The Theory of Inquiry*, he is careful to explain that: "The position taken implies the ultimacy of inquiry in determination of the formal conditions of inquiry." "Logic as inquiry into inquiry," he writes, "is, if you please, a circular process; it does not depend upon anything extraneous to inquiry." etc.[33] And thus he rejects as emphatically as possible "the assumption of a prior ready-made definition of knowledge which determines the character of inquiry."[34] Again it may be objected by some that Mr. Dewey has occasionally used his theory of *How We Think* in a manner which makes it in effect not entirely unlike a preliminary discourse.[35] But, however that may be, there can be no question of Dewey's determination to see everything of the kind eliminated from philosophy as he would have it *re*constructed.

To mention all reactions of this kind would be almost to call the roll of outstanding contemporary philosophers. This is hardly necessary, however, and it will serve our purposes to discuss only a few more, representative of different present-day groups, to show how omnipresent the tendency is. Among the writings of the self-styled "Neo-Realists", for example, it suffices to consider Mr. E. G. Spaulding's *New Rationalism*. Throughout this work, modern philosophy is so consistently interpreted in terms of the propaedeutic claims to which attention has here been called[36] that each of its reviews of the various positions which have emerged from the literature centers about an observation that this particular epistemological *-ism* is the one which assumes a certain particular "presupposition" as to "the nature of the knowing situation". But Spaulding's own conviction is that "*in order to know,* one need not first find the *how* and *whence* or *wherefore of* 'knowing'."[37] Observing that "the larger part of scientific development and discovery has been the work of men who have ignored this problem,"[38] he insists that "there are good reasons for examining the facts of knowing . . . only after, and not before, other facts are examined." "The former," he writes, "are but a small part of the total realm of facts, while the study of other facts seems to be more illuminative of the study of knowing than conversely."[39] Consequently, he finds that "up to the present time, opposed (epistemological) systems have not been consistently derived," but that, "in the method of arriving at their transforming conclusions, such systems depart from and contradict the very presuppositions on which, as philosophies, they depend."[40] And so, in direct contrast to the manner in which he defines them all, he defines the "Neo-Realism" he professes as that position which, taking account of the difficulties which arise in modern epistemology, contradicts their propaedeutic premises.[41] The details of his statement is put in terms of a considerable amount of formal dialectic concerning "solutions" of the so-called "Ego-centric" and "Value-centric predicaments" into which we need not go here; but it amounts, in effect, to a profession of belief that knowing is so of a piece that no part of it can be a revelation of what any other part essentially is in any terms which all parts do not equally well illustrate. We gather, therefore that Spaulding's "Neo-Realism" is a repudiation of the attempt at understanding preliminary to inquiry proper—*by explicit definition.* In this instance, the reaction against prolegomena to inquiry is so strong as to become the first and central article in a major creed of philosophic conviction.

It might be supposed from its title, perhaps, that A. N. Whitehead's *Enquiry Concerning the Principles of Natural Knowledge* runs counter to the general tendency illustrated here in the works of Carnap, Russell, Dewey and Spaulding. But at least so far as the design of this treatise of

Whitehead's is concerned, quite the opposite is the case. The text assumes the form of an unusually discursive account of mathematical physics, its pages splashed here and there with differential equations and geometric diagrams, rather than with the more familiar dialectic of prolegomena. And in the *Preface*, Whitehead is most careful to state that his argument is concerned "only with Nature, that is, with the object of perceptual knowledge, and not with the synthesis of the knower with the known," so that "none of our perplexities as to Nature will be solved by having recourse to the consideration that there is a mind knowing it."[42] Whitehead's "principles of knowledge" are to be regarded as incomparable to those of Descartes in that they are offered simply as exhibitions of what we may be said to know, the term "principles" being used only to indicate a belief in their exceptional importance or generality as instances of knowing. In his *Concept of Nature* too, moreover, after repeating that "no perplexity concerning the object of knowledge can be solved by saying that there is a mind knowing it,"[43] he specifically defines the "problem of natural philosophy" which he addresses as that of discussing "the relations *inter se* of things known, abstracted from the bare fact that they are known."[44] And in the *Preface* to his *Science and the Modern World*, it is explained that "on the philosophical side, any consideration of epistemology has been entirely excluded," since "it would have been impossible to discuss that topic without upsetting the whole balance of the work."[45] All in all, therefore, despite the title of his *Enquiry*, Whitehead's philosophical researches tend consciously away from any kind of epistemological consideration whatsoever. And it appears from remarks which he makes in *Process and Reality* that they tend most emphatically away from what is propaedeutic in the tradition. In this last mentioned work, he describes his concern to be with "the coherence of things known and knowable," frankly confessing his method to be none other than that of "imaginative generalization" confronted with the matters which are to be construed.[46] Seeking a scheme of ideas of as great an "interpreting power" as possible for this purpose, he emphasizes his belief that "the accurate expression of the final generalities is the goal of discussion and not its origin," and that "the verification of a rationalistic scheme is to be sought in its general success, and not in the peculiar certainty, or initial clarity of its first principles."[47] This, of course, is the exact opposite of the attitude assumed by theories of knowledge with propaedeutic pretensions.

Finally, F. J. E. Woodbridge's *Realm of Mind* expresses a similar rejection of epistemological considerations, with an even more emphatic disapproval of the propaedeutic turn to which they have tended. As its title indicates, this book is addressed to a theme which has figured prominently in propaedeutic literature. "Mind", like "method", "understanding", "knowledge", "reason", "logic", and the rest, has mediated many preliminaries to inquiry. But this discussion of the "realm" of mind is worked out in a radically different way which brings the soundness of the propaedeutic approach into most serious question. Its major thesis is that a consideration of *mind* does not properly lead to the kind of logical or physical analysis of a process or of an entity to which it is usually presumed to lead in modern essays in the theory of knowledge, but brings us rather to a consideration of the domain in which thinking occurs. Without going into the many implications of this idea, it is interesting to translate it into terms of inquiry. The fact of mind, as developed by Woodbridge, if not exactly equivalent to the fact of inquiry, most certainly includes it. His thesis, therefore, has the corollary that a consideration of the fact of inquiry does not lead to a prior apprehension of the logical or physical nature of the processes of inquiry, nor does it lead to a foresight of what inquiry somehow intrinsically is, but brings us rather to a consideration of the field inquiry obviously explores and evidently concerns. The latter undertaking, however, is nothing other than inquiry in the familiar sense. The thesis that "mind" must be construed in terms of its "realm" is also an insistance that inquiry must be construed in terms of its revelations. Hence the observation: "An examination of knowledge is apt to wear a strained and troubled look." And hence the conclusion: "What is so often called epistemology is not legitimate."[48] When we examine the reasons Woodbridge gives for his conviction of the unintelligibility of any alternative view, moreover, it develops that the kind of epistemology which he declares invalid is again the kind here termed propaedeutic. When we "confine our attention to those identifiable processes which occur when we know, we are not sensible of any peculiar difficulty," he admits; and, when we "confine our attention to such matters as classification, definition and consistency, we also know what we are about and expect a common understanding of what we do." "But," he adds, "when we take either psychology or formal logic as an exposition of what knowledge is rather than particualr illustrations of it like physics or chemistry, we may become acutely sensible that we have done a strange thing. Knowledge of one set of facts can hardly be taken as an account of what knowledge of any set of facts essentially is."[49] This is no mere dismissal of the importance of prolegomena to inquiry, no mere wariness of their associations, distaste for their exploitation for the purposes of conservative apologetics, or indifference to their concerns. It is a denial that prolegomena to inquiry make sense, a denial of their legitimacy in any terms whatsoever.

Notwithstanding the case that can be made for epistemology in the general sense of inquiry concerning inquiry, then, epistemology in the modern mode of prolegomena to inquiry meets special difficulties. Its propaedeutic undertaking is subject to persistent sidetracking, it tends to revert to more serious controversies than those at which it is directed, and its very conception is discredited by those contemporaries best able to understand its issues. Any study of epistemological literature today must take account of the fact that this important part of it is seriously suspect.

IV: THE FAILURE OF "PROLEGOMENA"

The likelihood is that, despite the patent soundness of investigations of inquiry in general, prolegomena to inquiry are justly suspect. Neither ability nor industry has been lacking for the accomplishment of their attempt if it were possible at all. For at least three centuries men of undisputed genius, not to mention many others, have labored hard and dreamed great dreams on their behalf. If these have failed, therefore, it is highly probable that something about their undertaking does not admit of accomplishment. The attempt to anticipate inquiry itself invites careful inquiry.

Its repeated sidetracking, for example, calls attention to the fact that it meets difficulty especially in the assumption that inquiry in the familiar sense *can* be held in suspense. After all, withholding inquiry to discern what it is is a strange procedure. It is not a little like trying to discern what seeing is before opening one's eyes. This analogy may be followed through instructively in terms of an analysis made by Professor Woodbridge of efforts fundamentally to construe vision in terms of physiological optics. To the extent that such efforts are intelligible, Woodbridge observes in his article on *The Universe of Light*, they are so only in terms of the revelations of seeing in its own right; for, in developing a theory of physiological optics, we are dealing with "a system which, if delineated at all, must be delineated in terms of optical models which its character imposes, but which are not replicas of that character. These models can not be placed side by side with the system and then compared with it. They serve in exploring the system, but they do not embrace it . . . optical frameworks are in the system, but the system is not in any framework at all."[50] In other words, Professor Woodbridge aptly points out, although the techniques of optics are excellent devices for exploring the activity and the realm which, by the testimony of their effectiveness, are most certainly optical, still they cannot *transcend* either. Whatever their power of penetration, they never get *through, above,* or *beyond* seeing and its conditions. The *grounds* of seeing, if you wish, are opaque to the light we see by. Seeing, therefore, is not ultimately explainable in optical terms. On the contrary, it is seeing which gives point to optics. And so, explore the universe of light as we may, we can never see seeing or what lies *behind* it. The attempt to do so finds us peeking. And much the same is true in the case of inquiry, which is seeing—or rather, looking—in the broadest sense of the expression. Analyses of inquiry are to its actual undertaking much what analyses of vision are to actual seeing. By the compulsion of the character of what they deal with, analyses of inquiry are logical, physiological and psychological, etc., just as analyses of vision are optical. Consequently they are testimonies that inquiry and the world inquired into are just as much logical, physiological, psychological, and whatever, as they are optical. But although such analyses serve to explore the fact of inquiry, they do not embrace it. Whatever their power of penetration, they never *transcend* inquiry. They never get *through,* or *beneath,* or *beyond,* its evident conditions. Inquiry, as a matter of fact, is not completely reducible to any terms comparable to those of logic, physiology, or psychology. On the contrary all of these disciplines are expressions of inquiry. They are hardly intelligible unless construed in terms of its usual revelations.

It is only natural, therefore, that the claims of most epistemological writings to preliminary relevance are not respected. In spite of the fact that they put inquiry itself in question, they obtain no immunity from the kind of subsequent development which inquiries usually receive if they are important enough to warrant attention. Indeed, it is precisely because inquiry proper does not admit of suspension in the first place that readers fail to realize the characteristic pretensions of allegedly preliminary investigations. Readers persist in regarding the mediating themes of these books as subject matters simply because it is so absurd that they should have none. The distinction between pursuits of inquiry and preliminaries to it is not a distinction supported by the facts. It is only a distinction of claims, and the claims of the latter are invalid. The seeming triumph of inquiry proper, therefore, though incontestable, is somewhat empty. It takes over preliminary investigations chiefly because they have no independence to begin with.

In view of this, it is not surprising that the attempts to get around controversy through preliminary consideration have also been ironically unsuccessful. These efforts have been based on a conviction that the very processes which lead both to agreement and to disagreement are themselves analysable in such a way as to yield a discipline which will make further contention unnecessary. They have bottomed on the belief that there is possible a kind of *a priori ethic of the intellect,* which, discerned, excludes all but willful error. But this confidence is undermined by the fact, already pointed out, that inquiry does not admit of suspension. Attempts to state *a priori ethics of the intellect* obtain no special immunity from questioning. They are subject to all the challenges to which other investigations are subject because, their claims to special status being unwarranted, they are caught up as much as any in the conflicts ordinarily caused by vying interests and differing slants on things. Not only do they thus fail to avoid the usual sort of disagreements, moreover, but they run into others of a peculiarly troublesome kind. After all, those who pursue ordinary inquiries rarely fall out completely with each other. Their disagreements are restricted by the fact that they necessarily involve a certain amount of common agreement on the basis of which to state their disagreements. They appeal to a common subject matter, for example, and to terms of mutual understanding, which they identify readily enough to give satisfaction that they are talking intelligibly about the same thing. But the case is sometimes different with writers of preliminary discourses. Their procedures, as will be shown in greater detail in later chapters, often tend to delimit in mutually exclusive ways the ultimate terms of possible agreement, or even of understanding. And thus the most serious arguments in which they become involved are totally irresolvable within the contexts defined for them by their own arguments.

The present-day reaction against prolegomena to inquiry, then, cannot be dismissed as a mere capricious fashion in our ways of thinking or a mere change in our philosophic style. But there is still another fact about such writings which this reaction compels us to take account of. Since their conclusions are represented in some sense or other as revelations of the underlying character of inquiry, they are offered as though they were arrived at by some way external to its usual processes. As has been remarked here, however, these processes are actually insurmountable and are not subject to the kind of circumvention which would be required for an investigator to arrive at a comprehension of inquiry *from an external point of vantage.* Consequently, the claims made for their conclusions are inconsistent with the procedures by which they are arrived at, and·their developments are therefore dogged by the kind of self-contradictions which invariably attend such offenses against sound logical practice. When pursued with candor these writings seem eventually to become associated with absolute *scepticism* and *solipsism.* But strictly construed, scepticism and solipsism of this sort are the signs of epistemological contradiction. They are the peculiar absurdities which terminate prolegomena *reductiones ad absurdum.* In their bare statements they undermine the arguments from which they issue, since their conclusions deny the cogency of the reasoning which derives them, thus excluding their arguments from relevance to any conclusions which they might have. To state the point briefly: Scepticism suppresses definitions of knowledge, and solipsism suppresses definitions of other minds. But definitions of knowledge and of other minds are indispensable premises, or enthymemes, of the very argument which enforce their suppression. The result, therefore, is that a process of reasoning effects a complete disjunction between its premises and its conclusion. If the premises are valid, the conclusion is not; and *vice versa.* When we require absolute scepticism to be accepted of itself and solipsism to admit its own isolation, both break down under the insupportable weight of their inherent absurdity.

It is clear enough, then, that notwithstanding what can be said in general for the appropriateness of inquiry into the fact of inquiry, the special, modern, propaedeutic preliminaries to inquiry are not only suspect, but in large part justly suspect.

V: PROPOSAL FOR A NEW APPROACH

The foregoing critique does not in the least imply, of course, that such long respected treatises as Descartes' *Discourse on Method* and *Metaphysical Meditations,* Locke's *Essay Concerning Human Understanding,* and Kant's *Critique of Pure Reason,* to mention only a few

of the greater, have been disposed of for any further serious consideration. To assume that would be stupidly to misunderstand their full
relevance. "Philosophies," it has been aptly said, "must be judged not
so much by their truth as by their power." And it cannot be imagined
that the essential power of these philosophical writings could possibly
be impugned by any analysis such as has been made here. The profound
manner in which they have stirred men's minds for centuries . . . their
still strong fascination even for those of us today who, *knowing better*,
re-read them again and again . . . their unquestionable place in world
literature—all unmistakably indicate that, even denied their fondest
claims, these treatises are still impressive and significant.

But although the critique made here must therefore be regarded as
primarily a work of candor undertaken in the interest of frank dealing,
it raises two sets of very important issues: the first, and more restricted,
concerning what is to be made of the modern prolegomena themselves
in view of the seemingly contradictory facts of their error and their
power; the second, and broader, concerning what clarification thus
results for the entire literature of inquiry concerning inquiry in which
these prolegomena have figured.

The former of these problems, although of less consequence than the
latter and subordinate to them, are by no means beneath attention in
their own right. The reaction against the grand prolegomena described
at some length above has been strongest among the more *creative* workers in the field of philosophy today. But students of world literature and
of the history of ideas still refer to the chief of these writings as the
most *required* part of their basic bibliography. Consequently, the clarification suggested would appear essential to the sound critical evalua-
tion, and hence to the intelligent appreciation, of fundamental texts
which illuminate the core of a liberal education as many of us still conceive it. Indeed, it may even prove necessary to the cultural survival
of these texts. There is no small danger that, if the reaction discussed
in this critique is sufficiently strong and un-challenged, it may eventually succeed in so turning attention from the grand prolegomena that,
notwithstanding what is important and valuable in them, they will
become lost to view as a part of our intellectual heritage. Despite the
obvious incomparability of our era to the early days of the modern period, we cannot altogether forget that at that time some of these very
writings, by their polemics against the scholastic tradition, so successfully distracted attention from the corresponding works of the me-

diaevals that these latter had to be completely *re-discovered* in the nine-teenth century, and many years of scholarship have even now only begun to bring them back to light of day. Doubtless it would not yet be re-garded as perverse obstruction of progress, to view a similar fate for all modern prolegomena to inquiry as most unfortunate. The issue is one of extremely wide cultural ramifications.

Closer to the central concern of the present essay, however, are the broader problems raised by the foregoing critique for the theory of knowledge more generally. Notwithstanding the special non-charac-teristic turn of the grand prolegomena to inquiry, it is not uncommon to find them wholly identified with *epistemology* in current accounts.[51] Regardless of the fact that this is in large part due to the exceptionally great interest which they have aroused by their provocative brilliance on other scores, therefore, their technical failures reviewed in the fore-going critique must be regarded as largely responsible for the disrespect which the theory of knowledge has incurred, and for the widespread misunderstanding which handicaps it today at a time when we stand in particularly great need of the kind of elucidation it might offer. Con-sequently, we are compelled to ask a number of fundamental questions concerning these writings and their relation to the rest of the literature of epistemology.

First, and most generally: What was the ironical inevitability in which they were thus caught up? How are we to construe failures so serious in the face of such confident attempts on the part of such competent investigators? What were the provocations, the compulsions, and the controlling circumstances, in terms of which these ventures may be made intelligible, if at all, to contemporary students of our intellectual past?

Then, more specifically, and in the light of the answers to the above: When discounted for their technical complications, are these writings left completely without relevance to inquiry as a going concern, and hence to the theory of knowledge in the sense in which it is here ac-cepted? Or, on the other hand, do they still retain some *residual* epis-temological significance?

Also in the light of the answer to the above: Exactly in what typical details of their arguments do these writings depart from sound proce-dure to become involved in technical difficulties? That is to say: What are the fundamental alternatives of procedure, if there be any, concern-ing which they presumably represent a mistaken choice?

And finally, in the light of the answers to all the foregoing: To what extent is epistemology in general subject to the same tendency? What is the lesson, if any, to be learned from all this by contemporary and future essayists in the theory of knowledge?

The rest of this study is addressed to such questions against the background of the observations made throughout the present chapter. Ideally, the fulfillment of its purpose would require a detailed review of the epistemological literature of modern and contemporary times, in contrast, perhaps, to that of ancient and mediaeval times. But that being impracticable within present limits, this study is confined, in *Part Two*, to an examination of modern epistemology in the crucial period of its early formulations, both before and during its propaedeutic development, with observations, in *Part Two* and especially in *Part Three*, as to the relevance of the conclusions which can thus be drawn, to issues of present day concern in both the quest and the theory of knowledge.

It goes without saying that the centuries of competent scholarship already expended on these books has disclosed a great many important and interesting facts about them. Such researches have brought to light, for example, many unsuspected doctrinal indebtednesses of their authors to each other and to previous writers. It has elaborately traced their discussions of such engaging themes as "method", "mind", "substance", "nature", "God", "soul", "religion", "value", and the like, in their respective technical terms. And its historians have recorded in impressive detail the development of the controversies to which they have given rise, and in some measure sustained, centering about the so-called *problems of philosophy*. But for the most part, such studies have been either footnotes to the texts of these books or else developments of those selfsame technical issues which tend to become secondary when we raise the question of their power and their relevance in the face of technical shortcomings. When we reconsider the great preliminary essays in the light of all that has been said above, we find ourselves challenged to take a broader view of their significance. We find ourselves challenged to read them as attempts to express convictions which cannot be dismissed as easily as the difficulties of their errant statements. We find ourselves challenged to follow their developments as explorations regarded, by the intellectual adventurers who undertook them, as bearing on broader issues than those by the technicalities of which their formal developments later become complicated. And we find ourselves challenged, finally, to regard them too in the light of the familiar considerations, and humane and practical intentions, which largely suggested and controlled them.

In such a reconsideration, however, the specifically propaedeutic works, when we come to them in their turn, cannot be accepted naively in terms of the claims by which they are defined above. There can be no further question of their being *absolutely propaedeutic* preliminaries to inquiry in the strict sense which they themselves suggest. They must be regarded, rather, simply as *prefaces to inquiry*. *Preface* is a comparatively neutral term. It has a familiar, commonsense meaning . . . to those, at least, who read books as their authors like them read, preface first. Consequently, it suggests a preliminary excursion only in the sense of an introduction. Although it comes before matters introduced, it presents them in such a way as to make no claims for *priority in the absolute order of knowledge*. Liberally construed, it does not evoke the kind of *a priori* presuppositions we have seen to lead to the peculiar perplexity and confusion of prolegomena.

With all these introductory points in mind, then, we turn now to a more detailed consideration of texts in *Part Two*. The first works to be considered in this analytic part of the essay are those of Francis Bacon, the earliest true epistemologist of note in modern times and the chief *forerunner* of the propaedeutic movement. Next to be examined are those of René Descartes and John Locke, who come partly before and partly in the movement. Then, in *Part Three*, two concluding chapters sketch subsequent developments to date and consider the implications of the entire study for the general relevance of the theory of knowledge . . . a relevance, it must be insisted once more, which is both broad and profound in this day when the quest of knowledge is undergoing fundamental transformations under the impact of recent events in major fields of research.

PART TWO

STUDIES IN THE LITERATURE

BACON ON THE ENTERPRISE OF LEARNING

I: THE "GREAT INSTAURATION"

SUCH WRITINGS of Francis Bacon as the *Advancement of Learning* and the *New Organon* are perhaps the earliest important treatises in the modern literature of inquiry to give explicit attention to the fact of knowledge rather than to its straightforward pursuit. Consequently there is a certain natural convenience, or historical appropriateness, in considering them at the outset of this study. Their chief claim to early attention here, however, rests on stronger grounds than their priority in mere point of time. It happens that these works are especially instructive in this context because of a very special relationship they bear to the crucially important propaedeutic part of the literature in question. Although they clearly are not attempted prolegomena to inquiry in the strict sense elaborated in the preceding chapter, they nevertheless have so much in common with such writings that they help us to understand the provocations which suggested them and the circumstances which controlled them. Both indicate the sounder sort of undertaking from which the more brilliant, but errant, prolegomena to inquiry tend to depart; and thus they help us to appreciate what these writings might have been were they differently attempted.

The relationship of *The Advancement of Learning* and *The New Organon* to the grand prolegomena is suggested by their organization about the themes of "learning" and "method", both of which have obvious affinities with the typical themes of ostensibly propaedeutic essays. But what underlies such surface associations is an important similarity of undertaking at bottom. In the *Announcement* of his *Great Instauration* which serves as an introduction to all his writings in this vein[1], Bacon does not call attention to the state or problems of any particular branch of inquiry, nor does he propose merely that certain particular investigations be pushed further in a few particular ways. His theme is the general "inquisition of nature" and the total "commerce between the mind of man and the nature of things". The question he raises concerns the way in which "the entire fabric of human reason" is "put together and built up". His aim is "to try the whole thing anew upon a better plan, and to commence a total reconstruction of sciences, arts, and all human knowledge raised upon the proper foundations." And so the main proposal he makes on behalf of his *Instauration* is essentially the proposal of all prefaces to inquiry—that inquirers leave off whatever special researches they are busied about to give thought to the general undertaking of inquiry itself.

Bacon's *Distribution of the Work,* which outlines the six phases of his grand project, merely details the manner in which he suggests this be done. It recommends to the investigators of his day that they: *first,* pause to survey the present general state of their work[2]; *second,* look to their ways and means of starting it anew[3]; *third,* gather together the facts and experiments they may be able to use thereafter[4]; *fourth,* work out a number of good examples of their improved technique as models to guide them further[5]; *fifth,* collect any good results that may have been turned up meanwhile[5]; and *lastly,* set to work again from the beginning in the light of all the preceding[6]. But obviously they could not do these things without leaving off the usual course of inquiry. This program is merely an explanation of how such routines are to be dropped for the while until the larger project, to which they are incidental, is thoroughly reconsidered.

Like the grand prolegomena which followed them, therefore, Bacon's writings subsidiary to his *Great Instauration* report attempts to inquire into the fact of inquiry itself. The special instructiveness with which they do so is the theme of the rest of this chapter and all of the chapter which follows.

II: A NOTE ON "NATURAL ORIGINS"

One question which comes naturally to mind when we take up any of the great prefaces to inquiry is: What provokes them? What makes their authors feel in the first place that they are imperatively called for? In many familiar instances, however, answers to this question are confused by the troubled fate of such writings on so many other scores. The view seems to have got about that because they have given rise to a multiplication of controversial -*isms* and have posed the so-called *problem of the reality of knowledge,* that it was specifically to accomplish these ends that they were first undertaken. But although there may be some soundness in this attitude with respect to the academic literature which followed them up in a critical, controversial vein, it is highly unsound with respect to the great originally conceived essays which gave rise to the genre. As has already been pointed out to some extent[7], most of these essays were attempts to dispose of controversy as a thing abhorrent. Most, moreover, and especially the earlier ones, were quite innocent of any awareness of knowledge as *problematic* in anything like the academic sense implied here. The compulsions which brought them into being were quite other than those so commonly assumed. And, precisely because of its comparative freedom from the confusions of the more technically complicated prefaces to inquiry, Bacon's *Great Instauration* makes this point strikingly clear.

Why should Bacon have called on inquirers in his day to take time off to survey their field, re-assemble their materials, overhaul their routines, and make a fresh start? Well, fundamental re-organization was *in the air*. As is shown by such works as John H. Randall Jr.'s *Making of the Modern Mind*, institutions generally were then being revamped. In the field of government, nationalism was replacing feudalism; in the field of religion, Protestantism was disrupting the mediaeval order of Catholocism; and likewise in the field of inquiry, men were finding themselves at a parting of the ways. When Bacon thought and wrote, the mediaeval scholastic tradition was still dominant in most of the schools and universities; but a new humanistic learning and a new experimental and mathematical investigation of nature, suggested by the revival of ancient Alexandrian science and the alchemy and wizardy of the middle ages, was being cultivated by scattered, independent workers. These independent investigators, although they were closer to the movements which were soon to become dominant in the intellectual life of Europe, were in serious want of the means and recognition necessary to them for doing their work most effectively. Thoroughgoing reconsideration of inquiry as a general undertaking was a need of the time, paralleling needs for reconsideration just as thoroughgoing in other fields. And quite on the face of it, the proposal of the *Great Instauration*, sound or unsound, is a proposal to recognize and meet this need. Bacon felt that the failing scholastic tradition, and the "delicate" humanistic tradition which was partly replacing it, must be cleared away so that the whole business of inquiry could be begun over in line with the more progressive tendencies of the time. And it is obvious that his grand project was the means by which he hoped to accomplish this end.

If bare inspection of the proposed six phases of his plan leaves any doubt as to this, examination of the language which introduces them removes it. The *Announcement* of Bacon's *Great Instauration* is a general indictment of the state of learning in his day, and the *Preface* follows up this indictment with a vigorous attack on its "triviality", "unproductiveness", "contentiousness" and "lack of sound direction". We find there, for example, the criticism that the knowledge then current is "but like the boyhood of knowledge and has the characteristic property of boys: it can talk, but it cannot generate: for it is fruitful of controversies but barren of works."[8] "If sciences of this kind had any life in them", Bacon writes, "that could never have come to pass which has been the case now for many ages—that they stand almost at a stay, without receiving any augmentations worthy of the human race; insomuch that many times not only what was asserted once is asserted still, but what was a question once is a question still, and instead of being resolved by discussion is only fixed and fed; and all the tradition and succession of schools is still a succession of masters and scholars, not of inventors and those who bring to further perfection the things invented."[8] In passages such as these, Bacon obviously holds up to stinging ridicule all the most familiar surface features of scholastic and humanistic practice: its successions of erudite commentaries, its raising and re-raising of disputed questions, its arrangements of arguments *pro* and *con* largely from sources of authority, its re-statements of issues in the light of further distinctions or new arguments, its attempts at resolution, then its endless recommencements of the whole procedure over again in the hands of new contenders. . . . And there can be no doubt but that it is primarily a strong feeling of need for replacing such a procedure with another, fundamentally different, which motivates Bacon in turning attention to the general undertaking of research.

In short, the most significant thing about the program of the *Instauration* outlined above is its ostensible culmination in a "legitimate, chaste and severe course of inquiry"; for this legitimacy, chastity, and severity Bacon obviously intended to be freedom from any of the features of scholasticism and humanism here lampooned. And the most significant part of the *Announcement* of the *Instauration* is its conclusion that, in view of the "manifold ignorance of the day", there was "but one course left—to try the whole thing anew upon a better plan . . ."; for by "a better plan" Bacon obviously meant one fundamentally different from that which sustained the respectable erudition of his time. His clear, explicit, literal words, viewed against their evident historical background, makes any other conclusion impossible. So it appears from consideration of this first great prefatory writing of recent centuries that, historically at least, the modern attempt to take thought about inquiry in its own right began as one of the many conscious efforts to remold social institutions which ushered in *the modern era*. Far from being the product of a finicky concern over whether we *really* know what we know, it was an expression of forces of social change, an articulation of one phase of a complex of historical movements which were then affecting all departments of living. Whatever may have been the motivation of later efforts of the same kind, that of this first one was simply an acute awareness of a most practical problem; the problem of how to launch anything like what we now know as the enterprise of learning in the halls of the mediaeval schoolmen, in the libraries of the humanistic literati, or in the dens of the Renaissance wizards and alchemists.

We may gather, therefore, that the characteristic twist of prefatory literature is not necessarily a freakish quirk given it by minds with an obstinate, but purely impractical, bent for queer questions; nor is it one that cannot be effected without impressive *metaphysical* jargon. That it does call for a kind of deflection of the inquirer's usual efforts, there can be no question. But as this special turn of attention is illustrated in Bacon's *Great Instauration,* it is exhibited to have a kind of natural origin in commonsense. That is to say, it is shown to be a reasonable, sensible expedient suggested by a fairly obvious state of affairs. And if it strikes us as . . . well, *unusual* . . . we can observe that the state of affairs to which it is addressed is not exactly ordinary either. It is not every day, nor every age, that inquirers find themselves faced with such fundamental differences or confusions as to what they are about; so we should not expect them always to be pondering what their proper business is, rather than doing it. But sometimes, as in Bacon's day, they do find themselves in such straits; and then we should not expect to find them doing nothing but what they are not entirely sure they ought to.

It need not be inferred from this that every preface to inquiry, or even a substantial number, arise from precisely the same kind of circumstance; namely, the emergence of a fundamentally different conception of learning in a society undergoing fundamental transformations. Indeed, one of the theses of this essay is that, in point of fact, such challenges have become less and less important, and less and less possible, from Bacon's time to the present. But that does not mean that the *Great Instauration* was altogether unique in provocation. Regardless of the more special circumstances under which it was worked out, the fact remains that the project was addressed to a kind of crisis in the affairs of men who scanned their surroundings inquiringly; and we shall take this as our main clue in considering the possibility of natural origins for other such ventures.

In making the foregoing observations, it should be noted, one has only begun to state the full significance of Bacon's writing in this vein. An inveterate rhetorician even when the business in hand did not call for rhetoric, Bacon might well have tried to achieve the practical purpose of his *Great Instauration* solely by further rhetorical elaboration of the passages already quoted from its *Preface* and *Distribution of the Work*, both of which, incidentally, are no more than prospectuses of his whole project. Yet, for all their gratuitous figurative language, neither his *Advancement, De Dignitate* nor *New Organon* can be called primarily a rhetorical document. All three are unmistakably attempts to get down to serious business and work out the first two phases of the larger undertaking in specific detail. And since there should presumably be much in the parts which cannot be included in the sketch of the whole, questions still remain open here as to what contributions, if any, each makes to it.   Besides, the historical rôle of these writings, although admittedly great, is after all only historical. Alone, it is not enough to explain the continued interest and fascination they have for many readers not especially concerned about what the historical careers of these writing have been. So just what is it about them which rises above consideration of their time and place? Then, too, it must be remembered that there have been many other attempts to take thought about such matters. And so the question persists as to what characterises Bacon's particular ways of doing so.

Furthermore, if Bacon's prefatory writings are considered in the light of the whole argument of *Chapter One*, there are also two standing questions which must still be answered. *First,* in view of their affinities with the propaedeutic literature analyzed at length in *Sections ii, iii,* and *iv* of *Chapter One,* must not these writings be caught up in all its characteristic difficulties? One might easily assume, in view of the comparability of their attempt, that they are also subject to sidetracking from the outset, that they get involved in worse controversial difficulties than those at which they are directed, that they issue eventually in such logical impasses as those of solipsism or absolute scepticism, and that they are repudiated now by the current reaction against such writings. Is this the case, or is it not? And *secondly*, if these writings are so involved, what in their procedures, or in the circumstances, which control them, brings this about? Or, if they are not, what in these same procedures or circumstances enables them to avoid such a fate?

For answers to all these questions we must go beyond the mere general prospectuses and historical provocations of the *Great Instauration* to consider those writings in which its parts are worked out more concretely.

IV: THE PRO'S AND CON'S OF "LEARNING"

Bacon's *Advancement* and *De Dignitate*, we have already mentioned, are devoted to the first phase of his ambitious project—the survey of "the intellectual globe" or of the state of *learning* in his day. At first approach, it is perhaps the theme of these works which here strikes the attention most forcibly. "Learning," as has been remarked above, has an obvious affinity with the "understanding", "knowledge", "pure reason", "mind", etc., of many of the better known propaedeutic essays. It shares with them what we might call a kind of common reference to the characteristic business of man as a searching, thinking being; and this fact has been taken here as one of the more obvious signs which suggest an intimate relationship between these writings of Bacon's and the main body of propaedeutic literature. As we shall now show in greater detail, however, the similarity is a similarity with an important difference.

To begin with, "learning" is a particularly comprehensive term. Its discussion is unusually hard to confine. One should not be surprised to find its development lead to questions of such diverse matters as the way to write history, the possibility of a science of languages, or the interpretation of myths. And both Bacon's surveys of learning become involved in all these issues, as well as in many others. Indeed, they are in point of fact small encyclopedias, and like the great encyclopedias of the next century, a good deal of their value consists in the insight and shrewdness with which they turn up information and suggestions about a great many such matters. But in following up all these developments, one would find oneself exploring Bacon's intellectual globe as he saw it inhabited in his day; and such an exploration is not called for in a study such as this. What is in question is only the bearing of the total discussion on inquiry generally speaking—that is to say, its bearing as a preface to inquiry. And it is to this that the following analysis of the *Advancement* and *De Dignitate* is strictly confined.

In *Book I*, which is much the same in both editions, we find Bacon beginning by reviewing some of the slanders against learning current in his day. The stilted platitudes of this preliminary part of the survey remind one so uncomfortably of the stiffness of Bacon's moral essays that the casual reader is likely to skip over it somewhat impatiently. But for the purposes of this study it is significant to note that all the "false accusations of learning" against which Bacon protests here take the form of "discredits and disgraces", attacks on its "worth" and "dignity". A typical instance of complaint is that learning is *bad* because its moral effects are bad.[9] And in much the same tenor are the objections that learning unfits men for action; that it softens their minds and leaves them incompetent in politics and arms; that it inclines them to leisure and love of privacy, thus making them slothful; that it lessens reverence for government, so undermining the state, etc. etc.

The interesting thing about all these criticisms is what they put in question. They do not raise what have become the issues of the *reality* or *validity* of knowledge. They are not in the least concerned with the question of whether it is an accurate transcript or report of what it is knowledge of. Such *problems* are foreign to the context in which the discussion moves. The issues which are raised concern matters like "worth", "usefulness", "value", "excellence", or "dignity". The basic question asked is: What becomes of men and their institutions when learning is cultivated?

Furthermore, for all their legalistic quibbling, the answers given are stated in terms appropriate to these questions. The justice of many of the accusations is in part recognized. The "diseases of learning" and its "peccant humors" are pointed out for treatment and correction. But the more serious accusations are denied in their own terms. To vindicate the excellence and dignity of learning, appeal is made to its role in effective living. Whatever the ill effects of its unsound forms, Bacon insists that when sound it can educate men to competence in affairs, that it is an instrument of moral culture, that it is a technique of control, and that it can serve as a bond of society. In answer to the questions put, he replies that learning is useful and worthwhile because men and their institutions flourish when it is cultivated. In *Book I* he repeats, in short, the central point of his essay *Of Studies*, which is that, although learning may "serve for delight and ornament", it also serves "for ability . . . in the judgement and disposition of business; for expert men can execute, and perhaps judge of particulars, one by one; but the general counsels, and the plots and marshalling of affairs come best from those that are learned".[10]

What, then, does this accomplish as a phase of a preface to inquiry? Quite independent of the *pro*'s and *con*'s of any particular part of the argument is the conclusion that inquiry is construed by it as a matter ultimately to be judged in terms of its working "for the benefit and use of men".[11] The first *Books* of the *Advancement* and the *De Dignitate* put inquiry in question. Almost by definition, that is what all prefaces to inquiry do. But more specifically, these introductory parts of Bacon's surveys of learning put inquiry in question as an activity that must be judged against criteria of social worth and usefulness. They make it a practical and moral matter, a matter of serving purposes and accomplishing ends. They bring inquiry to court, so to speak, and point it out as something which can be justified or condemned largely by what it does and promises yet to do for society on the whole. And thus they make its criteria the kind of criteria which arise from attempting social enterprises and judging whether they achieve or defeat social ends.

V: "ACTS" AND "WORKS"

The full significance of all this may not be apparent at first blush, but it becomes clearer when we turn to *Book II*, which concludes the *Advancement of Learning,* and to its expansion in *Books II to IX* of the *De Dignitate et Augmentis Scientiarum*. These books are usually approached as though they were primarily concerned with the complicated classification of the departments of knowledge which their argument elaborates. Outlines of them are usually confined to the bare structure of this schematism.[12] But although the texts suggest such an interpretation, they do not sustain it. It is true that Bacon makes use of his classification of the departments of knowledge as a device of exposition. But it is a serious misunderstanding to confuse such purely expository device with subject matter. The plan which does control their development is revealed at the very outset of their argument where, in dedicating the work of the King, Bacon writes that "the sum (of the treatise) will consist of these two parts; the former, concerning the excellency of learning and Knowledge, and the excellency of the merit and true glory in the augmentation and propogation thereof: the *latter*, what the particular acts and works are, which have been embraced and undertaken for the Advancement of Learning; and again, what defects and

undervalues I find in such particular acts. . . ."[13] The part of the treatises we have not already considered is here said to concern a review
and criticism of the "acts" and "works" which promote learning. And
that this is quite a different matter from pigeon-holing arts and sciences is clear from the discussion given such "acts" and "works".

Bacon describes them roughly as "conversant about three objects:
the places of learning, the books of learning, and the persons of the
learned"; for, "as water, whether it be the dew of heaven, or the springs
of the earth, doth scatter and leese itself in the ground, except it be collected into some receptacle, . . . so this excellent liquor of knowledge
. . . would soon perish and vanish to oblivion if it were not preserved
in books, traditions, conferences, and places appointed as universities,
colleges, and schools. . . ."[14] In more detail: the first group, concerning the seats and places of learning, include "foundations and buildings,
endowments with revenues, endowments with franchises and privileges,
and institutions and ordinances for government", etc. The second,
"touching books", are "libraries and editions of sound authors." And
the third, "pertaining to the persons of learned men," have to do with
the appointment of teachers and research workers.[15] In short, the "acts"
and "works" to which Bacon turns, after arguing the social value and
dignity of learning are books and schools and bodies of men devoted to
the pursuit of inquiry and to the publication of its findings—to education, one might say. Generally speaking, they are institutions of public
enlightenment, social organizations with society as the field of their
operation.

Accordingly, the program of the review which Bacon proposes is a
program of social criticism in the strictest sense, calling for a scrutiny
of learned institutions with a view to improving their social effectiveness. Bacon finds in his survey that colleges are devoted too narrowly
to professional training in law, medicine, and ministry, while neglect-
ing arts and sciences. And similarly he finds that there is too little sound
supervision of programs of study in the universities, that courses of
study are not adapted to changing requirements, that proper allowance
is not made for experimental equipment with which to "spy on nature",
that books are badly written and badly edited, that the faculties of different schools do not correspond enough to exchange views and co-
operate in their work, that those who devote themselves to all these
matters are not properly paid, and that no survey has been made of accomplishment in the various fields of inquiry to determine what has

been done and what might be done.[16] A complete working out of the plan of his project calls for following up each of these observations in as much detail as Bacon actually worked out the survey of what had been done in the various fields of investigation. It is only a circumstance beyond his control which compels Bacon to confine his attention chiefly to surveying what has been done and remains yet to be done in the several fields of scholarship. Most of the "defects of learning", he writes, "are *opera basilica:* toward which the endeavors of a private man may be but as an image in a crossway, that may point out the way, but cannot go it." That is to say, it is a public undertaking, a social enterprise. "But the inducing part of the last, which is a survey of learning", Bacon adds, "may be set forward by private travail."[17] And that is the only reason why he limits most of his discussion to but a single one of the many "acts and works of learning" which he enumerates: The task is so thoroughly social in character that this is the only part of it which he can attempt alone.

What, then, is the upshot of his argument in so far as it constitutes a preface to inquiry? What is its bearing on inquiry generally speaking? Briefly, it is this conclusion: Not only do these surveys of learning put inquiry in question against certain social criteria—the criteria of social worth and usefulness—but they also bring out the fact that its undertaking occurs in a comparable context which must be taken account of. They place inquiry. They place it in a context of human needs on the one hand, and of agencies for fulfilling them on the other—in the context of *society*, that is to say. Possibly a broader name for the context of inquiry is *nature*. But if *nature* be insisted on, Bacon's surveys of the acts and works of learning emphasize its character as the environment of men organized in society, the natural setting of institutionalized human living. And in so delimiting the context of inquiry, they also identify inquirers themselves as primarily the men who organize and carry on the business of institutions of learning. To be sure, Bacon is well aware of his private role as a lone pioneer in the working out of his ambitious project. On several occasions he is egocentric enough to announce that he publishes his ideas for fear that they will never occur to anyone else.[18] But his remarks concern primarily the state of literacy, attitude, intelligence, or education in society. As an individual critic, however self-assertive, he always presses his arguments in the role of a citizen in the commonwealth of learning.

Moreover, further examination of the *Advancement* and *De Digni-*

tate reveals that placing inquiry in a social context and identifying
its agents as men organized in social institutions are not the only consequences of his putting it in question in this way. Again and again
in these books we find Bacon running up against certain *problems*
which his manner of approach seems to make inevitable. A typical instance is his discussion of the state of medical science and practice.
Medicine, he complains with typical sarcasm, is "more professed than
laboured, and more laboured than advanced";[19] whereupon he
promptly looks into the practices of physicians for the errors of their
usual ways. He finds, for one thing, that medical men pay too little
attention to the preservation of health, confining their attention to
pathological conditions. And even when they attempt cures, he finds
their practices criticisable on a number of scores: they fail to keep accurate records of case histories, they vary their treatments without check-
ing carefully on the differences in results, they pay too little attention
to the variations in the constitutions and symptoms of their patients,
they make no study of comparative anatomy, they do not try out ways
of mitigating pain, they make no attempt to standardize prescriptions, and they do not study ways of reproducing artificially the cures
of natural medicinal springs.[20] So what does Bacon suggest doing? A
good example of his way of tackling such a situation is his suggestion,
in the longer account in the *De Dignitate,* that a physician's directory
be compiled to help in standardizing prescriptions on some sound basis,
and that a committee of competent members of the profession be appointed to supervise and edit the work; for, he writes: "It is a thing
that should not be undertaken without keen and severe judgement, and
in synod, as it were, of select physicians."[20] The important thing to
note here is Bacon's way of going about things. Having pointed out
a defect in learning, he traces its causes to defects in the functioning of
a specific institution, such as the practice of medicine in this case. Then,
having so traced it, he suggests a correction, also through institutional
agencies, as when he here recommends a committee of physicians to
standardize prescriptions. We may recall as an amusing, but instructive,
alternative to such a procedure that when Descartes learned his friend
Mersenne was sick with erysipelas in 1630, he wrote him an urgent letter
begging him to take good care of himself while he, Descartes, tried to
find a medicine "founded on indubitable demonstration" for the cure of
his disease.[21] In such a situation, Descartes evidently felt he must turn
to principles of demonstration. But Bacon turns to agencies of control.

The considerations which he makes have society as their context; they hinge on ways and means of organizing inquiry about an issue which challenges understanding; consequently, the obstacles they face are characteristically those which confront organized ways of doing things.

The problems of inquiry which develop in this critique of learning are the problems of the *"opera basilica"* that Bacon regards learning to be. As he writes in the last page of the discussion of his general project, we may take it that "those things are to be held possible which may be done by some person, though not by every one; and which may be done by many, though not by any one; and which may be done in the succession of ages, though not within the hour glass of one man's life; and which may be done by public designation, though not by private endeavor."[22] As they are delimited here, the problems of knowledge find development, not in schools of metaphysical contention, but in the work of societies . . . like the British Royal Society which as a matter of historical fact was largely inspired by Bacon.[23] Bacon's *New Atlantis* is a delightful phantasy. But it is no mere phantasy. It is a sketch of the kind of solving required by the problems delimited in his survey of learning. Its "House of Solomon" is an institutional device for focussing the means of society on the difficulties which lie between social needs and their fulfillment.

Then finally, there is still another consequence of Bacon's putting inquiry in question as a matter of learning. His social approach seems to make inevitable the social conclusion that knowledge should be "not as a courtesan, for pleasure and vanity only, or as a bondwoman, to acquire and gain to her master's use; but as a spouse, for generation, fruit, and comfort."[24] Just as *nature* is a general name for inquiry's context, *knowledge* is a general name for its issue. But Bacon finds himself constrained to repeat again and again that "knowledge is power". Whatever the difficulties which may be raised about this equation in other connections, and whatever more primary significance it may be found to have, in the light of all that has just been said it here takes on a perfectly clear meaning. When inquiry is placed in the context of society as an activity carried on by men organized in social institutions, and when its problems are circumscribed as problems of how to achieve social ends, its issue unavoidably becomes "power" in the sense of ability to arrive at those ends. It becomes a technique for approaching difficulties in terms of an understanding of the agencies they involve. Knowledge so arrived at may possibly be diverted by other purposes;

but most significantly, most essentially, it is the power of social capability. This conclusion may be troublesome when tampered with out of context; but in the context of Bacon's *Advancement* and *De Dignitate* it is the most inevitable outcome of the entire undertaking.

To sum up, therefore, we find, on analyzing this attempt to preface inquiry in terms of a survey of learning, that it tends to:

1. Put inquiry as a general project in question *by measuring it against criteria of social usefulness and worth.*
2. Identify the agents of inquiry *as groups of men carrying on the work of the social institutions devoted to inquiry.*
3. Delimit the context of inquiry *as society and its natural environment.*
4. Single out the problems of inquiry *as primarily those of how best to direct the social agencies which carry it on.*
5. Interpret the issue of inquiry *as power in the sense of ability to attain social ends.*

VI: "LEARNING" AND SOCIAL INSTITUTIONS

The schematism of conclusions arrived at in summing up the foregoing analysis has, perhaps, a kind of alluring simplicity; and this may lead the wary to suspect that it is a deceptive, if intriguing, formula. But the suspicion that Bacon's texts may have been somewhat forced to conform to a preconceived design ought largely to be allayed by consideration of the patent appropriateness of the five developments of Bacon's survey to which the schematism calls attention.

After all, both the treatises in question develop a phase of the *Great Instauration* by which Bacon attempted to replace the dominant scholasticism of his day with a fundamentally different approach to inquiry; and the opuscula which serve as prospectuses of this project were little more than general rhetorical diatribes. But attacks of that kind were faced with two serious disadvantages. *First* and most obviously, there was the fact that scholasticism, the principal tradition which Bacon proposed to do away with, enjoyed not only the sponsorship of the Church but also the tacit approval of prevailing *respectable* opinion which it were pointless to offend by mere name-calling. Then *secondly* and of greater importance, there is also the fact that the opposition which Bacon addressed to scholasticism and humanism was of so fundamental a character that all direct attack by either side was quite futile.

The gulf was so wide between his ideas and those he fought that, as in all such cases, they faced in different directions. There could be no direct contact between them, even for coming to grips, so long as he confined himself to generalities about "sterility" and "triviality." After all, how could the inquirer with strong scholastic sympathies, for example, possibly see Bacon's elaborate figures of speech as anything but stupid blathering, or expressions of misdirected zeal, when he saw his own work, in its own terms, so endlessly fruitful and important?

But the reason for this invulnerability of older traditions to such attacks lay precisely in the fact that their whole structure was based on fundamentally different assumptions as to the criteria by which inquiry can be evaluated, the role of the inquirer who undertakes it, the nature of the context in which it is pursued, the character of the problems which it chiefly encounters, and the nature of the results with which it comes eventually to fruition. It is difficult to make generalizations about so complex a tradition as that of scholastic inquiry, for example; but, despite instances which may well be pointed out to the contrary, it is fairly safe to say that, as Bacon himself viewed it at least, it exhibited the following features: (1) when called in question, it found its proper justification in its role as a supplement to faith and mystical intuition in bringing about man's salvation; (2) it assumed as its proper agents the scholars of the Church, dedicated by vocation to the Church's work of salvation; (3) it assumed as its broad context the world viewed as the setting of the drama of man's salvation: (4) it assumed as its broad problems the problems of how, through reason, to help achieve this salvation; and (5) it assumed as its broad aim the natural end of all mediaeval society, the enjoyment of eternal life.[25] Taken all together, these assumptions formed a complete and consistent system which, so long as it was held to, served as impenetrable armour against all the abuse and ridicule any number of Baconians could muster.

The underlying assumptions themselves, however, were more easily challenged; and it is at them that Bacon's prefatory account of inquiry as a matter of learning is addressed, without bitterness, without explicit mention, perhaps even without full awareness, but nevertheless with deadly effectiveness. Learning, as Bacon approaches it here, has implications which root it firmly in the context of society. It is hard indeed even to think of the theme very long without coming to think of the institutions which sustain it. And these institutions can be torn from their moorings with others only with difficulty. Their isolation, if it is attempted, must be forced. Indeed, aping the style of the Baconian metaphor, one might well say that when one examines the links in the chain of learning, one finds them securely fastened to the very pillars of society. It is quite inevitable, therefore, that in discussing inquiry generally as a matter of "learning", Bacon finds himself faced first of all with a kind of preliminary question appropriate to the discussion of such a theme—the question, namely, of whether, in view of what it involves, it performs a worthwhile function in society. And it is just as inevitable that, after declaring for its social worth and dignity as he sees it, he finds next that a survey of its state calls for a study of acts and works which it is beyond the ability of any single investigator to work out, but which must be referred for the most part to the King or to society at large. So bound up is the undertaking right from the outset with the whole social scheme of things that, as a lone worker, he must call on the whole system of learned institutions to come to his aid. From beginning to end, the whole undertaking is fated by the fact that learning is an enterprise with society as its background; and that is why Bacon ends by insisting on its role in social living. It does not matter that this was what Bacon wanted to do in the first place, as indeed he doubtless did. Whatever may be said about his original sympathies and intentions, the fact remains that the means he chose were appropriate for expressing them. Bringing to the survey of learning his bias for its advancement, he could not help but end by proclaiming its *enterprise* as primarily a social undertaking.

But in thus working out the implications of his approach to inquiry in the *Advancement* and *De Dignitate*, Bacon undermines the scholastic tradition in a much more subtle way than by ridicule or abuse; for he challenges its fundamental assumptions by constructive suggestions of alternative ones, and so sets up the whole business of inquiry on a basis which will not sustain the scholastic conception of it. In proclaiming the enterprise of learning, he champions an entirely different conception of what inquiry is about. Despite his tactful suggestions that divinity is a field of investigation which is well developed and most suitably pursued by the Church, he rests his positive case for the worth and dignity of the main body of learning on its usefulness to lay society for its worldly purposes. By implication, at least, he identifies its agents, its context and its problems as primarily those of this same lay society for these same lay purposes. And finally, he construes its aim to be that of achieving, not the eternal salvation of man in another world, but his dominion over nature for living a better life in this one. And it is quite clear, from the course of subsequent history, that the actual undertaking of this enterprise of learning was more effective in changing the historical development of inquiry than all the rhetoric he or any number of debaters could have marshalled against the strongly entrenched dominant academic traditions of his day.

From the legitimate point of view of scholasticism, of course, the whole procedure is both narrow-minded and unfair. It takes no account of the ends of scholastic inquiry in their own terms; and its method consists simply in bringing a foreign consideration to bear—namely: "the occasions and uses of this life" as contrasted to the occasions and uses of a soul facing its immortal destiny. But it happened that Bacon's age was one in which the pressure of events was turning men's minds from their soul's salvation to the world of things about them. In challenging the erudition of the scholastics on the score of its usefulness as an instrument by which men might control their living on this earth, Bacon's survey of learning gave vivid and forceful expression to the this-worldliness of an increasingly greater number of his contemporaries in all walks of life, and then measured the achievements of the learning dominant in his day against its demands. Such protests, therefore, are but further testimony to the effectiveness of his survey of learning as an instrument of social reconstruction, and, more generally, to the effectiveness of the preface to inquiry as a device for bringing about fundamental changes of attitude toward the larger undertaking which it directs back upon itself.

VII: THE ENTERPRISE OF LEARNING

Turning, then, to consider the *Advancement* and the *De Dignitate* against the background of the critique of propaedeutic epistemology presented in *Sections iii* and *iv* of *Chapter I* above, surely it would seem passing strange if they were now found to be faced with all the difficulties pointed out there at length. But in the light of the analysis that has here been made of the essential phases of their prefatory survey of learning, quite the opposite develops to be the case.

For one thing, it is now plain that in calling a halt in the regular course of inquiry, these writings of Bacon's do no more than propose that men engaged in a social activity leave off the regular routine of their work to stop and take stock of what they have thus far done and need yet to do. These books do not require that the inquirer attempt somehow to get *around* or *beyond* the usual familiar relationship between knower and known. They are not addressed to the so-called *problem of the reality of knowledge* as we often hear of it as an established theme of *metaphysical* discussion. They are addressed rather to a state of affairs in society. And the action they propose takes the form of a social program faced with none but practical difficulties—that is to say, difficulties concerning ways and means. Consequently, the discussion which they arouse cannot be regarded as a sidetracking of their original purpose, because their undertaking is itself admittedly a step in the actual procedure of inquiry proper, however "legitimate, chaste, and severe" it may be as afterwards attempted.

We may also conclude here, moreover, that although certain controversial questions are raised by these works, they are only the practical questions which concern such issues as the advisability of organizing this or that line of inquiry in this or that way, without raising purely *academic* debates about the *reality* of the outcome in any event. The undertaking from which they develop, even though it may not do away with controversies among inquirers, at least does not aggravate them. On the contrary, to a certain extent it decreases what is most objectionable about such controversies. In appealing from the "futility and sterility" of scholastic debate, this review of learning does suggest a practical way of setting about to investigate problems. It proposes that the energies of debaters, usually wasted in contention, be turned to the active cooperative study of matters hitherto only talked about. It calls upon men to cease attempting to defeat each other "in argument" in order that they might conquer nature "in action".[26] Indeed, it calls upon men to do this by working together, not only on a local or national scale, but even on an international scale. "For as the proficience of learning consisteth much in the orders and institutions of universities in the same states and kingdoms," Bacon writes, "so it would be yet more advanced, if there were more intelligence mutual between the universities of Europe than now is. . . ."[27] Thus, although his proclamation of the enterprise of learning may not supply a metaphysical touchstone which transforms disagreement to agreement on the basis of an inescapable certainty, it does suggest a program by which questions raised in debate may become incentives to the investigation of subject matters rather than of arguments.

It is only natural, therefore, that this survey should also remain practically untouched by the current trend in philosophy. As has been seen, its undertaking is not subject to the particular propaedeutic twist of which many people have become so distrustful today. Quite on the contrary, the enterprise of learning which it proclaims has been most instrumental in supporting the insistence that finicky preliminary hesitations about knowledge are absurd and pointless. It is beyond serious question that such institutions as the graduate faculties of our great universities, the British Royal Society, the Smithsonian Institute, the Rockefeller Institute, the Carnegie Foundation, the Guggenheim Foundation, the General Electric Company's Laboratories, and the like, are all dedicated to the enterprise of learning much in the sense that Bacon's *Advancement* and *De Dignatate* helped to popularize it. And it is equally beyond question that the unchallenged success of these institutions in piling up a formidable body of working knowledge has done much to destroy the original practical incentives for starting *How-do-we-know-that-we-really-know?* debates. The current tendency among philosophers to turn attention to the implications of knowledge, rather than to a preliminary questioning of its *reality*, may even be regarded as a kind of indirect consequence of Bacon's sponsorship of the enterprise of learning. In any event, it is significant that at least one branch of the current reaction in philosophy, that lead by John Dewey, pays specific tribute to Bacon as an important forerunner of the movement.[28]

Considered all in all, then, not only does the more detailed analysis of Bacon's survey of learning reveal something of the power of such a preface to inquiry as an instrument of criticism, and something of the kind of controls to which its development is subject, but it also demonstrates the legitimacy of such an essay when soundly undertaken. And this suggests that even those preliminaries to inquiry in the strict sense which are most vulnerable to the critique with which this study begins may be found to contain much that is equally sound and legitimate when they are considered in the same way. But that is a matter for further investigation in later chapters.

Of course, as many may still point out, it would be easy to deny the unique appropriateness of measuring inquiry against social criteria and identifying its agents as social agents, etc. etc. Evidence suggesting different conclusions could readily be produced. And it may possibly be that the most important criteria, agents, contexts, problems, and issue of inquiry are quite other than Bacon's survey of learning makes them out to be. For the purpose of this study of prefaces to inquiry, however, the important point is that, even though inquiry is subject to scrutiny in other ways, its appraisal in terms of its social worth and usefulness does call attention to an important function it does fulfill. It happens that inquiry and society *are* mutually relevant to each other. Regardless of what other services he may perform, the inquirer does perform a social service, and he may well be called to account for how he performs it. The agencies of inquiry, on the other hand, are part and parcel of the social organism. As a general activity, inquiry cannot afford to be indifferent to that part, at least, of its context which is social. Neither can it afford to be indifferent to those of its problems which are due to the fact that society is part of its context. Nor can it ignore the fact that, whatever else more commonplace or more exalted its issue may be, it is, among other things, "power" in the sense of social capability. Whatever other roles it may have, inquiry has a social role. Whatever other ends it may serve, it serves social ends. Whatever other contexts of consideration may add to our understanding of it, we cannot overlook its social context. And whatever other issue it may have, it has a social issue.

Inquiry has social significance. From a non-historical point of view, the chief power of Bacon's survey of learning as a preface to inquiry is that it calls attention to this fact for his age, for our age, and for any age.

BACON ON THE TECHNOLOGY OF RESEARCH

I: THE "ART OF INVENTION"

IMPORTANT as are the *Advancement* and *De Dignitate* to the plan of Bacon's *Great Instauration*, their survey of the state of learning and their proclamation of the social enterprise of learning belong only to the first phase of the larger project. Inquiry, it seems, is more than a matter of organization. Whatever its sponsorship, it still must be brought to bear on subject matters. Neither ecclesiastical blessing nor the support of lay society is, in itself, all that is necessary to set it going. As Bacon himself observes, "Though all the wits of all the ages should meet together and combine and transmit their labours, yet will no great progress ever be made in science by means of anticipations; because radical errors are not to be cured by the excellence of functions, etc."[1] So, after exhibiting the social character of the learning he champions, and after arguing for institutional support on its behalf, he finds he has yet to take up the question of detailed ways and means before he can make the proposal of his *Great Instauration* definite and concrete. And this brings us to the *New Organon* which he presents as expounding "a kind of logic" which is to be an "art of interpretation" or an "art of inquiry and invention".[2]

How, now, does this second part of the *Instauration* supplement the first? And what more does its analysis contribute to our understanding of literature prefatory to inquiry?

II: A SURVEY OF TECHNIQUES

It will be recalled that the *Advancement of Learning* and the *De Dignitate et Augmentis Scientiarum* begin with a review of criticisms of the social usefulness of learning,[3] and that in doing so they put inquiry in question as an undertaking which has a social bearing.[4] In the *New Organon* there is nothing, to be sure, which is inconsistent with such an approach to inquiry; but there is, on the other hand, a comparable, if more special, critical review which has comparable, if more special, consequences.

Bacon's many comments in this treatise on traditions of inquiry turn sooner or later on criticisms of their "methods". When mentioning such Greeks as Plato, Aristotle, Zeno, Epicurus, and Theophrastus, for example, Bacon here concedes that most of the science of his day derived from them, but with the complaint that they turned matters "into disputations" like the sophists, and battled for "philosophical sects and heresies", rather than set to work on the investigation of nature.[5] His concession that still earlier inquirers, such as Empedocles, Anaxagoras, Democritus, and their fellows did more substantial work, evokes the explanation that they actually "betook themselves to the investigation of truth" with results which unfortunately did not survive the subsequent course of history.[6] His crediting of "the sceptics of the New Academy" with better sense than the "dogmatizing Greeks" is modified by the important reservation that they went too far to the other extreme in that they wasted their time arguing whether anything could be known, rather than putting the issue to the test by actually trying it out.[7] His mention of the empirics and alchemists finds him immediately commending them because they consult experience by making experiments, but at the same time objecting that they do not go about this properly.[8] And his principal comment on the scholastics is that their method is "altogether erroneous and impassable", leaving everything "either to the mist of tradition, or the whirl and eddy of argument."[9] The discussion of this last group in the *New Organon*, indeed, is an elaborate critical dissection of their whole methodology, and especially of their "syllogizing", which, he writes, "serves rather to fix and give stability to the errors which have their foundation in commonly received notions than to help the search after truth."[10]

The important thing to note about these various comments is, not their specific details, but the fact that all are variations of a single basic criticism—that the procedures in question are merely ways of setting up "systems for the nice ordering and setting forth of things already invented," and not "methods of invention or direction for new works."[11] Bacon seems to have no objections to "dogmatism", "scepticism", "alchemy", and "scholasticism" as such. His complaint is simply that, as they are attempted, the science each issues in is sterile like "a plant torn up from its roots," rather than like one that "had remained attached to the womb of nature and continued to draw nourishment from her."[12] His chief indictment against them is that each, in its own peculiar way, gets nowhere so far as substantial "works" and "inventions" are concerned. His protest always amounts at bottom to a protest against their unproductivity in terms of gradually accumulating means of controlling natural forces. Despite all the details of his minor criticisms, the important underlying reason why he finally rejects all the traditions of inquiry he here reviews is that their methods are not well adapted for the development of instruments of control. He sets them aside because, for the purpose he has in mind, their routine procedures are inefficient, unproductive.

Like many similar critical observations in Bacon's other writings, of course, these might well be challenged on a number of scores. For example, his understanding of some of the Greeks and of some of the experimentalists of his day are both extremely questionable. But such matters are not at issue in this analysis. Regardless of their *pro*'s and *con*'s the important point for this study is the way the whole critique puts inquiry in question. In reviewing traditional techniques, Bacon here calls attention to inquiry as an undertaking that must be judged by its fruits, not only in the broad social sense which concerns its worth and dignity, but also in a more limited sense which concerns its efficiency or productivity. This review puts inquiry in question, not only as a social matter, but also, one might say for lack of a better word, as a *technological* matter. So thoroughly does it do so, indeed, that just as the corresponding consideration of the worth and dignity of learning makes the survey of the *Advancement* and *De Dignitate* primarily an account of the institutions of inquiry, this consideration of the efficiency and productivity of its methods makes the "Art" of the *New Organon* primarily an account of its technology.

III: AN APPEAL TO "INDUCTION"

Whither are we led, then, by this attempt to work out the technological art of invention? The obvious formal answer, suggested by a literal reading of the text, is that we are led to "induction." As an alternative to the vanity of dogmatism, the pointless despair of scepticism, the carelessness of unorganized empiricism, and the endless disputing of scholasticism, Bacon proposes "a new kind of logic"—"systematic induction". But this term can mean, and has meant, many things. What does it mean as Bacon here develops it?

If we are to be guided by the "Tables of Presence", of "Deviation", of "Degree or Comparison", and of "Exclusion or Rejection", illustrated in the example of the study of heat, and by the accounts of "Perogative

Instances", all in *Book II* of the *New Organon*, "induction" means for Bacon a careful, methodical scrutiny of the evident world about us by any device it offers for its own probing. It means making observations of such things as the rays of the sun at different seasons and under different circumstances, and also of meteors, thunderbolts, volcanoes, flames, ignited solids, natural warm springs, boiling or heated liquids, fumes, furnaces, air, caverns, wool, animal skins, bird down, solid bodies, sparks, bodies in friction, green and moist vegetables, quick lime, and scores of other such things.[13] Furthermore, it means comparing these observations, and subjecting them to all kinds of variation and further development, as when one tries to see whether concave lenses have a different effect on the sun's rays than convex, and whether both have the same effect on heat radiating from other sources than the sun.[14] Still further, it means exerting all possible ingenuity in the special selection of these observations;[15] it means implementing them by every possible device coming to hand, such as microscopes, telescopes, measuring rods, astrolabes, etc.;[16] it means making exact measurements whenever possible;[17] and it means always paying special attention to those experiments and observations which might be crucial in leading to increased possibilities of practical application.[18] In short and in sum, for Bacon "induction" means turning attention from "the little cells of human wit" to "the greater world" about us,[19] from the library armchair and the debate auditorium to the experimental laboratory and to nature.

But to *nature* in what sense? As is pointed out in *section v* of the preceding chapter, *nature* is but a general name for the context of inquiry. The important thing is how it is delimited. In Bacon's survey of learning, for example, it is delimited as the environment of society, so that its most significant features are the institutions that are the acts and works of men socially organized. In Bacon's discussion of the "art of discovery", however, it is delimited somewhat differently as the realm having as its most significant feature the fact that technological ways of doing things can be set up in it and made to work. It is delimited as the order of things which yields to systematic, instrumented ways of probing. It is delimited as the nature which, in the most common use of the term, we call *physical*—the familiar nature in which men find out things by collecting flora and fauna, keeping records of weather observations, peering through telescopes and microscopes, cutting tissues, injecting serums, poking thermometers here and there, timing balls rolling down inclined planes, and reflecting light back and forth between spinning mirrors set on a revolving disc.

Bacon's appeal to "induction" places the exercise of the "art of invention" in the experimental workshop and in the nature which supplies the raw materials for the experimental workshop. And at the same time, too, it calls on men fit to staff such a shop and practice such an art. It calls on the technologists of inquiry, on men like Archimedes, Galen, Galileo, Harvey, Newton, Pasteur, Faraday, Darwin and Edison. "True sons of knowledge" Bacon terms them.[20] *Natural scientists* is our common name for them today.

IV: "IDOLS" AND "FORMS"

These implications of Bacon's account of "induction" are further developed in his "doctrine of idols" and "doctrine of forms" which are inseparable in most readers' minds from the *New Organon*.

Throughout the discussion of his "new logic" Bacon frequently complains, as in *Aphorism I, xviii*, that: "The discoveries which have hitherto been made in the sciences are such as lie close to vulgar notions, scarcely beneath the surface."[21] And he usually explains this state of affairs, not only in terms of the shortcomings of common methods, but also in terms of the tremendous difficulty of the task of inquiry and the comparative inadequacy of our unaided means for undertaking it. He writes in *Aphorism I, x*, for example, that "the subtlety of nature is greater many times over than the subtlety of the senses and understanding."[22] And so, in addition to criticising the technological unsoundness of the common ways of research, he also calls attention to the natural fallibility of man's faculties, and to the peculiar complexity of the fabric of the things he explores with them.

It is primarily to take account of the first of these difficulties that Bacon introduces into the *New Organon*, as a kind of supplementary analysis of the inquirer himself, a review of the "idols", or "false notions", which complicate investigation.[23] The interesting thing about these "idols"—quaintly classified as those of "the tribe", "the cave", "the market-place", and "the theatre"—is that they do not concern so much the technological routines and instruments of inquiry, considered in their own terms, as the fitness of inquirers to make use of them. They do more than point out, as Bacon repeatedly does, that sense "fails us" in that "sometimes it gives no information" and "sometimes it gives false information".[24] They go so far as to suggest that "the minds of men are strangely possessed and beset, so that there is no true and even surface left to reflect the genuine rays of things".[25] And thus they raise questions as to the competence of men to carry through so strictly technological an undertaking as the *New Organon* interprets inquiry to be.

By his criticism of the senses, however, Bacon does not undermine the whole preceding account by confronting it with sceptical doubts similar to those to which it is proposed as an alternative.[26] He does not make insuperable obstacles of the difficulties he finds with our sight, hearing, touch, taste and smell. As he says in his sketch of the *New Organon* in the *Distribution of the Work*, "certain it is that the senses deceive, but then at the same time they supply the means of discovering their own errors; only the errors are here, the means of discovery are to seek."[27] Consequently, his criticism of the senses amounts to no more than a warning that, in scientific research, observations cannot be made as casually as men are often wont to make them. Its principal outcome is an insistence on the importance of instrumenting observation with precision devices; and of not stopping even at that, but letting such refined observations be leads to even finer experimentation. That, at least, is what seems to be implied by his statement that "the subtlety of experiments is far greater than that of the sense itself, even when assisted by exquisite instruments," and by his determination that "the office of the sense shall be only to judge of the experiment, and that the experiment itself shall judge of the thing."[27] The chief consequence of Bacon's critique of the senses is no more than a recommendation that we do such things as we have since done in reflecting light back and forth between the teeth of a spinning gear to measure its velocity unapparent to ordinary sight, or in making time exposures with cameras to discover nebulae otherwise invisible even with a telescope. Its main upshot is its challenge to inquirers to make more refined use of the technology of inquiry.

And much the same is true of the doctrine of "idols". Bacon develops it, not to confound the inquirer, but rather to put him on his guard and prepare him properly for the kind of task he has before him. As is said in *Aphorism I, xl*, "the doctrine of idols is to the Interpretation of Nature what the doctrine of the refutation of Sophisms is to common Logic."[28] Bacon discusses these categories of deception only as wayward tendencies to be avoided. His mention of them cautions the inquirer that, if he is to be fit to handle the technology of inquiry, he must be careful how he plays his own role in its highly refined processes. To escape the deceptions of the tribe, the cave, the marketplace, and the theatre, the inquirer must detach his work as much as possible from those traits of his kind, of his own peculiar personality, of his common use of language with his fellows, and of his previously elaborated conceptions, which are not consonant with the extreme impersonality of a technological procedure. He must beware of possible miscarriage due to un-technological conduct on his part. Like Bacon's critique of the senses, then, this doctrine amounts to a refinement of his account of the technology of inquiry. It is a challenge to the inquirer to come properly prepared to his work, with his understanding "thoroughly freed and cleansed"—"the entrance into the kingdom of man, founded on the sciences, being not much other than the entrance into the kingdom of heaven, whereinto none may enter except as a little child."[29] In other words, the doctrine of "idols" developed in the *New Organon*, together with the accompanying critique of the senses, is a doctrine of *technological salvation,* and therefore a refinement of the identification of the inquirer as a technologist, remarked in *Part iii* of this chapter. Since it requires of the inquirer that he be properly adjusted to take part in technological work, it is an identification of him as an agent who must be just as carefully controlled as his techniques and instruments; and thus it assimilates him to the very process itself as part of its machinery. It would not be too much even to say that the final upshot of this doctrine is to identify the inquirer as the primary instrument of inquiry.

Moreover, the parallel "doctrine of forms" has a very similar function. To cope with the formidable "subtlety" which he finds in nature, as well as with the lack of "subtlety" which he observes in human sense and understanding, Bacon makes frequent appeals in his account of the "art of discovery" to what he calls "the facts" and "things themselves."[30] Indeed, his last comment on the total project of the *Great Instauration* in the *Distribution of the Work* is the remark that "all depends on keeping the eye steadily fixed on the facts of nature and so receiving their images simply as they are."[31] The original purpose of these appeals is simply to call the investigator's attention to the world about him. It is to liberate research from the tyranny of mere ideas and books, and to direct it to the examination of the world at large. But Bacon proposes to "sink the foundations of the sciences deeper and firmer", or to "begin inquiry nearer the source than men have done heretofore";[32] and when he thus tries to come to grips with "facts" or "things themselves", he invariably writes of them as "forms".

Perhaps Bacon is occasionally loose enough in his discussion of these "forms" to leave considerable doubt as to what he actually means by them. His language with regard to them is even sometimes a little disturbing, as, for example, where he remarks in *Aphorism II, xiii*, that "the form of a thing is the very thing itself, and the thing differs from the form no otherwise than as the apparent differs from the real, or the external from the internal, or the thing in reference to man from the thing in reference to the universe."[33] In passages like these he almost seems to refer to a kind of entity altogether inaccessible to the kind of inquiry which the *New Organon* develops. If such expressions are read as *manners of speaking*, however, and in the light of others unmistakably appropriate to the entire argument of the book, they give no real difficulty. As early in the *New Organon* as his account of "abstraction" as an "idol of the tribe" Bacon rules out *super-realistic* interpretation of his "forms" by explicitly stating that "matter rather than forms should be the object of our attention, its configurations and changes of configuration, and simple action, and law of action or motion; for forms are figments of the human mind, unless you will call those laws of action, forms."[34] It is only in this last sense which he here allows as legitimate that Bacon himself uses the term constructively. "For though in nature nothing really exists besides individual bodies, performing pure individual acts according to a fixed law," he writes, "yet in philosophy this very law and the investigation, discovery and explanation of it, is the foundation as well of knowledge as of operation. And it is this law, with its clauses, that I mean when I speak of Forms; a name which I rather adopt because it has grown into use and become familiar."[35] In directing inquiry to the study of "forms", then, Bacon here directs it to the study of the regularities with which things act; he calls the inquirer's attention to the entire universe as primarily a universe of things affecting each other according to definite discoverable laws. As a phase of the preface to inquiry in which it occurs, this doctrine serves simply to identify further the context which the entire argument of the *New Organon* delimits for inquiry; for it calls attention to the evident world of nature as one which invites technological probing because it is dynamic in structure.

At the same time, moreover, this doctrine also serves to define the problems of inquiry more specifically. *Book II* of the *New Organon* begins with the generalization: "On a given body to generate and super-induce a new nature or natures, is the work and aim of Human Power. Of a given nature to discover the form is the work and aim of Human Knowledge."[36] But in view of all that has been said above, making the task of knowledge the discovery of forms is equivalent to defining the problems of inquiry in technological terms, which, of course, is no more than appropriate to the whole procedure of the account of the "art of invention" out of which it arises. After identifying the agents of inquiry as its technologists and delimiting its context as the nature which is the proper working place of such technologists, Bacon quite inevitably finds himself confronting problems which, although tying together with those of social organization, are at closest approach chiefly concerned with ways of setting up the techniques and instruments of research.[37] The most important difficulties which confront Bacon in this work all center about such matters as special techniques in laboratory procedure[37] and such devices as vacuum chambers,[38] high temperature furnaces and low temperature refrigerators,[39] compression machinery; and potentially, electroscopes, centrifuges, vaccines, cameras, "electric eyes", and spectroscopes. In short, the difficulties Bacon singles out as primary for inquiry here are practically the same as confront all technological undertakings, be they so widely different as those of growing better crops, manufacturing goods on a larger scale, constructing stronger bridges with less material, or prolonging life. At bottom they are the problems of how to get a physical leverage in things so as better to be able to manipulate them.

Then finally, the doctrine of "forms" serves also to interpret the issue of inquiry in comparable terms. The parallelism between "Human Power" over bodies and "Human Knowledge" of forms, with which *Book II* of the *New Organon* begins, soon converges into an identity. It is in defining "forms" as laws of action, that Bacon arrives at his famous pronouncement, "From the discovery of Forms . . . results truth in speculation and freedom in operation",[40] and hence at the conclusion that "What in operation is the most useful, that in knowledge is most true."[41] Nor should it be surprising that this doctrine returns us to the same formula as the survey of learning, equating knowledge and power. *Book II* of the *New Organon,* which is the one mainly devoted to whole question of "forms", bears the subtitle: "Concerning the Interpretation of Nature *and the Kingdom of Man*", and like the *Advancement* and the *De Dignitate* it constantly repeats that the "main

object is to make nature serve the business and conveniences of man".[42]
Technological power is social power, with perhaps this single difference: the ways of man being many and strange, his business need not
always be his fellow's welfare. His command of nature may possibly be
power to build railroads, to restore tissue, to check epidemics, to send
music broadcast, or simply to measure the galactic system or to see the
other side of the moon. And then again, it may be power to sink ships,
to bomb cities, and to gas civilian populations. But regardless of its
social good, ill, or indifference, the power which the *New Organon* interprets to be the outcome of inquiry is nevertheless the power "to conquer nature by works"—the power of technological competence.

To sum up, then, we find from this examination of Bacon's prefatory
account of the art of discovery in terms of a survey of methods and discussion of "induction", "idols", and "forms", that it tends to—

1. Put inquiry in question *against criteria of technological efficiency*.
2. Identify the agents of inquiry *as the natural scientists who are its
   technologists and its primary instruments*.
3. Delimit the context of inquiry *as the familiar world of dynamic
   things subject to general laws of action and to exploration by
   technological ways and means*.
4. Single out the problems of inquiry *as those of how to devise and
   apply technological ways and means to the discovery of controlling laws of action*.
5. Interpret the issue of inquiry *as power in the sense of technological command of things through control of their laws of action*.

V: MODELS—INSTITUTIONAL AND MECHANICAL

Despite the fact that the *New Organon* is committed very largely to
the general notions of the *Advancement of Learning*, then, it gives those
notions quite a different development which results in different conclusions. And it is instructive to note that such differences as thus emerge
between the two undertakings are largely expressions of different controlling ideas which underlie their very conceptions.

The commonsense observation which prompts the first, we observed
in the preceding chapter, is that the general undertaking of inquiry is
profoundly affected by the form of its organization and the character
of its sponsorship: hence the approach to inquiry in the *Advancement*
and *De Dignitate* chiefly as a matter of learning institutionally con-

ceived, and hence its result in a proclamation of the social enterprise of learning. The difference of the underlying ideology of the *New Organon*, however, is clear from Bacon's very first reference to the "art of discovery" in his review of "intellectual arts" in the *Advancement*. In deploring its deficiency in his day, he is moved to exclaim: "And like as the West Indies had never been discovered if the use of *the mariner's needle* had not been first discovered, though the one be vast regions, and the other a small motion; so it cannot be found strange if sciences be no farther discovered, if the art of invention and discovery hath been passed over."[43] Here Bacon writes of his proposed "art" on analogy to a guiding mechanical device; and this is not due to any chance imagery. Similar language reappears again throughout the *New Organon*, as, for example, in the famous *Aphorism I, ii*, which reads: "Neither the naked hand nor the understanding left to itself can affect much. It is *by instruments and help* that the work is done, *which are as wanted for the understanding as for the hand*. And as *the instruments of the hand* either give motion or guide it, so *the instruments of the mind* supply either suggestions for the understanding or cautions."[44]

So fundamental, indeed, is mechanical analogy to the very conception of the *New Organon* that Bacon employs it in the *Preface* to introduce the fundamental idea of the whole work. In there comparing the general task of inquiry to that of raising a huge obelisk, he likens unmethodical inquiry to men's attempts to do the job with their bare hands, and usual methodical ways to their attempts to do it by increasing the number of workers, by using only the strongest ones, and by exercising and oiling their muscles. But his own recommendation is to use such aids as levers and pulleys; and the suggestion carries over to the general project of inquiry. "Certainly if *in things mechanical* men had set to work with their naked hands," he writes, "without *the help or force of instruments*, just as in things intellectual they have set to work with little else than the naked forces of the understanding, very small would the matters have been which, even with their best efforts applied in conjunction, they could have attempted or accomplished." Whence he arrives at the conclusion: "There remains but one course for the recovery of a sound and healthy condition,—namely, that the entire work of the understanding be commenced afresh, and the mind itself be from the very outset not left to take its own course, but guided at every step; and the business be done *as if by machinery*."[45]

Accordingly, just as Bacon's earlier work ends in proclaiming the enterprise of learning, the *New Organon* ends in calling attention to the technology of research by putting inquiry in question, identifying its agents, delimiting its context, singling out its problems, and interpreting its issue, all in the technological terms appropriate to a mechanical conception of its procedure. The foregoing analysis must be taken as a first piece of evidence that there is no unique way of prefacing inquiry, and that there is no unique set of conclusions or unique ground of appeal in doing so. The attempt develops to be one which admits of such variation at least as is here illustrated.

Moreover, as another contribution to our understanding of prefatory literature, this analysis also helps us better to appreciate the variety of ways in which such writings can serve critical functions of historical consequence. Bacon's *New Organon* not only contributes to the program of his *Great Instauration* in its positive aspects, but also increases its effectiveness as an instrument for undermining the prevailing order in learning. Considering only the chief tradition under attack, we may note that Scholasticism was not only a function of a social regime, but also a way of inquiry; and that it was therefore founded, not only on the assumptions outlined in the last chapter, but also on others of a *methodological* character. As Bacon viewed it at least, Scholasticism not only found the broad justification of inquiry in its role as a supplement to faith and mystical intuition in bringing about man's salvation, but also, on closer approach, put its procedures in question in terms of their appropriateness to the discernment of the structure of eternal truth underlying this work. Not only did it assume as its proper agents the scholars of the Church; but when it considered these men in their technical roles, it identified them principally as skilled dialecticians. Not only did it assume as the broad context of inquiry the world viewed as the setting of the drama of man's salvation; but it also delimited the part of this world most significant for inquiry as, on the one hand, a structure of "eternal truth" embodied in or adumbrated by it, and on the other, seeds or first principles of this truth to be found in the traditions of wisdom deriving from the scriptures, from the ancients, or from subsequent authority, and in faith and the dictates of commonsense. Not only did it assume as the broad problems of inquiry those of how to help achieve men's salvation through reason; but it also viewed the technicalities of these broad problems as concerning, first, the ferreting out of the first principles of truth from their sources in authority, faith, and commonsense, and second, the dialectical development of these first principles by chains of reason to include them within the structure of the total system of truth. And finally, not only did it assume as the broad end of inquiry the enjoyment of eternal life; but more specifically, it attempted to achieve this end through a kind of approximation to the system of eternal verity that might produce understanding and contemplation, foreshadowing the beatitude of salvation, and so turning men's attention to God as the proper object of all their study.[46] So long as these assumptions of scholasticism as to the technique of inquiry were unchallenged, it still retained a certain validity no matter what was said about other aspects of it. As Bacon himself observes: "Demonstrations truly are in effect the philosophies themselves and the sciences. For such as *they* are . . . established, such are the systems of philosophy and the contemplations which follow."[47] Despite the tremendous undermining effect of his account of the enterprise of learning on scholasticism, therefore, he had still to challenge its assumptions as to the method of inquiry before he could expect its superstructure to collapse altogether.

But it is now apparent that this is precisely what the *New Organon* does. In this treatise Bacon demands "works and inventions" of inquiry, rather than a system of eternal truth. He calls on technologists to pursue it, rather than on documentary scholars and dialecticians. He places it in the context of experiments and dynamic events, rather than in one of traditions of wisdom and schemes of ideas. He confronts it with problems of systematizing and instrumenting exploration of the natural world, rather than with those of conning manuscripts, probing the faith of the soul, or linking syllogisms. And he announces the outcome of the whole undertaking to be power to control the forces which affect this life, rather than contemplation which prepares for another life to come. Consequently, in placing the technique of inquiry on a purely technological basis the *New Organon* does more than hold up the scholastic tradition to scorn on a number of particular scores. Not only does it in passing ridicule general scholastic attitudes, but in its general outcome it sets up the working routines of inquiry in terms which make scholastic ways appear wholly irrelevant. In calling the inquirer to an entirely new conception of the nature of his task, it takes the very underpinning from beneath scholasticism by setting up the routines of research on a basis which will not sustain it. And needless to say, the same argument is equally destructive to the other traditions which it challenged.

VI: THE FABLE OF THE "NEW ATLANTIS"

Another generalization suggested by the analysis of Bacon's *New Organon* is the conclusion that prefaces to inquiry differently suggested, differently attempted, and differently controlled, need not necessarily be inconsistent or incompatible with one another. It is quite clear from the foregoing expositions that putting inquiry in question in terms of its productivity or efficiency as a technological way of doing things is not fundamentally different from putting it in question in terms of its dignity or usefulness as a social way of doing things. Technological ways and means need not be regarded as any other than social ways and means more closely examined. Any doubt which the *New Organon* may leave as to this point, Bacon's fable of the *New Atlantis* readily removes.

This Utopian idyll presents an imaginative picture of the whole of the *Great Instauration* as it might ideally be realized. And to take account of that phase of the larger project to which the *New Organon* is devoted, it tells of the pursuit of inquiry with the aid of "preparations and instruments" such as "large and deep caves of several depths," "burials in several earths," "high towers," "great lakes both salt and fresh", "artificial wells and fountains," "fair and large baths of several mixtures for the cure of diseases", "large and various orchards and gardens", "parks and enclosures of all sorts of beasts and birds", "divers mechanical arts, and stuffs made by them", "furnaces of great diversities and that keep great diversities of heats", "perspective houses for demonstrations of lights and radiations", similar "sound-houses", and "perfume-houses", "engine-houses where are prepared engines and instruments for all sorts of motions", and "a mathematical house where are represented all instruments, as well of geometry as astronomy, exquisitely made", etc., etc.[48] In short, the story tells of the pursuit of inquiry with all the means of "induction" available which Bacon can imagine as necessary to the technological exercise of his "art of invention".

But where does Bacon locate this ideal set-up for the instrumented probing of the wide world? Even for the purposes of this purely fabulous account, he places it in an ideal society on an unknown continent in the Pacific Ocean. All these "preparations and instruments" are the equipment of "Solomon's House", the "noblest foundation" in a system of institutions which all depend on it for their well being.[49] The kingdom itself, moreover, is most conspicuously ideal in its relationship to learning. It is one which sends ships to the rest of the world "whose errand is only to give us knowledge of the affairs and state of those countries to which they were designed; and especially of the sciences, arts, manufactures, and inventions of all the world; and withal to bring unto us books, instruments, and patterns in every kind."[50] Its trade with others is "not for gold, silver, or jewels; nor for silks; nor for spices; nor any other commodity of matter; but only for God's first creature, which was light".[51] And its "merchants of light", who carry on this trade in learning, are fellows of "Solomon's House", which conducts such import business only as a minor part of its general work as the "lantern" of the kingdom. This institute of technological research is intimately part and parcel of the learned society which it serves. Its "Merchants of Light", "Depradators", "Pioneers", "Lamps", "Compilers", "Inoculators", "Dowry-men", and "Interpreters", are both citizens of the state which sustains such an institution and the technologists whose work makes such a state possible.

Surely, then, the technological roles of these men are not inconsistent with their social roles. Their technical ways of going about their work can be judged in terms of the more special technological criteria appropriate to them, without our losing sight of the broader social criteria with which they can also be required to comply. The former are merely the latter viewed in a more restricted way. The nature examined in the physical, chemical, or biological laboratory is not discontinuous with the nature which has society as its most prominent feature. It is simply this same nature more closely or more specially viewed. And likewise, the technological conception of the problems of inquiry, and the technological interpretation of its issue are perfectly consistent with their social conception and interpretation. In each case the one is but a more special, or technical, view of the other.

Bacon's surveys of learning and accounts of the art of invention, although quite distinct as prefaces to inquiry, therefore, tend mutually to illuminate each other. A study of each helps us to understand the other better, for each illustrates the same basic attempt in different terms. And realization of this fact brings us to the more general conclusion that, however much some prefatory accounts of inquiry may conflict with each other, their incompatibility is not inherent in the general nature of such undertakings. Even when they are widely different in conception, they can jointly contribute to a common task of clarification, not only of the broader undertaking to which they point, but also of each other as prefaces to it.

VII: THE TECHNOLOGY OF RESEARCH

Besides illustrating further the kind of development and control of which the preface to inquiry admits, the kind of critical function it can perform, and the kind of relation possible between different illustrations of it, this analysis of the *New Organon* also demonstrates further that the preface to inquiry need not become involved in the difficulties which have been seen in *Chapter I* to confuse propaedeutic preliminaries to inquiry.

In calling a halt in the regular processes of natural investigation to take account of its technological organization, Bacon raises no more difficulties than in calling such a halt to take account of its social organization. Just as his discussion of the enterprise of learning is addressed to a familiar state of affairs in society, his account of the technology of research is addressed to a familiar state of affairs in the experimental laboratory. The action it proposes is faced only with difficulties that are practical in the sense of those which face the earlier proposal. The discussion it arouses cannot be regarded as a sidetracking of its purpose, because its undertaking is obviously a step in the actual procedure of the regular course of inquiry. Bacon himself frequently points this out in describing the manner in which he expects his "art of discovery" to develop. Despite his concern to have it formulated as much as possible in the second preparatory phase of his great instauration, he is nevertheless careful to indicate that he regards its technique to be one which must be worked out, not only by forethought, but also by progressive development in inquiry proper. He assures his reader, for example, that "he must be a trifler and a man of narrow mind who thinks that the perfect art of invention of knowledge can be devised and propounded all at once; and that then it needs only to be set at work. Let men be assured that the solid and true arts of invention increase as inventions themselves increase; so that when a man first enters into the pursuit of knowledge, he may have some useful precepts of invention; but when he has made further advances in that knowledge, he may and ought to devise new precepts of invention, to lead him the better to that which lies beyond."[52] Had Bacon subsequently arrived at the last phase of his "Instauration" which was again to take up the regular course of inquiry, then, he could have regarded it as finally "legitimate, chaste, and severe" only in the sense that it would presumably have its social sponsorship better organized and its techniques better planned, better instrumented, and better illustrated.

Moreover, this study of the *New Organon* also illustrates further the fact that, although a preface to inquiry may not supply a metaphysical touchstone to transform all controversy to agreement, it may, like the *Advancement of Learning* and *De Dignitate et Augmentis Scientiarum*, offer a sensible alternative to the less fruitful kinds of dispute. It is significant that in his very first announcement of the art of invention in the *Advancement*, Bacon discusses its objects as "of two kinds, much differing; the one of *Arts* and *Sciences*: and the other of *Speech* and *Arguments*".[53] The latter of these two, he then says, is not really invention at all, but only a kind of "recovering or resummoning of that which we already know",[54] and he reports it as well enough developed. The other, however, he reports as seriously deficient; and so, it is to the art of inventing arts and sciences, as an explicit alternative to the art of inventing arguments, that he dedicates the *New Organon*.[55] This is quite appropriate, for just as his account of the enterprise of learning suggests that debaters turn their energies to cooperation in the study of matters previously only talked about, his account of the technology of inquiry suggests that, when they do thus get together, they thenceforth proceed with techniques which will minimize the intrusion of their fretful, wishful, contentious personalities. And it is a matter of historical fact that the technological approach to inquiry has done as much as its organization as a social enterprise to turn hairsplitting to investigation, and so to turn debates about the possibility of knowledge to studies of its implications.

Some may remark, of course, that for all his enthusiasm for technology, Bacon himself was so little apt at it to make practically no worthy contribution of his own to its actual development. And the observation is sound enough; it would be hard indeed to point out many specific technical advances for which the real technologists of inquiry have been indebted to Bacon. But this fact is not very important here. Prefacing inquiry is, after all, quite different from pursuing it in the ordinary sense. The important thing for our purpose is the inescapable fact that the *New Organon* does develop the total conception of the technology of inquiry which has proven abundantly fruitful when worked on by men more competent than Bacon to follow up his suggestions. The general undertaking of inquiry does have a technological aspect which has been overlooked as often as its social aspect. And whether or not the *New Organon* contributes much to our actual technological skills, it does call attention forcefully to the role of these skills in all research.

Inquiry is an activity which can be criticized in terms of technological criteria, which does require controlled and instrumented ways and means, which does require workers competent to use such ways and means, which does confront a world that yields to probing by such ways and means, which can result in the power of technological control of things. And it is part, at least, of the power of the *New Organon* as a preface to inquiry that it gives strong and significant expression to these facts.

4

DESCARTES ON THE WAY OF CERTAINTY

I: A HANDBOOK OF SCIENTIFIC PRACTICE

ALTHOUGH Francis Bacon's prefatory writings express the point of view toward inquiry characteristic of epistemology, we cannot presume that they were primarily intended as contributions to that discipline. In the course of their arguments Bacon raises the issues typical of the theory of knowledge without the conscious purpose of doing so. Only a critical analysis of what their attempt involves brings them within the scope of a study such as this and restates them in terms of the more technical terminology we usually associate with such literature. Consequently, on now turning to the related works of René Descartes, we are considering in detail for the first time a body of writings in which the formal theory of knowledge is explicitly addressed and systematically developed in its own terms. But before discussing those of Descartes' writings of which this is most true, we may profitably examine first his early *Rules for Directing the Mind*, which serves somewhat as a transition from unpremeditated to fully deliberate epistemological speculation, and which consequently is most instructive as to the considerations which gave rise to the latter in the modern era.[1]

Like Bacon's *Advancement* and *De Dignitate*, Descartes' *Rules* introduces the kind of broad perspective from which we are here viewing matters of inquiry simply by directing attention to the total enterprise of learning rather than to any special limited field of investigation. Its very first precept, "that the aim of studies ought to be to direct the mind so as to make solid and true judgements concerning *everything* which presents itself to it,"[2] is based on the conviction "that all the sciences are so inter-connected that it is easier to learn them all at once than to isolate one from the others; so that if one wishes seriously to search for truth, one ought not to choose the study of any particular science, for all are bound together and dependent on each other."[3] And its insistence that the "discipline" which it expounds is one which "ought to contain the first rudiments of human reason, and to serve to extract from any subject matter whatsoever the truths which it contains,"[4] is provoked by such observations as that "nearly everyone studies with the greatest care the customs of men, the properties of plants, the movements of the heavenly bodies, the transformation of metals, and other similar objects of study, whereas hardly anyone gives thought to commonsense, or that universal wisdom, although all other things ought to be valued less on their account than because they contribute something to it."[5]

Like Bacon's *New Organon,* moreover, Descartes' *Rules* thenceforth approaches inquiry as a unified undertaking through a generalized discussion of the manner in which individual researches are carried on. In *Aphorism II, ix* Bacon had stated the main issue between his account of the technology of research and what he found in "the play books of philosophical systems and perverted rules of demonstration" to be "only as to the way". "For as the saying is," he had explained, "the lame man who keeps to the right road outstrips the runner who takes a wrong one. Nay, it is obvious that when a man runs the wrong way, the more active he is the further he will go astray."[6] But this is precisely the idea which is central in Descartes' *Rules.* We may recall that in the first part of his *Discourse on Method,* Descartes almost paraphrases the foregoing quotation from Bacon where he writes that "it is not enough to have a good mind, but the main thing is to apply it well . . . ; those who proceed only very slowly get a good deal further ahead if they always follow the right road, than those who speed and depart from it."[7] And it appears that it is primarily in terms of such a consideration of the way in which inquiry is gone about that Descartes addresses his *Rules for Directing the Mind* to the discussion of its total project. The fourth precept, which reads "that method is necessary to the search for truth",[8] is as fundamental as the first to the definition of the project of the entire book. Descartes writes in its explanation that "if we are ignorant of something which we are capable of knowing, that is due either to our not having discovered any way leading to such knowledge, or else to our having fallen into the contrary error;"[9] whereupon he adds that what he understands by "method" is "certain and simple rules, the rigorous observance of which will prevent one ever from supposing as true that which is false, and will enable the mind, without consuming itself in useless efforts, but always, on the contrary, gradually increasing its science, to arrive at the true knowledge of all things to which it can attain."[10] By "method" he means simply: precepts that direct our inquiring *along a way,* μετὰ ὁδός, which brings us to its proper completion. And it is to the exposition of such a "method" that the bulk of the treatise is devoted.

So far as its conscious purpose is concerned, therefore, Descartes' *Rules* is simply an attempt to instruct the investigator as to how to go about his work. Far from being an attempt to promote an academic discipline, it is a volume of advice to the inquirer as to the ropes of his job, a manual to guide him in the routines of his workaday tasks. At bottom there is little essential difference between its "rules" and the "aphorisms" of Bacon's *New Organon*. Both relate to the discipline of research as handbooks of scientific practice.

II: THE CRITERION OF "CERTAINTY"

Notwithstanding the very great similarity of conception and structure between Bacon's *New Organon* and Descartes' *Rules*, however, they differ very greatly as to the specific developments they undergo and the specific results at which they arrive. Descartes, it seems, was a man of a very different stamp from Bacon; and his peculiarities of intellectual habit and habitation are immediately reflected in the kind of criticisms which he tends to make of the scholarly practices of his day.

The object of attack being the same, some of the critical remarks in the *Rules* are of course almost identical with corresponding ones in the *New Organon*. At the beginning of *Rule iv*, for example, Descartes comments on the careless, unsystematic habits of the experimentalists of his day in words which might easily be mistaken for Bacon's. But whereas the fundamental criteria against which Bacon eventually evaluates the work of all other investigators in the *New Organon* concern its technological efficiency or productivity, Descartes' chief complaint here is that it is somehow "obscure" or "ill assured". At times his objections take the mild form of complaints against obscurantism in works reporting on the results of investigations.[11] But when he follows up these charges, he explains them in terms of the failure of inquirers to keep to the "certain" and "assured" in the first place. Descartes attributes the confusion which he finds in the literature of inquiry to "the fact that everyone allows himself to affirm things by divination in an obscure question," and to "the fact that it is a great deal easier to make conjectures on any question whatsoever than to get at the truth itself in any single question however easy it may be."[12] This deliberate courting of ambiguity, moreover, strikes him as thoroughly invalidating the whole super-structure of learning. "The chief reason why in ordinary philosophy one finds nothing sufficiently evident and certain to

be above controversy," he explains, "is that savants, not willing to recognize clear and certain things, have first off dared to affirm obscure and
unknown things, at which they arrived only by probable conjectures;
and that then, gradually coming to have complete faith in these and to
mix them indifferently with true and evident things, they have ended
by not being able to conclude anything which did not seem to depend
on some obscure proposition, and which, for this reason, was not uncertain."[13]

The question which naturally occurs to the present-day reader of
such criticisms, of course, is what Descartes meant by the "clarity" and
"certainty" he found so lacking in the erudition of his age. Descartes
himself gives no direct answer, but we can have little doubt of what it
should have been when we consider what remains unaffected by his
sweeping critique. Despite the brilliant promise of the mathematics
of the early seventeenth century, it was still so little developed that
Bacon could almost entirely overlook it in his ostensibly comprehensive
survey of the "intellectual globe". Yet Descartes restates his second
"rule", that "we must occupy ourselves only with object of which our
minds are capable of a certain and indubitable knowledge,"[14] as an insistence that "those who seek the road to truth should not concern themselves with any object of which they cannot have a certainty equal to
that of the demonstrations of arithmetic and geometry."[15] And his
critique of the traditions of inquiry, most of which occurs between these
two statements, is summed up by the conclusion that "if our calculation
is correct, of all the sciences already known there remains only arithmetic and geometry to which the observation of this rule reduces us."[16]

The main issue, then, which Descartes raises at the outset of the
Rules concerns, not the social worth or technological efficiency of inquiry, but its mathematical perspicuity. This preface to inquiry centers
about the theme of *mathematical* "certainty". Ostensibly its instructions
to the inquirer are instructions as to how he can, and must, achieve
the mathematician's self-assurance in his work.

III: "INTUITION" AND "DEDUCTION"

In proclaiming the way of inquiry to be the mathematically certain
way, Descartes does not of course intend that it should be confined to
the special field of mathematics. Indeed, at places in the *Rules* he writes
of arithmetic and geometry as very trivial subjects unworthy of much

attention, reconciling this disparagement with his account of them as the only satisfactory science of his day by the explanation that the full possibilities of clear and evident knowledge are not even suspected by most savants because they have never taken the trouble to search it out. And accordingly, he attempts to develop his distinction between the ways of certainty and of uncertainty in more general terms by explaining the former to be "intuitive" and "deductive", and the latter merely "experiential".

But what do "intuition" and "deduction" mean as Descartes here writes of them? What do they lead to as he develops his recommendation of them to the inquirer? We may recall that, as an alternative to the kind of inquiry to which he objects in the *New Organon*, Bacon had appealed to "experience" and "induction"; and we may recall too that in Bacon's development of these conceptions they lead chiefly to a broader, freer, better controlled, and better instrumented examination of the whole wide world about us. What comparable undertaking, then, do Descartes' appeals to "intuition" and "deduction" suggest? In the course of his explanation of *Rule iii* Descartes takes the trouble to define both these terms very carefully. He tells us that by "intuition" he means "not the changing testimony of the senses or the deceptive judgement of a lying imagination, but the conception of a pure and attentive mind, so simple and so distinct that no doubt remains concerning what we understand by it."[17] And in the same place he also tells us that he means by "deduction" the "operation by which we understand all that is necessarily concluded from other things known with certainty."[18] These definitions, however, are merely *formal*. They put the terms defined into other words, but those other words in turn need just as much *pragmatic* definition as the original ones. They still leave unanswered the question of what, in use and outcome, the appeals to "intuition" and to "deduction" in the *Rules* really amount to.

Descartes' illustrations of the use of these "operations" are far more instructive in this respect than his definitions. His most characteristic examples of "intuition" center about the inquirer's knowledge of such matters as that a triangle is bounded by only three lines, that a sphere is bounded by only one surface, and that 2 and 2, and 3 and 1, being both equal to 4, must be equal to each other.[19] And since to amplify his meaning of "deduction" Descartes refers simply to long series of such "intuitions" reviewed in sequence[19], we gather that he offers the actual procedures of geometers and arithmeticians as the best available working illustrations of what he means by both. Moreover, the remaining rules devoted specifically to this matter tell us little more of importance about it. Except for some further mathematical examples and a few untypical digressions to be considered in the next chapter, they merely manipulate terms already introduced. Despite Descartes' pleas that we be persuaded to the contrary, his appeal to "intuition" and "deduction" returns us eventually to the distinction which introduces it—the distinction between certain and uncertain ways of inquiry as respectively mathematical and non-mathematical.

Consequently, these appeals not only reaffirm the essentially mathematical significance of Descartes' basic criterion of "certainty", but they also have the effect of identifying the inquirers who are to use his handbook, and of delimiting the context of their work, in comparable terms. Since the only significant illustrations which Descartes gives for "intuition" and "deduction" are mathematical, in calling upon inquirers strictly to confine themselves to such means, he requires them to regard themselves as primarily mathematicians. And likewise, since the only significant objects he points to for such treatment are of the same kind, he meanwhile confines these mathematical inquirers to the range of the mathematical sciences, strictly excluding from their pale and ken, not only most of the traditions of inquiry, but also most of the frontiers of natural exploration which Bacon had so enthusiastically advertised in his *Advancement of Learning* and *New Organon*.

By the same token, moreover, this beginning also commits the rest of the text to singling out the problems of inquiry and interpreting its outcome in similar mathematical terms. But the gradual steps by which these developments actually take place in the remaining rules, despite Descartes' strenuous attempts to broaden their scope and relevance, are so highly instructive as to the fated character of the whole work that we may profitably trace them in some detail.

IV: "PERFECT AND IMPERFECT QUESTIONS"

Towards the end of the explanation of *Rule xii*, which completes the first part of the treatise, Descartes makes a second attempt to establish greater generality of application for his "method". "In order that the linking of our precepts shall escape no one," he writes here, "we divide all that can be known into simple propositions and questions."[20] "Simple propositions," he adds, are those which "present themselves spontaneously, and cannot be sought out", wherefore the first twelve rules already expounded, are the only ones necessary for their study.[20] Then, "as for questions," he continues, "some are perfectly understood, even when we do not know their solution: . . . while others are imperfectly understood"; whereupon he announces that the next twelve rules of the treatise are intended for the study of the first group and the last twelve for the study of the second.[21] Thus, by these new distinctions Descartes restates his "intuitive and deductive" way of "certainty" as a systematic way of dealing with three different kinds of issues; namely: "simple propositions", and "perfect" and "imperfect questions". What, now, do these new terms mean? And what do they add to our understanding of the *Rules* as an account of a "certain" way of inquiry which is more than mathematical?

As in the case of his formal definitions of "intuition" and "deduction", those which Descartes gives of "perfect" and "imperfect questions" afford the reader very little notion of what the conceptions actually involve. For example, in his explanation of *Rule xiii*, which states in substance that the advice of the preceding rules should be applied to "questions we understand perfectly",[22] he writes simply: (1) that "in every question there is necessarily something unknown, for otherwise it would be pointless to raise it": (2) that "this unknown must be indicated in some way or other, for otherwise there would be nothing to determine us to seek it rather than something else"; and (3), that "it (the unknown) cannot be so designated except by something known".[22] Then to distinguish further his two main types of "questions" he adds that "in order for a question to be perfect, we want it to be completely determined, so that nothing more is sought than what can be deduced from what is given;"[23] from which we gather that, if what is sought cannot be deduced from what is given, the question is "imperfect". But all of this is quite vague and general. We can make of it either nothing at all or almost anything we please.

Again, however, Descartes' use of his language gives it a more definite signification. At the beginning of his explanation of *Rule xiv* he begins to consider more specifically the relations between the "known" and "unknown" matters which figure in his definitions of "questions"; and the outcome of this is the generalization that "all knowledge which is not acquired by pure and simple intuition of an individual object is acquired by the comparison of two or more objects among themselves."[24] Thus the problem of solving "questions" is reduced to one of making "simple comparisons" between things. When their relations are so obvious as to be inescapable, Descartes writes, such comparisons are the mind's natural response. But when these relations are so complicated to begin with as not to be obvious immediately, it is the task of methodical investigation to reduce them to so simple a form as to make simple comparisons possible.[24] "Nearly all the work of human reason consists in preparing for this operation (of comparison)" he says; "for, when it is clear and simple, there is no need of any help of method, but only of the light of nature to have the intuition of truth which it reveals."[24] And the "comparisons" which he thus makes the *atomic units of knowledge,* so to speak, he in turn develops as "proportions", construing their difficulties to be difficulties of reducing "proportions of inequality" to "proportions of equality".[25]

But this reduction of the comparisons by which knowledge is said to be acquired to terms of proportionality has the effect of making the first major step in the "methodical" solution of "questions" a reduction of matters to quantitative form. "Let us note," Descartes continues, "that nothing can be brought to this equality except those things which involve comparisons of *greater* or *lesser,* and that these things are included under the name of magnitudes; so that, once we have abstracted from any subject the terms of a difficulty according to the preceding rule, we understand that we have nothing further to be concerned with except magnitudes in general."[24] It turns out that the technique of handling "perfect questions" is primarily the technique of handling mathematical problems, since "perfect" questions are simply those which, when stated in their essentials, are quantitative in form to begin with.

Quite inevitably, therefore, the second dozen precepts of the *Rules* tend to become successively more and more mathematical in character[26]: *Rule xiv* itself tells us that perfect questions ought to be referred to plain diagrams in order to be much more distinctly understood by the intellect;"[27] *Rules xv* and *xvi* tell how these diagrams are to be drawn;[28] *Rule xvii* explains the algebraic device of supposing unknown quantities to be known and then developing the consequences; *Rule xviii* explains the geometric representation of the basic mathematical processes of addition, subtraction, multiplication and division;[29] and *Rules xix* to *xxi* state basic theorems of the theory of equations. These last precepts, indeed, except for a few unimportant technical details, are practically indistinguishable from corresponding parts of the *Geometry* which Descartes published as a purely mathematical treatise some nine years later. And thus it appears beyond any doubt that Descartes' account of the "intuitive" and "deductive" way of certainty as a way of treating "perfect questions" leads exclusively to the study of quantities in general by the devices of what we now call *analytic geometry*. The "perfection" of his "perfect questions" consists solely in their perfectly mathematical form.

What, then, are we to make of his proposal to treat of "imperfect questions" in the wholly unattempted third part of the *Rules?* Even though numbers and figures reappear so persistently in precepts *xiii* and *xxi*, Descartes still insists on minimizing the importance of such subject matters. Despite his concession that these maxims are more appropriate for the study of mathematics than for any other science, he adds that their utility is also so great for the study of a "higher wisdom" that he does not hesitate to say "that this part of our method has not been invented to resolve mathematical problems; but rather, that mathematics hardly ought to be learned except to cultivate this method."[30] What does the account of "imperfect questions" lead to, then, beyond the subject matter of the *pure* mathematics of "quantities in general"?

The suspicion arises that, whatever the concern of "imperfect questions", their study must depend somehow on the mathematics of "perfect questions";[31] and the nature of this dependence is quite clearly indicated in certain generalizations which emerge in the course of the explanation of *Rule xiv.* "It must be noted," Descartes there remarks, "that every time we deduce something unknown from something known, we do not thereby find a new kind of being; but all that happens is that the knowledge which we have is extended so as to show us that the thing sought participates somehow or other in the nature of those things which are given in the question."[32] Thus, for example, if there exists in the magnet "some kind of being of which our understandings have never perceived the like", then "we cannot possibly even hope to know it by reasoning," since to do so would require "either some new sense or a divine mind".[33] And so, Descartes concludes: "All these things already noted, such as extension, figure, motion, and others similar . . . are known in different subjects by the same idea—for we do not imagine the shape of a crown any differently whether it be silver or gold—and this common idea is transferred from one subject to another only by means of a simple comparison by which we affirm whether the thing sought is in some respect similar, identical, or equal to the thing given; so that in all reasoning it is only by comparison that we know the truth precisely."[33] What Descartes suggests in this passage is that, no matter what subject matters we investigate, we can gain genuine knowledge of them only in so far as we can construe them in terms of relationships among certain of our basic conceptions best illustrated off hand by those of "extension, figure, movement, and others similar." And this suggestion is followed immediately by his account, already reviewed, of how all knowledge not absolutely elementary derives from comparisons ultimately taking the form of quantitative equalities; which in turn is followed by the exposition of his famous "theory of dimensions", the main point of which is that any aspect of things, in so far as it is measurable, may be placed on a par with its size and subjected to essentially the same kind of quantitative treatment.[34] Consequently, we can infer from Descartes' parenthetical remark that "all imperfect questions can be reduced to perfect questions,"[35] only that all "questions" must eventually be reduced to mathematical form if they are to be considered at all.

It seems that, just as Descartes' "perfect questions" prove to be "perfect" chiefly in so far as they are perfectly mathematical, his "imperfect questions" prove to be "imperfect" chiefly in so far as they are imperfectly mathematical, but mathematical ultimately just the same. By his account of "perfect questions" as those of a kind of pure mathematics, he commits the treatment of the only other kind of questions he allows to becoming a kind of applied mathematics, or mathematical physics, having the same relationship to his treatise on *The World,* or to *Books II, III* and *IV* of his *Principles of Philosophy,* that his account of "perfect questions" has to his *Geometry.* The "higher wisdom" which he promises the student who will put up with the pain of studying mathematics is nothing more than a further study of the same basic science as it can be variously applied.

This last phase of the *Rules,* then, unmistakably singles out the crucial problems which confront the inquirer as those primarily mathematical in character. It fixes the inquirer's eye on the quantitative aspect of the world, challenging him to approach nature as a context of things of which the most significant aspects are their measurable "dimensions" which can be explored successfully, not so much by being probed by technological devices under the auspices of institutions of learning, as by being referred to diagrams and equations which can be developed algebraically. We may finally conclude that the advice which Descartes gives in his *Rules* as to the way of certainty tends, at bottom, to—

1. Put inquiry as a general project in question *by measuring it against criteria of mathematical certainty.*
2. Identify the agents of inquiry *primarily as mathematicians.*
3. Delimit the context of inquiry as, *most importantly, nature in its quantitative dimensions or mathematical aspect.*
4. Single out the problems of inquiry *as problems primarily of seizing on the quantitative dimensions of things and developing them mathematically.*
5. Interpret the issue of inquiry *as knowledge ultimately expressible in terms of mathematical formulae.*

V: ANOTHER NOTE ON ORIGINS

In the foregoing analysis many indications have been encountered that the *Rules* is as fundamentally controlled by mathematical conceptions as Bacon's prefatory writings are controlled by institutional and mechanical conceptions. Even its basic criterion of "certainty", not to mention its notions of "intuition and deduction", "perfect and imperfect questions", finally depend for their very intelligibility on illustrations in terms of numbers and figures. Descartes' reference to arithmetic and geometry as "a kind of envelope" of his "science"[36], therefore, may be readily translated into the language of this study to the effect that mathematics constitutes the model under the control of which he formulates his general account of the "certain" way to undertake all inquiry.

The most notable thing about the influence of this special discipline on the *Rules*, however, seems to be its suggestiveness of the very idea of such a treatise. At the outset of this chapter we observed that in its very first precept the *Rules* adopts the typical perspective of literature prefatory to inquiry by proposing to investigate the common use of intelligence in all researches regardless of the diversity of the matters with which they are concerned. But what led Descartes to think of such a project? What sustained his confidence that much was to be gained from its preliminary accomplishment? Descartes' early intellectual development is not sufficiently well documented for us to be able to pronounce on these questions with complete assurance; but at the end of his explanation of *Rule iv* he gives an account of his early mathematical researches which strongly suggests that that is where the answers are to be found.

According to this narrative, Descartes was attracted to the mathematical sciences from the time of his youth because of their reputation for simplicity, certainty, and usefulness; but he was not much impressed with what the standard authors had to say about them. The "superficial demonstrations" of existing texts seemed to him "worked out more often by chance than by art, and addressed more to the eye and to the imagination than to the intellect", for which reason they struck him as tending to hide, rather than show, how they actually had been found, and to be confusing, rather than helpful, in the search for new truths.[37] On recalling the ancient tradition of respect for mathematics, however, he suspected that men in olden times must have known a mathematics quite different from that which was subsequently handed down to his own contemporaries, but which they concealed, somewhat as a secret of the craft, in order to make their discoveries seem more remarkable.[37] These reflections leading him "from the study of arithmetic and geometry in particular to a more general study of mathematics", he decided first of all to determine what the mathematical sciences, including music, optics, mechanics, etc., essentially were; whence he arrived at the conclusion that what constituted their mathematical character, and distinguished them from other disciplines, was their common concern with "order and measure . . . no matter whether these were sought out in numbers, figures, stars, sounds, or any other objects."[38] And this "science of order and measure in general", or "universal mathematics", he then made his chief study up to the time of his writing the *Rules* as a broad summary of his findings to date. . . .[39]

We know, of course, that in this autobiographical note Descartes refers to his personal experience of the epoch-making generalizations of mathematical technique which the development of geometry, and especially of algebra, had made almost inevitable in his age. In the present connection, however, the interesting thing is not his reference to technical achievement as such, but is rather the special form which he describes his reaction to them as taking. Other men, such as Viéta, arrived at much the same technical results; but Descartes placed a highly imaginative construction on them which would hardly have occurred to a pure technician like Viéta. In the foregoing account, Descartes reports having begun with the several mathematical sciences in their traditional

formulations as a group of related but distinct disciplines; and his criticisms of these several disciplines as he found them at hand are directed
at precisely those of their features due to their separate developments.
It appears that his complaints that proofs are worked out "more often by
chance than by art", etc., have as their object demonstrative procedure
in *synthetic, Euclidean* form, which requires, as a special point of rigor
or style, that the properties of each type of mathematical object be
developed as exclusively as possible in terms of relations among its
own special differentia. To appreciate this we need not go into the very
involved problem from Pappus which Descartes himself makes use of
in his *Geometry* to show the limitations of the classic approach. We
know from his personal correspondence that he purposely made the
whole of that work unnecessarily difficult as a kind of *tour de force* to
confound his critics.[40] It is enough for our purposes to consider any
simple example of mathematics in the form in question: for instance,
the fourth proposition of *Book II* of Euclid's *Elements*, which states
that—

> If a straight line be divided into any two parts, the square on the
> whole line is equal to the squares on the two parts, together with
> twice the rectangle contained by the two parts.

Not only is the wording of this proposition lengthy and awkward from
the *analytic* point of view, but its demonstration, requiring some twenty
odd steps, is much longer still and much more cumbersome. Moreover,
it is clear that each proposition of this type depends so greatly for its
discovery on the ingenious contrivance and sheer good luck of the investigator mainly because the entire procedure out of which it develops is controlled by a deliberate confinement of attention to terms and
conceptions peculiar to the special subject matter in question—in this
case to axioms, postulates, definitions, theorems, and constructions
concerning lines, squares, oblongs, gnomons, etc. An important feature
of the technical achievements referred to above, however, is the discovery that when mathematical procedures are not so strictly confined
they can often be greatly expedited. As Descartes writes in *Book I* of
his *Geometry*, "often one has no need of tracing lines . . . on paper,
and it suffices to designate them by certain letters, each by a single
one . . .";[41] whereupon he proceeds to show that problems which are
difficult under other circumstances can thus be solved with considerable
ease, and that others which defy more restricted treatment can be com-

pletely disposed of. For instance, the above theorem from Euclid can be restated in the form:

$$(a + b)^2 = a^2 + b^2 + 2ab.$$

In this case the derivation follows from one algebraic operation. Indeed, it is so elementary as hardly to require explicit mention, except possibly in definition of the meaning of the symbols employed.

But whereas mathematicians like Viéta regarded developments such as these primarily as technically more elegant ways of pursuing research in the various mathematical sciences, it appears from the foregoing account of his studies that Descartes regarded as the most important thing about them what he took to be their implication that the several mathematical sciences can be best advanced by being approached, not as distinct fields of investigation, but as particular parts of a more general and comprehensive discipline. The conception of his "universal mathematics" goes far beyond the merely formal discoveries of his *Geometry*, that geometric analysis can be greatly facilitated by algebraic devices, and that algebraic analysis can be helpfully interpreted by geometric devices. In essence it is a generalization of these technical facts as implying that the "order and measure" which each of the various mathematical sciences considers in its own peculiar subject matter should be studied "in general"—that is, as they appear in any subject matter whatsoever.

But this "universal mathematics", at which Descartes arrived by technical consideration, is to the several branches of traditional mathematical science from which he started much what the general project of his *Rules* is to the various traditional branches of inquiry as they are ordinarily approached in their own terms. There is even a great deal of exact parallelism of language between his account of the relation of his "universal mathematics" to the popular mathematical sciences and his account of the relation of the general discipline of his *Rules* to all the usual fields of investigation. His "universal mathematics", therefore, might well be described as a kind of *special preface to mathematical inquiry*. And since Descartes finds it relevant in the course of the explanation of his fundamental *Rule iv* to report his almost sole concern with this prefatory consideration of the mathematical sciences up to the very time of his writing the *Rules*, it is difficult to escape the conclusion that it was under the control of his conception of a "universal mathematics" that he conceived this work as a kind of *universal science of all inquiry.* So obvious is the relationship between (1) the various mathematical sciences, (2) Descartes "universal mathematics", (3) all the usual fields of inquiry, and (4) the *Rules* as a unified, prefatory approach to all these fields—and so well established is the fact of their consideration in just this chronological order by Descartes—that we cannot but conclude that his thinking moved inevitably to the conception of the fourth when in the course of his intellectual development he passed from the first and second to the third.

It seems, furthermore, that the special form of Descartes' mathematical researches suggested to him not only the general idea of the *Rules* as a universal approach to all inquiry, but also the particular conception of it as such an approach worked out in terms of the *way* in which investigations are undertaken. Perhaps we cannot be quite so confident of this conclusion as of the previous one, but it is strongly suggested by a consideration of the kind of treatise in which Descartes eventually summed up the researches in which he tells us he was chiefly engaged for some years before writing up his *Rules*. Briefly, the structure of his *Geometry* is as follows:

After a general statement that "all problems of geometry can easily be reduced to such terms that afterwards one need only know the length of certain straight lines", *Book One* begins with a short explanation of how algebraic symbols can be made use of in the subject, and of how the statements of geometric problems can consequently be reduced to equational form.[42] Then, with this as preparation, it announces that all problems of ordinary plane geometry, in the classical sense, reduce to problems in terms of equations of no higher than the second degree; whereupon methods are given for the solution of these equations and for the geometric construction of their roots, it even being indicated when the construction is "possible" (i.e. when the roots are positive) and when "impossible" (i.e. when the roots are negative).[43] *Book Two* is next a general account of the nature of curved lines and the order of their equations, and *Book Three* is a discussion of problems involving equations of higher order in essentially the same form in which *Book One* treats those involving quadratics.[44]

This procedure contrasts most sharply with that of typical pre-Cartesian treatises on mathematics in that it develops more than anything else a way, or method, of analysis rather than a sequence of propositions of mathematical fact. The work does contain some brilliant theorems which historically were important contributions to the study of algebra

as a body of mathematical knowledge, and no doubt Descartes was glad
of this occasion to publish them. Nevertheless, such theorems are not
introduced in their own right or for their own sake, but only to instrument the technique of analysis which is the central object of concern.
After Descartes explains in *Book One* a general method for the algebraic solution of the problems of traditional plane geometry, he does
not then proceed to exhibit the properties of geometric figures which
can thus be found. He presents the solution of only one problem to illustrate his meaning and display the power of his method, but aside
from that his only remark is: "As for the rest, these same roots (of quadratics) can be found by an infinite number of other means, and I wished
to set these forth here only as very simple ones, in order to make it
evident that one can construct all the problems of ordinary geometry
without doing anything else than the little that is involved in the four
figures which I have explained."[45] It is perfectly clear from this that
Descartes regards all the problems of traditional plane geometry to be
adequately disposed of for his purposes by his account of a general
method for their treatment. And since he is just as cavalier in *Book III*
in his disposal of problems involving equations of a higher order, it is
equally clear that he conceives the whole of the work, not as a presenta-
tion of theorems in traditional style, but as an account of a way of arriving at such theorems whenever one has need of them. Descartes may
have been rash in thinking he had pretty much exhausted all that mat-
tered in the science of geometry in his comparatively few pages on the
method of research in the subject. Yet this much is sound in his attitude:
the important thing about the mathematics of his age, of which his
Geometry is a brilliant example, was not its discovery of new propositions, but its discovery of new techniques for arriving at them. Whereas
the accomplishments of most mathematicians of previous ages are measurable primarily in terms of the number and difficulty of the specific
new theorems they discovered, Descartes and the mathematicians of his
day distinguished themselves chiefly by the power and scope of the
new *methods* they devised.

Consequently, there is a very great likelihood that in turning to
write his *Rules* as a summary of what was "worthy of note" in his
studies along these lines, Descartes must have been profoundly convinced that his brilliant success in mathematics, through reconsideration of the way of inquiry into it, was an important lead to the possibility of still more brilliant success in the broader field of inquiry into

all possible matters. Just as his conception of a "universal mathematics" was to the many possible partitions of the Euclidean mathematical sciences a kind of prefatory consideration of certain general characteristics common to all, his analytic geometry was to the many propositions possible within the set-up of Euclidean geometry a discussion of the methods of investigation by which all might be discovered. In view, therefore, of the intimate connection between his "universal mathematics" and the methodology that goes along with it, and in view of the dependence of both for their justification on their common technical success within the technical field of mathematics, it is difficult not to conclude that, just as the former served as a provocative example of the soundness of a generalized approach in inquiry, the latter served as a provocative example of the usefulness of working out this generalized approach in terms of an examination of the way in which it is undertaken. Perhaps one cannot go so far as to say that, without his experience of the conception of a "universal mathematics" and the actual working out of his analytic geometry, Descartes would never have conceived the idea of attempting some sort of prefatory account of inquiry. But in view of the close parallelism in conception and structure between these mathematical ventures and his *Rules for Directing the Mind*, it seems extremely unlikely that without his experience of them, he would have worked out such a preface in the particular form that he did. And thus, this last piece of analysis, we should note, removes the origin of the preface to inquiry farther than ever from the professional sceptic's fretful brooding or the solipsist's lonely reverie.

VI: THE WAY OF CERTAINTY

How, now, does Descartes' *Rules* survive the critique of propaedeutic prolegomena to inquiry outlined in *Chapter I*, above? Does it, like Bacon's prefatory writings, remain practically untouched? Or does it, like many which follow, develop to be seriously suspect? To proceed in the order followed in the last two chapters, let us consider first its relation to the alleged *modern problem of the reality of knowledge*.

It must be admitted that, in its account of the way of inquiry as the mathematical way of certainty, the *Rules* does give rise to a problem of a kind concerning knowledge. There is no great difficulty in saying that only "certain" knowledge is worth inquiring into; that, of traditional learning, only the mathematical part is "certain"; that the "certainty" of mathematics derives only from the "simplicity" of its objects and from the "clarity" and "evidence" of its steps; and that, therefore, one should consider only objects of equal "simplicity', and take only steps of equal "clarity" and "evidence". But when one has said this, one has done a rather strange thing. One has paid understandable tribute to the formal elegance of mathematical science. But one has also invited some curious questions. If we confine ourselves to such a procedure and allow only its outcome as the legitimate result of inquiry, what then is the status of all the information which is usually gathered from what Descartes calls "deceptive experience"? If it is not the proper business of inquiry, what is the result of our many investigations into such matters as history, geography, ethnology, morals, government, language, and literature, which men like Bacon would have us examine "inductively" along as broad a front as possible? Questions such as these follow naturally and inevitably on the reading of Descartes' *Rules*; and they may be said, in a sense, to constitute a problem of knowledge to which it gives rise.

This problem, however, is not necessarily the academic sort of preliminary problem mentioned in *Chapter I*. Against the background of the argument sketched above, at least, it is not the kind of problem which casts artificial doubts on *whether we really can know we know what we know*, etc. In the main line of the argument of his *Rules* outlined above, Descartes does attach special importance to the kind of results which can be cast in a form comparable to that of mathematics; and in doing so, he does give the kind of results which cannot be cast in this form a less important, somewhat ambiguous, status. But so long as we confine our attention to his main line of argument and leave out of consideration for the while certain side-developments to be taken up in the next chapter, we have no difficulty in understanding the distinction between the two in terms of Descartes' own procedure. So long as he does not depart from the main project of the *Rules*, Descartes never makes statements which presuppose an impossible detachment or exemption from the usual circumstances of inquiry. His initial distinction between "certain" and "doubtful" knowledge is made in terms of the evident differences between the mathematical and non-mathematical parts of traditional learning. And likewise, save for the exception just mentioned above, all he subsequently has to say in behalf of the way of the former, as contrasted to the way of the latter, is worked out in terms of a further analysis of the same evident differences. Indeed, so strictly confined is the development of the *Rules* to considerations of the actual procedures of the mathematical part of traditional inquiry that, as we have already had occasion to recall, at the point where Descartes left it off it bid fair to become an actual pursuit of mathematical research. Consequently, its distinction between "certain" knowledge and "doubtful" knowledge invokes no act of super-knowledge which dichotomizes existence, and relates the one to the stuff of its *reality*, the other to the mere shadow of its *appearance*. All Descartes here implies about the two is what he says of them—namely, that the one is "mathematically derivable" and that the other is not. And if, in his zeal to call men to the cultivation of the former, he neglects to make clear what is his precise opinion of the latter, that must be understood as an oversight of enthusiasm. Although the theory of knowledge implied in this prefatory account of inquiry may be criticised as unsound, wrong, or fanatical, it cannot be criticized as absurd or unintelligible. The current dismissal of *the propaedeutic problem of knowledge* affects it no more than it affects Bacon's *Advancement of Learning* or *New Organon*.

To consider next the relation of the *Rules* to the second phase of our critique of prolegomena to inquiry, it should be noted that this work is even more explicitly directed at the traditions of disputation than either the *Advancement* or the *New Organon*. In the case of the *Advancement* the rejection of controversy is incidental to the more general rejection of all socially unsound ways of pursuing inquiry, and in the case of the *New Organon* it is incidental to the more general rejection of all technologically unsound ways of pursuing inquiry. But the fundamental distinction in the *Rules* between "doubtful" and "certain" matters seems to amount to a direct distinction between controversial and non-controversial issues as such. Descartes writes in the course of his explanation of the second precept of this treatise that "each time two learned men are of different opinions concerning the same matter, it is certain that at least one of them is deceived; and it even seems that neither of them possesses (genuine) science: for, if the reasons of one of them were certain and evident, he could expound them to the other in such a way as to convince him in turn."[46] Here Descartes treats the fact of controversy as indicating a lack of "certain" knowledge because he assumes that, were it to be had, all parties to disputes would inevitably come to common acceptance of it; and thus the "doubtfulness" to which he objects in most matters of inquiry is made equivalent to *con-*

trovertability, and the "certainty" which he attempts to cultivate is made equivalent to *incontrovertability*. There can be no misunderstanding about his way of certainty being intended, not only as a way of slighting controversy, but also as a way of directly disposing of it. The project is not a little ambitious on this score. How, then, does it succeed?

It will be recalled that Bacon attributed the contentiousness of the scholastics largely to their dependance on syllogistic reasoning, and that his chief suggestion for avoiding their quibbles was to have recourse to "inductive" reasoning, or "experience", which is precisely what Descartes finds to be the source of "uncertainty", and hence of controvertability. Nevertheless, although he formulates his own recommendations for an indisputably certain way of inquiry in terms of an appeal to "deduction", Descartes repeats much of Bacon's critique of scholastic syllogizing in his *Rules*, protesting, for example that the syllogism is essentially an unproductive device, perhaps useful for telling others what one thinks one already knows and therefore for promoting arguments, but absolutely useless as a way of discovery.[47] The kind of "intuition" and "deduction" of which he writes, on the other hand, he presents in quite Baconian terms as a "logic of discovery" leading to new truths. But his is a very different kind of "logic of discovery". At the beginning of the explanation of *Rule xiii* Descartes contrasts his way of treating perfect questions to the scholastics' general procedure by saying: "We imitate the dialecticians only in that, just as they assume the terms or matter of their syllogisms to be known in order to teach their forms, we also demand here that the question be perfectly understood. But we do not distinguish, like them, two extreme terms and a mean. . . ."[48] And thereupon, he gives as a substitution for such distinctions the requirements already summarized above: that a "question" must involve both knowns and unknowns, and, in order to be "perfect", must have its unknowns completely determined in terms of the knowns. These requirements, however, amount to nothing but conditions for the determination of quantitative equalities. Descartes himself points out that, once they are satisfied, "the only artifice consists simply in supposing known what is unknown, in such a manner as to give us an easy and direct means of research even in the most complicated difficulties," etc.[49] It appears, then, that it is the algebraic devices of solving equations which Descartes here opposes to argumentative use of the syllogism; and it is his own brilliant success with such devices which supports his confidence that his way of certainty leads to discovery of knowledge beyond argument. His *Rules* is neither more nor less successful as a way of disposing of controversy than mathematical science can be said to be.

It may well be observed that one of the questions by which modern thinkers have been most puzzled, and on which they have been most divided among themselves, is the question of how to interpret what comes of the exploration of the quantitative aspects of nature with the techniques of mathematical analysis. Kant's *Critique of Pure Reason*, for example, which has perhaps provoked more controversy than any other treatise of modern times, is in large part a commentary the fact that five plus seven quite unmistakably equals twelve. And we must not forget the bewilderment evoked by the host of mathematical prodigies which have appeared with each new advance in mathematical science. Today it goes without saying that the mathematical way of certainty does not lead nearly so far beyond the domain of controversy as Descartes apparently imagined. But in its main line of development Descartes' *Rules* does not lead to these troublesome problems of the nature of mathematics. It calls attention, rather, to problems of the mathematics of nature. It focusses the main drive of the inquirer's energies on just those techniques of quantitative analysis which our technologically equipped "houses of Solomon" have made most brilliant use of, and without which their fine institutional organization and mechanical instrumentation would have been immeasurably less successful. Although it may not be all that Descartes seems to have thought it was in this respect, the *Rules'* account of the mathematics of inquiry is no less important than the *Advancement's* account of its social organization, and the *New Organon's* account of its instrumentation, as an influence turning hairsplitting to investigation, barren contention to fruitful research. The sheer fact of the vast bulk of the mathematics and mathematical physics of the last few centuries, beyond any possibility of merely argumentative challenge in its own terms at least, is ample evidence that the *Rules* must be included among those works which have helped to minimize pointless dispute.

Finally, we are also brought by this analysis to the more general conclusion that, notwithstanding all the criticisms which can be made of it, Descartes' *Rules* does illuminate the fact of inquiry by calling attention most forcibly to its genuinely mathematical aspects. Whatever the other criteria in terms of which inquiry can be examined and evaluated,

quantitative criteria are of the greatest importance. When we first pick
up a research report today, whether it be on the density of stars, the
treatment of disease, the intelligence of apes, the quality of soap suds,
or the literary style of Plato, we are driven by deeply ingrained habit
to look for its graphs and formulae. To the great annoyance of the
Weak Willies among many generations of students, *math* courses have
long been the most unwaivable requirements in our schools. And not
only physicists and engineers, but economists, historians, sociologists,
physicians, artists, educators, and literary critics often find themselves
driven by the course of their work to go back and brush up on the cal-
culus and statistical methods they may have glossed over too noncha-
lantly as undergraduates. There seems to be an important core of truth
in the ancient Pythagorean precept, τὸ ὅλον ὄργανον ἁρμονίαν εἶναι καὶ
ἀριθμόν; for it is obvious that the world is one which lends itself to
probing at least as much by equations as by instruments. Not only the
tides, the seasons, the life of the sun, and the strength of bridges, are
numerically calculable and predictable, but also, within limits, the
cycle of business prosperity and depression, the rise and fall of price
levels, the birth rate, peculiarities of literary style, and numerous other
such matters. When equations can be set up to express the structure
of a situation, their solution produces knowledge in its most brilliant,
most spectacular form, if not in its profoundest.

Whatever else the criteria of inquiry, the qualifications of its agents,
the nature of its context, and the character of its crucial problems and
significant issue, they are most certainly mathematical too. And much
of the power of the *Rules* as a preface to inquiry is due to the forceful-
ness with which it expresses this fact.

5

DESCARTES ON THE FIRST THINGS OF KNOWLEDGE

I: PREFACES TO PREFACES

ONE might well suppose that with an account of "the way of certainty" behind him Descartes would feel free thenceforth to follow its advice and devote himself to the mathematical researches he had so partially recommended. Although he did do this to a considerable extent, however, he also kept going back to additional prefatory considerations. It seems that Descartes was not altogether satisfied with the main argument of his *Rules*; and this for good reason.

Assume, hypothetically, that we were to accept in its essentials all the advice given in its precepts. That would require us to concern ourselves only with matters of which we can have as "certain" knowledge as we have of mathematics, to elaborate these only by "intuitions" and "deductions" such as we find in mathematics, and consequently to confine our attention strictly to the relations of magnitudes in general and to other things only in so far as they have measurable dimensions which can be examined in purely quantitative terms. Thus disposed, what should we then be able to make of the very text by which we were so constrained? Concerning its many assertions about faulty ways of inquiry we should have, as for other such matters, only the hearsay evidence of Descartes' own word, which we must immediately rule out; to be convinced of the sameness of intelligence no matter to what it is applied, we should have only an analogy between its operation and that of sunlight presumed to remain unchanged no matter what it may shine on, which we should similarly have to reject; and so on for the rest of its instruction. Its arguments might have considerable cogency for the ordinary reader; but for us, as the hypothetical readers figuring in this supposition, they would have none at all. Our supposed convictions would hardly let us get through the first sentence in explanation of the first rule before we should find ourselves compelled to dismiss the whole work in exactly the same manner in which Descartes dismissed practically all the teachings of his predecessors and contemporaries. The exposition, in other words, does not rigorously comply with the requirements it itself exacts.

This complication might well be taken as evidence that the conclusions of the *Rules* are too restricted, or too exclusive, to be as generally applicable as Descartes presumed them to be. Discourse, after all, is not to any large extent the purely quantitative matter they seem to require it to become. In order to bring readers or listeners to follow one to a conclusion, one must first of all make contact with them as comprehending recipients of one's ideas; one must evoke an intelligent response to one's mode of expression; one must establish a tacit agreement that meaningful communication is taking place. But in order to do this one must use terms which refer significantly to the common context of all our thinking—the familiar, but most uncertain, setting of our common day-to-day existence. The language of the *Rules*, therefore, is quite above suspicion. It is the kind of language which is sooner or later inevitable in this world—so inevitable, indeed, that any other kind of language in any other kind of world is quite inconceivable.

However, it is his mode of exposition which Descartes tended to distrust rather than his conclusions. In a digression which interrupts his line of argument in explanation of *Rule xii*, he remarks that the greater part of his manuscript establishes its points "only in a confused and artless manner"; and this is obviously a concession that it does not comply with the criteria expounded in it. But instead of reconsidering these criteria, Descartes thereupon proposes to introduce new explanations through which they may be "expounded clearly and . . . by a sufficient enumeration"[1].

These new explanations, interestingly enough, constitute a more explicit essay in epistemological theory than anything thus far discussed in this study. Despite the fact that an elaborate account of such matters may be found in the rest of the *Rules*, Descartes begins his digression with the remark, "Concerning knowledge we need consider only two things: namely, we who know, and the things themselves which are known," whereupon he proceeds to elaborate on both in totally different terms than hitherto. Indeed, so discontinuous is what follows with everything that has gone before, that, although Descartes writes he would "like to explain here what the mind of man is, what the body is, how the one is informed by the other, which in this whole composite are the faculties which serve to know things, and what each of them does," he is compelled to remark that space is too short for "all the preliminaries which are necessary in order for the truth of all this to be evident to all."[2] Consequently, he presents only a few conclusions with regard to these things. He begins his account of "the knower" with the remark: "It will be enough for me to say as briefly as I can which is the manner most useful for my purpose in which to conceive all of our faculties made to acquire knowledge. Do not believe things to be so, if you do not wish; but what will prevent you from accepting these hypotheses, if it is evident that they do not alter the truth in any way, but only make all much clearer? It is just as in geometry where you make hypotheses concerning a quantity which does not weaken in any way the force of the demonstration, although often in physics you have a different idea of the nature of this quantity."[3] And he begins his account of "things known" with the very similar remark: "we must admit here, as above, certain things which perhaps are not accepted by everyone; but it matters little if one believes them to be no more true than those imaginary circles with which the astronomers describe their phenomena, provided only that with their aid one can distinguish in every question which knowledge can be true or false."[4] The ensuing sketch of a theory of knowledge which presumably validates the *Rules,* therefore, must be taken as so fundamentally prior to the rest of the argument that its proper development belongs to an account prefatory even to that which tells of the way of certainty. We must accept its conclusions here merely as "hypotheses" which we can legitimately challenge only as to their usefulness in making other matters intelligible. Where, then, are they more properly taken up in their own right?

It appears that when Descartes actually set about to find a proper place in which to take up the questions originally posed in this digression of the *Rules,* he found, not one, but many, as different occasion and different demands suggested different forms of exposition. In *Part Four* of the *Discourse on Method* he takes up essentially the same question within the context of his famous "fable" of the quest of "certainty", referring to it there as the "foundations" which his inquiring hero took when, having encountered many adventures with more commonplace, but dubious, matters, he finally set about to be really "certain". This account is brief to the extent of being cursory and sketchy; but its entire argument is repeated in *much* greater detail in the *Metaphysical Meditations* where Descartes again refers to the project as one which develops when one tries to "begin anew from the very foundations" in order to "establish something firm and constant in the sciences,"[5] and in *Book One* of the *Principles of Philosophy* which, as has been mentioned in the first chapter above, he devotes to the "principles," or *first things,* "of knowledge". These last two works are Descartes' chief discussions of his second prefatory theme, and they greatly overshadow both *Part Four* of the *Discourse* and the hypothetical digression of the *Rules*. There are still two more brief accounts, however, which shed additional sidelights on it. One is a "demonstration" of the principal points of the others in "geometrical order", appended to the end of the *Replies to the Second Objections* to the *Meditations*. The other is a fragmentary beginning of a dialogue titled *The Search for Truth by Natural Light* in which Descartes repeats the first part of the argument in a somewhat dramatic form.[6] In the following analysis, therefore, we shall consider, not only the main line of argument, common to these works, but also the special kind of contributions made by each form of its expression.

II: THE "DEMON" OF "DOUBT"

The general features of Descartes' "metaphysics" are so well known that they hardly call for detailed repetition here. His own texts, as well as many excellent critical summaries and explanations of them, have made the reader of philosophical literature well acquainted with his procedure from "systematic doubt", aided and abetted by the supposition of a "wicked deceiving demon", to the discovery of the "indubitability" of the "cogito"; thence, through the examination of "ideas", by the aid of "natural light" and its revelations as to the "nature" and "axioms" of "substance", to the "discovery" of "God" as an "absolutely perfect being"; thence, finally through "clear and distinct perceptions" that to admit otherwise would be inconsistent with the "undeceiving perfection" of "the Creator", back to the discovery that the "mind" is an "unextended thinking substance" to which is appended a body inhabiting a kinetic world of other bodies all of which are "substances" consisting of "pure extension".

After so many years of astonished disbelief and angry challenge on the part of countless readers, it would be pointless to examine this argument for literal truth or logical rigor. Quite aside from all the merely technical objections which have been pointed out so often, we must admit that its language was quaint at best and became archaic even as it issued from the press; that its many assumptions allowed by "natural light" in most statements, or made explicit as the "definitions", "axioms" and "postulates" of the "demonstrations in geometric order", are more challengeable than most of the matters placed in doubt by them; and that the fundamental distinctions of the whole procedure are invalidated by the implications drawn from them, since the whole argument which leads to the unique "indubitability" of the "cogito" rests so fundamentally on analogies drawn from the apparent world, and on evident differences between sleeping and waking, health and sickness, deception and veracity, that dismissal of their context leaves the conclusion pointless to the extent of unintelligibility. All that can appropriately be said here on such scores is that the "metaphysical" part of the "fable" of which Descartes writes in his *Discourse* is by far the most fabulous part of it. On other scores, however, there are many interesting things which can and should be pointed out concerning this "metaphysics" as a preface to inquiry. Fantastic as the whole argument is, there is much about it which provokes attention. If it lacks plausibility when examined for what we might call *literal truth*, it still has a great measure of the kind of telling cogency which all great fables have even when thoroughly fictitious.

For one thing, it is interesting to note that the "preliminary" considerations which Descartes feels he has to make in this justification of his way of certainty are most ironical in that they begin not with certainty, but with "doubt". The first of the *"Philosophical Meditations"* is titled, "Of the things which can be put in doubt."[7] The first of the *Principles of Human Knowledge* reads: "That in order to examine the truth it is necessary once in one's life, to place all things in doubt as far as possible."[8] The first "postulate" of the "reasons disposed in geometrical order" is a "request" of readers that they consider "how feeble are the reasons which have hitherto led them to repose faith in their senses, and how uncertain are all the judgments which they afterwards founded on them," etc., etc.[9] The first requirement which Eudoxus, the Cartesian *Socrates* of the dialogue on *The Search for Truth*, makes of his *slave boy* subject, Poliander, is that he rub out from his "imagination" all the "imperfect ideas" engraved on it by the teachings he received in his youth and the impressions he since got from his many experiences in the world of affairs.[10] And so thoroughgoing are these "doubts" that Descartes feels himself driven by them to suppose in his *First Meditation* "that a certain wicked demon, as deceitful as he is powerful, has used all his ingenuity to deceive me, . . . that sky, air, earth, colors, figures, sounds, and all other external things, are only illusions and dreams by means of which he has set snares for my belief . . . and that I myself have no eyes, no flesh, no blood, no senses, but falsely believe myself to have all these."[11]

What is to be made of this abundant doubt confronting the seeker after certainty as he attempts to take the first steps along the way of certainty? Surely its implication is the same as that of Descartes' critique of traditional learning and experience in the *Rules,* and of his accounts of his early adventures in the *Discourse.* It leads us just as unmistakably to the conclusion that, if *total certainty* is what we demand, the familiar world is hardly the place in which to look for it. The setting of life is normally fraught with risk and perplexity, illumined only at infrequent intervals with glimmerings of things of which the critical can feel assured. Sky, air, earth, colors, figures, sounds, hands, flesh, blood, and senses are as much the matter of the poet and gambler as they are of the mathematical investigator.

But although this fact might seem off-hand to defeat the attempt to state "first things" about knowledge which will set it on unchallengeable "foundations", Descartes exploits it for another purpose. As in the early parts of his *Rules* and *Discourse,* his persistence in holding up his pet criterion here against a context which will not sustain it turns the inquirer's back to all traditional learning. The "wicked demon" of this exercise in doubt is the genius of Descartes' own bad intentions with respect to all that the erudites of his day cherished. Indeed, it is Descartes himself, disappointed by his education and disabused by his wanderings. And the chief outcome of invoking it is the insinuation that the way of certainty in inquiry passes neither through the corridors of traditional schools and libraries nor across the fields of worldly experience. As Eudoxus plays the demon to Poliander in the *Search for Truth,* Epistemon, the learned man of the age becomes more and more a speaker of erudite irrelevancies exploited in the dialogue to clear away popular misunderstandings, until finally he is eliminated as a significant personality and becomes a mere by-stander more embarrassed by every new turn of the argument. The "demon" which this prefatory account of inquiry addresses is a profound suspicion as to the acceptability of the very foundations of traditional learning. And if it also raises questions as to the intelligibility of language such as Descartes himself employs throughout his "doubtings", that is only an accident which he did not foresee and conveniently overlooked, since practically no one of his age, except possibly Hobbes, thought in such terms.

III: THE "COGITO" AND THE "PERFECTION OF GOD"

The Cartesian "demon" of "doubt", however, serves other ends too. The review of beliefs in the shadow of this spectre confronts the inquirer with his subject matter, since the convictions examined cover all the things men usually probe. But it does so in an unusual way. First of all, it addresses the inquirer, not as he is usually involved in the context of inquiry as part of its very texture himself, but as somehow detached from it as much as he can possibly be imagined to be. And then it addresses the subject matters which this *depersonalized* inquirer examines, not in terms of their *internal relations* with each other, but only in terms of their *external* relation to such a detached investigator in "opinion".

After a brief word of general introduction Descartes settles down to business in his *First Meditation* by saying: "Now, since, appropriately to this plan, I have freed my mind of all sorts of care, and since I fortunately am not disturbed by any passions, and since I have assured myself of rest in peaceful solitude, I shall apply myself seriously and freely to generally destroying all my old opinions . . . ;"[12] whence he comes easily to the conclusion that "if, by this means, it is not in my power to arrive at the knowledge of any truth, at least it is in my power to suspend my judgment; that is why I shall diligently take care never to believe any falsehood, and I shall prepare my mind so well for all the ruses of the great deceiver, that, however powerful and deceptive he may be, he will never be able to impose on me."[13] Here Descartes turns attention, not to the stuff of the familiar context of his life's difficulties, but only to his state of conviction with respect to it. The preceding narrative of the *Discourse* makes it only too clear that the former is a matter of risk and uncertainty. So he selects an opportune moment free of ordinary concerns, when the insistences of the problems of living are least pressing, and then in the privacy of his own thinking reviews his "opinions" about its matter, which in a certain sense he is free to command. We should note, however, that in doing this he takes no more account of the inquirer than the fact of his holding opinions, which might be called more simply the fact of his thinking, and no more account of subject matter than the fact that it is thought about. That is to say, he sets the stage for a kind of *one-man instauration* such as the "hero" of the *Discourse* earlier decided he could make wholly his own without becoming a reforming crank—an instauration, namely, of the structure of

his own "beliefs". And in this setting, the "demon" of "doubt" assumes
the role of wrecker, tearing down the old structure so that Descartes
may lay aside the materials until he has put them together again more
securely.

This, however, is a rather unusual delineation of knower and known,
leading to rather unusual consequences. With the stage thus set, the
destructive activity of the demon in the *Second Meditation* amounts
to an artificial suppression of the usual context to which inquiry relates, until only the bare insuppressible fact of doing so is left. The
dialectical development of the "cogito" proves only this: *Do violence
to commonsense as much as you will by suppressing the subject matter
which thinking implies, it is too utterly absurd that the procedure should
be self-annihilating. The fact of the suppression remains. However
doubtful, doubting is still doubting. And if no other account is taken
of the inquirer, when pushed far enough the process strips his personality to the bare fact of doubting, or of doubtful thinking, within the
resultant universe of discourse.*

Although the fact of inquiry can thus be reduced artificially to the
bare fact of thinking, however, nothing can be accomplished by keeping it there. The seeker after certainty could remain thinking only
about the inescapable fact of thinking until death resulted from the
physical impossibility of doing nothing else indefinitely. But that would
get him nowhere. So, after twice taking time off from such strenuous
doubting for a night of relaxation in the body and world he felt himself constrained to question so radically, Descartes again confronts the
fact of thinking with subject matter in the *Third Meditation*, this time
as a context of "ideas" which he reviews in his well known manner as
to their "causes", "perfections", and "objective and eminent realities",
till he is led "by natural light" to find that an "absolutely perfect God"
exists in addition to his own thinking.

As to the soundness of the whole procedure as literally acceptable
demonstration again, it is perhaps enough to mention that pious-
minded contemporaries of Descartes indignantly denounced it as a
subtle attempt to undermine religion by advancing "absurd and in-
credible proofs" for the existence of the Deity. But considerably more
can be said of it as a phase of a prefatory account of knowledge. Spinoza,
the most careful student and conscientious developer of Descartes'
"metaphysics", it is well to remember, interpreted the "God" thus
demonstrated to exist, as the substance of the entire universe. And

although Descartes himself never gives the term such a literally pan-
theistic construction, it is quite clear that he conceives it as the total
implication of all things if not their actual stuff. "By nature considered
in general," he writes in the *Sixth Meditation*, "I understand nothing
other than God himself, or rather, the order and disposition which God
has established in created things."[14] Furthermore, under the pressure of
the *Second Objections* to the *Meditations*, Descartes attempts to make
his meaning clearer by remarking: "From the fact alone that I perceive
that I can never in numbering arrive at the greatest of all numbers,
and that from this I know that there is something in the matter of numbering which surpasses my powers, I can necessarily conclude, not to be
sure that an infinite number exists, but that this power which I have of
understanding that there is always something more to conceive in the
greatest of numbers which I can ever conceive, does not come from
myself, but from some other being which is more perfect than I." And
this observation he generalizes to the same end. "It matters little
whether one gives the name of idea to this concept of an indefinite
number," he writes, "but to understand what this most perfect being is
which I am not, . . . one must consider all the other perfections which,
besides the power of giving me this idea, can be in the same thing in
which this power is; and thus one will find that this thing is God."[15]
In other words, "God" here appears to be something which is to all
inquiring much what the indefinite range of the number system is to
all numbering. It is the infinite sphere of man's thinking, which has its
center everywhere and its outer surface nowhere. And the "demonstration" that such a being exists is as inevitable an outcome of the assumptions of Descartes' dialectic as the *"cogito"* itself.

To repeat the main points of the preceding analysis: *Inquiry, even
when viewed only in its restricted character as thinking, implies a context. The supposition of the wicked demon, therefore, is an imaginative
excursion which willfully suppresses the context of thinking, even
though in doing so it suppresses the force of the notion of deception
which has meaning only in terms of the context suppressed. And so, the
discovery of the "indubitable truth" of the "cogito" is a recognition
that, absurd as is the whole procedure of suppression, the fact of it remains itself insuppressible.* But now with his review of his "ideas"—
of subject matters, that is, regarded only in their special character as
dwelt upon in a kind of detached and impersonal contemplation—and
with this decision that all these "ideas" save only that of "God" could

be mere "fictitious inventions" of his own thinking, Descartes repeats the previous procedure of suppression in reverse order to show how the process breaks down of its own absurdity at the other extreme: *The contextual implications of thinking we may manage to deny, instance by instance, without feeling that we have done a strange thing,* Descartes says in effect. *But we cannot persist in the artifice to the extent of suppressing the implications of all thinking, which is what is here denoted by the "absolutely perfect being of God". And so, the discovery that "God exists" is not so much a "proof" of existence as a failure of the attempt ultimately to deny the context without which the fact of thinking is unintelligible.*

But how does all this serve to preface inquiry? What first things does it exhibit which set knowledge up on a firm foundation? Allegedly, all of the "metaphysical" argument thus far reviewed is strictly "preliminary", since no part of it is mentioned in the hypothetical digression of the *Rules* which is presumed to contain only conclusions of immediate application to the account of the way of certainty. The bearing of such "preliminaries" becomes clear, however, when Descartes makes the obvious deduction, "God" cannot be a "deceiver". To follow him in this we need not trouble with his quaint anthropomorphic language to the effect that "to deceive" is an "imperfection" which cannot be admitted of an "absolutely perfect being". The following is clear enough on the face of things: *If there is little sense in saying that this or that object of thought is such as always "to deceive" our thinking about it, there is absolutely none at all in saying that the same holds for the total system of what we think about, since it is hard to see what "deception" could possibly mean in that case.* "Meditation", after raising a great "metaphysical" dust, has the interesting result of confirming the common assumption of all actual inquiry—*that there is point to the undertaking.* This is the inference we may draw from this speculative excursion through the fells and dens of the "demon" of "doubt" to the discovery of the "cogito", of "God," and of his "undeceiving perfection".

Descartes, however, does not leave the conclusion in this general form to which assent is quite inevitable when his language is stripped of its more metaphorical phrasing. As he states it himself, he seems to feel it gives a special certification to his "belief" whenever he sees it illumined by "natural light"; that is to say, whenever he can say: "It really does seem to me that such and such is the case!" But, as we already know from the *Rules,* one of his most fundamental convictions is that inquiry is essentially a mathematical project. So far as he is concerned, therefore, the "undeceiving perfection of God" is a guarantee that only the mathematical is profoundly significant in inquiry. The text of his dialogue on *The Search for Truth* breaks off before reaching this point of development, but all his other accounts of the first things of knowledge end so as to delineate the project of inquiry as one allowing of proper pursuit only in the mathematically certain way of it already reviewed. His "clear and distinct perceptions" inform him that the difference between *thinking* and *being thought about* is a difference between two underlying "substances", the former of which consists solely in "pure intellect or conception", and the latter of which consists solely in "pure extension."[16] He reconciles all his previous grounds for "doubts" as to stars, earth, color, sound, flesh and blood with the "veracity" of "God" by saying of these things: "Although they are perhaps not altogether such as we perceive them by the senses, for there are many things which render this perception of the senses very obscure and confused, nevertheless, it must at least be admitted that all the things which I conceive in them clearly and distinctly, that is to say, all those things generally speaking which are comprised in the object of speculative geometry, are truly in them."[17]

As to the other details which fill in this account, there is no point in going into all of them here. It is enough to mention that, everything considered, they reduce the inquirer to a being as specially adapted to mathematical investigation as a fish is to swimming or a bird to flying, and at the same time they reduce nature inquired into to a realm as appropriate for sustaining this kind of investigation as water and air are appropriate for sustaining the characteristic activities of the creatures which inhabit them. The "purely spiritual, unextended thinking substance" which Descartes tells us "mind" essentially is, he locates at a point within the skull of a kind of "man-machine" body, from which it views the world through the medium of configurations brought to its sensorium by ripples of motion along the nerves of its senses. And the "purely physical extended substance" of which he tells us the world primarily consists, he locates wholly outside of such "minds", although it includes the bodies to which these "minds" are transigeantly attached, and informs them of its patterns and motions by various kinds of impact on the nervous systems of their mechanical organisms.

Meanwhile, of course, the investigator who is directed to consider his ways of using his eyes in the *Rules*, the *hero* who finds himself disappointed in his education and disabused by his travels in the early parts of the *Discourse*, the "metaphysician" who must free himself from cares to summon the "demon of doubt" in the *First Meditation*, and the characters who meet to talk things over in the dialogue on *The Search for Truth*—the personalities of all of these are dismissed as accidental circumstances of their "minds" being somehow so intimately attached to their bodies that, in a state of ignorance, they would perish from this life were they not informed of its exigencies by something other than "true knowledge". And at the same time, the world in which such inquirers seek education, travel, fight, view the sun and the stars, and abhor the thought of demons and their wickedness—this world is dismissed as merely a systematic delusion deriving from the same accidental circumstance in the *real* order of things.

To invoke the "perfection of God" to substantiate all this may well seem like taking liberties with Divinity. Since Descartes uses such language, however, it is well to remember that by all the traditions of religion "God" is always an object of faith; and it is not too much to suggest that in thus appealing to Him for certification of what he "clearly and distinctly perceives by natural light", Descartes does commit an act of pure faith. Only this one additional remark should be made: *In view of what he invokes God to certify, Descartes' faith in Him is essentially a confidence in the power of human reason totally to comprehend the world in mathematical terms.*

IV: A TRANSFORMATION OF COORDINATES

In the light of the most practical consequences of Descartes' several excursions into "metaphysical meditation" or "first things of knowledge", then, one might well say that, for all their apparent differences from the *Rules* as a handbook of scientific practice, they are identical with it in their general outcome as prefaces to inquiry. After all, Descartes regarded them as clearing the way for exactly the same kind of research that he actually began to undertake in the last part of the earlier work. He explicitly digresses into such matters in the *Rules*, it is well to remember, in order to "show in a general way" what formerly "had to be explained only in particular".[18] It would be reasonable enough, therefore, to regard the general construction they place on inquiry to be the same in effect as that already outlined in the preceding chapter. But although this is all perfectly true, the fact remains that in certain respects the language of the latter part of Descartes' "metaphysics" is so fundamentally different from that of the main argument of his *Rules,* and so much more special than the general conclusions of that earlier work require, that many readers have since felt compelled to regard it as maintaining much more.

To begin with, although the first part of these latter excursions into a more explicit theory of knowledge places inquiry in question in terms of the same kind of criteria as Descartes' handbook of scientific practice, at their outset they also tend more explicitly than either of those works to—

2. Identify the agent of inquiry *simply as that perplexed, uncertain sort of individual man usually appears to be.*
3. Delimit the context of inquiry *simply as that familiar locus of contingency and uncertainty, the workaday world.*
4. Single out the crucial problems of inquiry *as problems of finding certainty at all in a world where most matters are uncertain.*
5. Interpret the issue of inquiry *as concerning hardly anything more than "trivial" matters like numbers and figures.*

By the particular manner in which they invoke the "demon" of "doubt", however, the arguments go on to restate this general situation, more in line with the plan Descartes proposes in the second episode of the "fable" of his *Discourse,* by tending to—

2. Identify the agent of inquiry *as a thinker, or holder of "opinions", somehow detached from the familiar locus of his perplexity and uncertainty.*
3. Delimit the context of inquiry *as the sum of the "ideas" this opinionated thinker "holds" in a sense subject to his acceptance or rejection by his "doubt" or "belief" in them.*
4. Single out the crucial problems of inquiry *as the problems of such a thinker in finding his "opinions" concerning his "ideas" to be "indubitable".*
5. Interpret the issue of inquiry as *"indubitable ideas".*

But although both these general delineations of the project of inquiry fall very much short of that of the *Rules* as a preparation for mathematical research, the one which follows from the ensuing "metaphysical" discussion goes considerably further, in that it tends to—

2. Identify the agent of inquiry *as a "purely spiritual thinking substance" supplemented by a "man-machine body"; that is to say, as a kind of pure mathematical intelligence.*

3. Delimit the context of inquiry *as a world of "purely physical extended substances" in motion; that is to say, as the subject matter of mathematical physics in a pure kinematical sense.*

4. Single out the crucial problems of inquiry *as the problems of this purely mathematical intelligence in setting aside the deceptive appearances due to the requirements of its attachment to a body, and in penetrating beyond them to their underlying mathematical truths.*

5. Interpret the issue of inquiry *as direct grasp upon the mathematical nature of the world as it really is, in contrast to how it merely appears.*

It is these last conclusions by which Descartes feels he has finally prepared for the kind of inquiry in which he is most interested; for it is essentially they which he presents in the *Rules* as the means by which the mathematical way of certainty can at last be expounded "distinctly and sufficiently", which he refers to in the *Discourse* and *Meditations* as the "foundations" of "something firm and constant in the sciences," and which he classifies in the *Principles* as the very "first things of human knowledge."

That the argument from which these last conclusions derive is even more caught up in fundamental problems of exposition than Descartes' account of the way of certainty is of course abundantly clear from what has already been said above as to the unintelligibility of the doubts it invokes when they are viewed against the considerations which give rise to them. Yet it is interesting to note that, whereas the text of the *Rules*, and of the early parts of the *Discourse*, is simply confused by such remarks, the texts from which these three successive sets of conclusions emerge are fairly explicit, if unsatisfactory, rejoinders to such criticisms. We may soundly say that, although we can understand Descartes' arrival at the third in terms of his development of the second as a restatement of the first, we have difficulty in construing the first in the light of the third; And we can give as our reason for this the fact that the third places such restrictions on our universe of discourse that, although it originally derives from the first, the first cannot be adequately comprehended within the scheme of its limitations. Yet, whatever the soundness of all this from what is sometimes termed a *natural-istic* point of view, Descartes' argument here is a direct challenge to the so-called *assumptions* on which such a point of view *rests*.

In the course of his "metaphysical" reasoning Descartes discounts our familiar acquaintance with the sort of individual described in the first parts of his *Discourse* and in his *Rules* as going to school, traveling, fighting, and pondering over the ways of his fellows. At the same time, too, he also dismisses our familiar acquaintance with the sort of things this much disappointed individual usually considers in the world in which educations miscarry, popular opinions conflict, and doubts are positively demoniacal. He discounts both as cases of mistaken identity, so to speak. But by the same token, he also discounts reference to the likes of them as legitimate grounds for the intelligibility of discourse. He refers to his re-identifications of both as explaining his way of certainty better largely because his final accounts of knower and known, if we accept them, bring about a kind of *reorientation* of attitude toward everything about which we think. After all, if the familiar world in all its qualitative richness were really constituted by nothing but relations between the termini of vibrations in the sensorium, itself only a matter of extension in motion, and a thinking thing which somehow translates such stimuli into color, sound, feeling and smell, there would be little point in grounding the sense of discourse on reference to it. A much more reasonable appeal for assurance that one was speaking intelligibly would be reference to the subject matter of pure mathematics and pure kinematical physics. It would then happen, of course, that intelligible discourse would doubtless consist solely of algebraic equations and geometric diagrams, rather than of words such as we ordinarily use. Modern symbolic logic, by its tendency in that general direction, gives us a hint of what such discourse might be like. And Descartes probably did not himself realize very clearly this formal implication of his "metaphysics". Yet there can be little doubt, when we consider his use of his final "metaphysical" conclusions, that he explicitly attempts to bring about by them such a fundamental *transformation of coordinates* for all our thinking.

In most of the text of the *Rules* and in the first part of the *Discourse* Descartes discusses his "method" as a technique of investigation, with the general result that there he simply gives inquiry a special emphasis by pointing to a particular aspect of the world as most fruitful for exploration and to a particular kind of finding as knowledge *par-ex-*

cellence; what is left over is not an inaccessible excess, but merely a less significant hinterland of the intellectual globe. As a result of the *transformation of coordinates* just mentioned, however, Descartes' method becomes more than technique of research. It becomes a way of understanding what investigation and discovery essentially are, and therefore a kind of *principle of certification*. If we are willing to run the risk of a most precarious use of language, we may say that it becomes *an absolute definition of* REALITY, since all that is not accessible to probing by it is relegated to a domain of "deception" and "illusion".

Not to go further into the remoter implications of this development for the present, however, it is enough to note here that it is a prefatory consideration of inquiry that Descartes attempts to effect such a fundamental transformation, and that the device therefore lends itself to such purposes; although of course, as has amply been illustrated in the three preceding chapters, it need not necessarily be so worked out.

V: THE PROVOCATIONS OF "MIND" AND "STRUCTURE"

That this all takes place under the same mathematical controls as those which affect the *Rules* is quite obvious from the entire foregoing analysis. It seems that Descartes' accounts of the first things of knowledge are, from one point of view, but varied expressions of the compulsions under which his accounts of the way of certainty are worked out. In his so-called "metaphysical writings", however, Descartes seems somewhat more responsive to broader aspects of the provocativeness of mathematics than in his earlier handbook.

Although the discovery of the *"cogito"* in these writings can be construed very largely in terms of the implications of "doubt" arising out of the attempt to apply the criterion of "certainty" universally, it is hard fully to understand the very great importance they attach to it unless we also take account of the expectations which they attach more generally to the fact of thinking or "mind". Even in his explanation of the fourth precept of the *Rules*, Descartes remarks with obviously profound respect: "The human mind contains I know not what divine, in which the first seeds of useful thoughts have been thrust, so that often, however neglected and stifled they may be by contrary studies, they produce fruits spontaneously. We have evidence of this in the simplest of the sciences, Arithmetic and Geometry," etc.[19] Here Descartes interprets the basic mathematical sciences, not only as developments of subject matters, but also as spontaneous expressions of man's power of thought. He construes "mind", not only as man's way of responding to thought-provoking things, but also as itself a fecund source of knowledge in its own right. And accordingly he develops his "method", not only as a device for the exploration of things thought about, but also as a means for the cultivation of the power of thinking about them. The precepts of the *Rules* are "Rules for the Direction of *the Mind*"; and the title which Descartes first intended to give his *Discourse*, we may do well to remember, was: "Project of a Universal Science which can raise our nature to its highest degree of perfection."[20] In the *Introduction* of the *Search for Truth by Natural Light,* moreover, Descartes announces its motivation to have been a wish "to display the true riches of our souls, by showing to each one the path which will enable him to find in himself, without borrowing anything from others, the science which is necessary for the regulation of his life and for the acquisition, by its own means, of all the most curious knowledge which the human mind can possess".[21] And in the preface of his *Principles,* he writes of the kind of wisdom with which he is concerned as "the nourishment of the mind", and of the "philosophy" from which it derives as the opening of the eyes of the soul.[22] In short, the central role of the *"cogito"* and of "thinking substance" in Descartes' first things of knowledge is in part a consequence of the fact that for him inquiry is significant, not only as a matter of institutional learning, technology and mathematical technique, but also as a matter of sheer thought. The pivotal importance of both these conceptions in this prefatory account of inquiry is largely due to his conviction that the undertaking is a function of the mindful personality of the individual who engages in it.

Moreover, there is another important point on which Descartes finds the significance of mathematics to lie in implications beyond itself. It seems that there is something about this subject matter which relates most particularly to the fact of mind in the sense in which it has just been discussed here. At a crucial point in *Part Two* of his *Discourse* Descartes writes: "Those long chains of very simple and easy reasons, which geometers usually make use of to accomplish their most difficult demonstrations, have given me occasion to imagine that all things which can fall under the knowledge of men are inter-related in the same way, and that, provided only one abstain from accepting any for true which are not, etc. . . . there can be none so remote that one cannot eventually arrive at them, nor none so concealed that one cannot discover them."[23] This is why, at the first crisis of his fable of the quest for certainty when he addresses himself to his "beliefs", Descartes finds something about them which invites him to think of them on analogy to such things as buildings, cities, and codes of laws. So obviously do they hang together that it occurs to him that, if properly adjusted to each other, they ought all to be of a piece. Together they ought to constitute a structure not incomparable to the structure of a well designed building, a well planned city, or a well framed code of laws. And since that is the case, he reasons, then certainly the commonsense considerations which apply to buildings and cities and laws, should also apply to the beliefs we organize into a body of knowledge. Like other structural things, beliefs should rest on secure foundations; they should be assembled systematically; they should be free of discontinuity or irregularity; they should have some unifying principle or plan; they should, in short, comply with all the usual requirements of good structural organization. Hence the very idea of the "metaphysics" as "first things of knowledge" taken as "foundations" on which to build all the rest of what we may be said to know. The fact of *structure* controls, not only the form which this preface to inquiry takes, but helps to inspire the very conception of it as a way of preparing for further inquiry.

VI: THE FIRST THINGS OF KNOWLEDGE

To the extent that Descartes' accounts of the first things of knowledge serve merely to reassert his earlier emphasis on the mathematical element in inquiry, all the final comments hold for them which were made in the last section of the preceding chapter. But to the extent that they go so far beyond the *Rules* and first parts of the *Discourse* as to demand what we have called in *Section iv* above *a kind of reorientation of all our thinking,* they stand in quite a different relation to the general critique made in the first chapter.

The "doubts" which Descartes invokes at the outset of his "metaphysics" do more than direct suspicion at the main forms of traditional inquiry; by implication, at least, they set aside all previous investigation as irrelevant. And subsequently they offer their conclusions as more fundamental insights into what inquiry essentially is than the ordinary pursuit of it could possibly reveal. We need no very special discernment to see that inquiry is significantly an institutional, technological, or mathematical matter; so we need go through no special dialectical acrobatics to follow the arguments of the *Advancement*, the *New Organon*, or the *Rules* into their details. And potentially the same holds for arguments concerning inquiry as significantly thoughtful and structural; for it takes only the ability to focus one's ordinary observations to see the sense of such conclusions, however much one may question their importance. But the kind of insight required of us if we are to grant that the inquirer is *only* a "thinking substance" and that the world inquired into is *nothing but* a system of extension in motion, is quite another matter. These conclusions do such violence to the revelations of most of our inquiring that, while he offers them to us, Descartes has to invoke a fantastic, not to mention unintelligible, "demon" to hold off the whole world of contradictory evidence.

In short, despite all their obvious similarities to the prefaces to inquiry which we have seen in the last three chapters to avoid such difficulties, Descartes' accounts of the first things of knowledge are open to construction as trying to effect the kind of break with the regular course of inquiry which we have seen in *Chapter I* to lead eventually to the sidetracking of their main undertaking. It is not surprising therefore, that, whereas his *Rules* leads directly into mathematical analysis of monumental importance, his *Metaphysical Meditations* is followed by seven long sets of *Objections and Replies* which make practically no reference to the preceding argument for the active investigation of nature, but refer rather to its themes of "doubt", "thinking", "ideas", "substance", "perfection", "God", "cause", "substance", and "extension", considered in their own right. Nor is it surprising that the same sort of consideration that was begun in these lengthy appendices was continued until it appeared that a distinct line of special investigation was in question, and Cartesian *metaphysicians* appeared as well as Cartesian scientists, who as time went on regarded each other with less and less mutual recognition or interest. The mathematical research Descartes urged proceeded of its own momentum. But these "metaphysical" arguments he gave to draw attention to it lead to entirely different lines of speculation, not infrequently by people who never solved an equation in their entire lives. If the hand of irony brushes over all preliminaries to inquiry, it descended on these of Descartes' with a particularly resounding blow.

The fate of these writings is ironical, too, with respect to their relation to the traditions of controversy. Fully as much as his *Rules*, Descartes' accounts of the first things of knowledge are explicit attempts to do away with endless disputing. Despite the many *Replies* he himself gives to the *Objections* to his "metaphysics", he writes in the *Preface* of his *Principles* that one of the main "fruits" which he believes can be gathered from its precepts, is "that the truths which they contain, being so clear and so certain, will free all subjects of dispute, and thus dispose minds to sweetness and agreement."[24] Such was his confidence in the incontrovertibility of his "first things"! Yet, of all he wrote, they have proved the most debatable. His *Geometry* was incorporated practically at once and in whole into the store of scientific knowledge which men examine only to learn or to develop further. But his "metaphysics" was the beginning of a controversy which lasted for centuries and lured so many great thinkers to take sides in it that the history of philosophy since has rarely been thought of except in terms of the many successions of positions taken with respect to it. Once men got sidetracked by Descartes' suspension of the usual course of inquiry, and therefore free of the controls of specific subject matters which usually set limits of a kind on contention, every man was his own prophet and it was any man's argument. Others than Descartes could see "God" by "natural light", but they found different images on His "absolutely perfect" reflecting surface.

What is more, not only did this attempt to dispose of controversies actually multiply them, but those which it brought about tended to become more profoundly irresolvable than any at which it was directed. The scholastics of whom Descartes complains so sarcastically usually understood what others of their kind said at least as well as they understood what they said themselves; and so they debated, however vigorously, according to rules which they were willing to observe in order to keep in argumentative contact with one another. But in effecting what we have called a kind of *transformation of the coordinates to which all our thinking relates*, Descartes' metaphysics sets up a very serious limitation on the mutual comprehension possible with a challenger who refuses to accept the *transformation*. Most of the *Objections* to his *Meditations* hinge on minor points made by men who either tacitly accepted such a *re-orientation* or did not comprehend the whole argument well enough to realize that it had any such implication. But this is hardly true of the *third* set. Thomas Hobbes grants the soundness of the "*cogito*", for example, but he cannot admit that it is any less certain to say: "I walk, therefore I am", afterwards to discover that he is not only a thinking thing but a walking one as well. He refuses to dismiss the wandering hero of the fable of the *Discourse* or the familiar world in which this hero wandered for so many trying years before invoking the "demon" of "doubt". When his objections are all made and answered, therefore, the reader does not feel that the arguments *pro* and *con* have really got down to considerations fundamental enough to bring the opposed positions into genuine contact with each other. And from this it is only a short step for Locke to claim that Descartes' arguments are not so much false as meaningless, and for Leibniz to protest that it is really Locke's which are so. But of all this we shall say more in *Chapters VIII* and *IX* below. It is enough to note here that by the very prefatory treatises with which he proposes to "dispose minds to sweetness and agreement", Descartes best illustrates the hyper-controversial preliminary literature discussed above in *Sections iii* and *iv* of *Chapter I*.

It would seem, furthermore, that however much Descartes' other writings contributed to the enterprise of learning in the Baconian sense, those on the first things of knowledge also helped to give rise to the approach to knowledge as presenting an academic *problem* of explanation. Whereas the difficulties which are singled out as the crucial ones for inquiry in his *Rules* are simply those of getting nature related to diagrams and stated in equations for subsequent formal treatment, it is possible to construe the difficulties which emerge in his "metaphysics" as those of explaining how a mind which is not extended can possibly get into contact with a world which is. Although Descartes himself may never have had occasion to question whether it was in such contact, others who followed his argument began to wonder; and some of the lines of division which appeared among the controversialists who debated the kind of "metaphysics" he started were based on just the kind of answers they gave to this question which they found posed for them by these writings of Descartes. The reasons for all this we shall consider in greater detail after reviewing Locke's attempts to preface inquiry in terms of the "history" of "understanding". But now there are a few observations in a more appreciative vein which the analysis of the last three chapters suggests as relevant.

Despite their technical difficulties, and despite the ironical destiny which those difficulties forced upon their later interpretation, the writings of Descartes examined in this chapter unquestionably rise above both. Perhaps one of the chief reasons for this is the fact that forcibly, if somewhat fantastically, they do draw attention to the important fact that inquirers are, not only social animals, manipulators of mechanical devices, and solvers of equations, but also, in a broader sense than any of these facts about them alone would imply, minds as well. Philologists are inclined to believe, on the grounds of purely etymological evidence, that *minds* and *men* were originally one; and by identifying inquirers as most essentially "thinking substances" Descartes seems strikingly to express the underlying truth of this etymological affinity. Whatever else may be important about inquirers there is something about them which does provoke the term *mind* so strongly that one is tempted to forget what other terms they also provoke. And on the other hand, there is something in things too which seems to respond to the fact of men as minds. Whether that something is "structure" only in the sense of the geometrical framework of a universe of "pure extension" in motion is perhaps extremely doubtful. Nevertheless, the discussion of that kind of structure in these writings does draw attention just as forcibly to the fact that this something in things is the most proper concern of inquirers as sheer thinkers, and that such thinkers respond best when, whatever else they are, they are aware of this most special characteristic, and are disciplined accordingly. Knowledge, after all, is not only a social acquisition made by instruments and equations. It is also, in a sense, a private possession too, a fulfillment of the thoughtful personality of the thinker in his grasp of that aspect of things which lends itself most readily to such comprehension. And it is perhaps the chief *power* of Descartes' "metaphysical" instauration that it will never let us forget that fact.

6

LOCKE ON THE HISTORY OF UNDERSTANDING

I: EPISTEMOLOGY IN A "KNOWING AGE"

THE place of John Locke's *Essay Concerning Human Understanding* in epistemological literature has already been mentioned in *Chapter I*, above, where it is introduced as a venture in the theory of knowledge which, although formulated largely as a criticism of Descartes' prolegomena to inquiry, tended nevertheless to parallel them so far as also to assume propaedeutic form. On closer examination, this parallelism may now be observed to extend to very basic details of conception.

The *Rules'* discussion of knower and known has been reviewed in the preceding chapter principally as it develops out of Descartes' proposal to expound the "certain" way of inquiry more "satisfactorily" than in his main argument. At one point, however, Descartes introduces the same discussion in more independent terms. "Before one attempts the knowledge of particular things," he writes during the course of his explanation of *Rule viii*, "one should have examined once in one's life what knowledge human reason is capable of, in order not to be always uncertain as to the ability of the mind, and so work mistakenly or rashly";[1] whereupon he comes around to the same project as a kind of preliminary survey of the possibilities of knowledge in order to inform the inquirer in advance of his competence.[2] But this is precisely the main idea of Locke's attempts "to set the understanding at a distance and make it its own object". We have already quoted the anecdote from the *Epistle to the Reader* of the *Essay* in which he ascribes its origin to an early determination to see what our "understandings" are "fitted to deal with" before attempting to explore issues which might be beyond their competence;[3] and in its *Introduction* he parallels Descartes' exact words even more strikingly where he explains as "the occasion of this essay" his decision that "the first step towards satisfying several inquiries the mind of man was very apt to run into, was to take a survey of our own understanding, examine our own powers, and see to what things they were adapted."[4] It would be absurd, of course, to claim that hesitation about our scope as inquirers is as important in Descartes' prefatory writings as in Locke's. It is obvious enough that the question was only a secondary feature of the former as attempts to reason about "reasoning" and a primary feature of the latter as attempts to understand "understanding". Yet it can hardly be anything but an accident that some of Descartes' prolegomena did not take the form of an *Essay Concerning Human Reason* very much on the plan of Locke's *Essay Concerning Human Understanding*. Even though it be true of each to a different degree, both are appeals to theory of knowledge to confine inquiry within proper bounds.

Locke's efforts to determine the "extent of understanding", it should be noted nevertheless, are responses to a very different kind of situation than that which lay back of any work thus far considered in *Part Two* of this study. The state of things in the early seventeenth century had been such as to provoke Bacon to call for radically different approaches to the entire enterprise of learning along institutional and technological lines, and such as to provoke Descartes to undertake the task of an instauration in learning completely on his own without waiting for the reform of traditional institutions to catch up with his pioneer explorations into the rediscovered fields of mathematics and mathematical physics. But by the latter part of the century when Locke reached full maturity, the great discoveries of the preceding era had begun to bear fruit and a fairly substantial body of new learning had been built up by research workers who had responded either to the challenges of these discoveries or to the interests which had prepared men's minds for them. Consequently, whereas Bacon and Descartes had little but scorn for the work of their predecessors and contemporaries, Locke is quite conscious in his *Essay* of "pretending to instruct this our knowing age".[5] Although he claims for himself the "satisfaction to have aimed sincerely at truth and usefulness", it is with the admission that he does so only "in one of the meanest ways"; and this is no mere show of modesty, for he has reason enough to remark that "the commonwealth of learning is not at this time without masterbuilders, whose mighty designs in advancing the sciences, will leave lasting monuments to the admiration of posterity".[5] Far from leading up to an ambitious proposal to undertake the total project of inquiry anew, Locke's unreserved tributes to "an age that produces such masters as the great—Huygenius, and the incomparable Mr. Newton, with some others of that strain," comes around to the simple suggestion that, since "everyone cannot hope to be a Boyle or a Syndenham," it is "ambitious enough to be employed as an underlabourer in clearing ground a little, and removing some of the rubbish that lies in the way of knowledge".[5]

With Locke's treatment of the preface to inquiry, therefore, the de-

vice is made to serve new purposes. From his time on the crises which
developed in the enterprise of learning became more and more unlike
that which disturbed the age of Bacon and Descartes. And much of
the significance of Locke's writings to this analysis is due to their illustration of how prefatory literature is adjusted to that fact.

II: THE "STUDY DURING A JOURNEY"

The difference of initial emphasis in Locke's reflections on the general project of inquiry is strikingly illustrated in his *Study during a
Journey*, a lengthy memorandum entered in his *Journal* in 1677 when
his *Essay* existed as yet only in general plan. This opuscule records
merely passing thoughts by a busy traveler, and consequently its argument is stated without any of the abstruser dialectic which complicates
the *Essay* Locke later devoted to its theme of "human understanding".
The *Study* centers, for example, simply about a number of comments
on certain kinds of scholarship which Locke says "it may not perhaps
be amiss to decline" as likely to bewilder us, or at least lie out of our
way"[7] . . . namely: (1) "all that maze of words and phrases which
have been invented and employed only to instruct and amuse people
in the art of disputing;[7] (2) "an aim and desire to know what hath been
other men's opinions"[8]; (3) "purity of language, a polished style, or
exact criticism in foreign languages"[9]; (4) "antiquity and history, as
far as designed only to furnish us with story and talk"[9]; and (5) "nice
questions and remote useless speculations, as where the earthly paradise
was"[10], or such as "the nature of the sun or stars, . . . and a thousand
other such speculations of Nature"[11]. Whereas comparable criticisms in
the writings of Bacon and Descartes lead to the formulation of rather
exact criteria for distinguishing what those men regarded to be sound
or unsound in research, the above seem merely to express a kind of
irritable impatience on Locke's part with the way some inquirers spend
their time. As one might expect of a traveler giving only incidental
attention to such matters, Locke was busy when he jotted down his
thoughts concerning them; and so the upshot of his criticisms is the
general comment that the kinds of inquiry at which they are directed
interfere with work. That a man should "acquaint himself designedly
with the various conceits of men that are to be found in books even
upon subjects of moment" strikes Locke as an "idle and useless thing"
which "will not seem much his business" when one considers how much

he has to do "both in his general and particular calling"[12]. And "to spend much time" on linguistic niceties, even though it may "serve to set one off in the world and give one the reputation of a scholar", offends him particularly because it "makes most of those who lay out their time this way rather as fashionable gentlemen than as wise or useful men"[13]. Thus, in almost every case Locke's objections reduce to the kind commonly made against liberal arts and sciences curricula in our universities today by a certain type of undergraduate who, without the least bit of intellectual curiosity, can tolerate nothing which does not obviously contribute to the cash value of his diploma as a certificate of qualification for that *good job* he is so bent on getting. Like such an undergraduate, Locke the traveler is obsessed here by a strong sense of having much else to do besides being curious or well informed; and the general effect of his criticisms is to demand that inquiry accommodate itself to this fact. He may at times echo Bacon's exact words in speaking of knowledge as subservient to "the use and advantage of men in this world"; but whereas Bacon had used such expressions in the hearty, robust manner of an expansionist statesman of the commonwealth of learning, calling enthusiastically for the conquest of new regions of the "intellectual globe", Locke repeats them merely to demand help in other matters which he regards to be more important. If he asks that inquiry be *practical*, it is not in the glad, almost romantic sense of Bacon, but in the grim, joyless, hard-headed sense of the fretful undergraduate who fears that he may lose his time on knowledge which is merely knowledge. In this *Study*, Locke is seventeenth century, middle-class Puritanism, freezing the sense of high adventure out of the enterprise of learning.

Whereas Bacon had called on investigators aggressively to attack nature "by works", therefore, here Locke merely cautions his fellow travelers to plod along in step with their noses to the grindstone of their everyday tasks. He attempts no elaborate identification of the inquirer or of the context of his work; nevertheless he addresses those who would inquire, in a manner which implies a very definite conception of their proper role and place. His most characteristic salutation is to men "on a pilgrimage through this world"[14]; and his chief advice to such is naturally that they take "the straightest and the most direct road"[14]. Anything else would be a waste of time. "If a traveler gets a knowledge of the right way," he says, "it is no matter whether he knows the infinite windings, by-ways, and turnings where others have been misled; the knowledge of the right secures him from the wrong, and that is his great business".[14] Locke's insistence here on the importance of keeping to the "right road" may remind one strongly of Descartes' very similar concern; but it has very different consequences. Advising the seeker after mathematical certainty, Descartes had pointed to the right road as one leading *from* the world of man's usual business eventually to a vast structure of mathematical subject matter confronted by pure mathematical intelligence. Locke, however, addressing men of worldly affairs, bids them eschew all such extravagances and keep their minds on their business. Escapades of this kind, he warns them, are not what they were meant for. The very first sentence of his *Study* states: "Our minds are not made as large as truth, nor suited to the whole extent of things; amongst those that come within its reach, it meets with a great many too big for its grasp, and there are not a few it is fair to give up as incomprehensible".[15] This conclusion, moreover, is not presented as a pessimistic one. From Locke's point of view, nothing is lost as a consequence, since he does not see that men have anything to do with such matters anyway. He finds no reason to "bemoan our want of knowledge in the particular apartments of the universe," since in his opinion "our portion here lies only in the little spot of earth where we and all our concernments are shut up".[16] "What need have we to complain of our ignorance in the more general and foreign parts of nature," he asks, "when all our business lies at home?"[16] But this is simply to demand what use great visions of the intelligible structure of the universe could possibly be to the *practical*, Protestant, English businessman who, having gained political power, was next turning calculating eyes to cultural and intellectual matters. And so, it is such a person whom Locke primarily addresses as the one most interested in inquiry, and it is such a person's natural sphere of interest which he delimits as its proper context.

None of the dialectical fireworks of the Marxian *class-angling* technique is required to show that the considerations which influence Locke most in this little work are thoroughly *bourgeois*. If a much overworked phrase may be exploited a little further, and we may write for a moment with tongue in cheek, Locke's very language is saturated with *bourgeois* ideology.[17] The whole thing is a tentative gesture at a *capitalist coup*, a proposal on the part of a middle-class champion to seize the enterprise of learning, which Bacon had proclaimed for all mankind, and conduct it in the interest of business entrepreneurs.

Bacon, of course, could not too often insist that the knowledge he wished to promote was equivalent to the power of making nature subservient to our wants; and Descartes also came eventually to see his "true philosophy" as "wisdom" which serves practical needs. But for Descartes this was an afterthought, a somewhat belated observation which he made with a kind of glad astonishment, and which he used to help *sell* to others ideas on which he had already been *sold* himself for other reasons. And for Bacon the notion was conceived from the outset in more heroic, Utopian terms. Regardless of the eventual use made of it by the citizens of his *New Atlantis,* the commodity for which the "merchants" of his "house of Solomon" exchange all others in "light". From "truth in speculation" to "freedom in operation" is the sequence of ideas in Bacon's thinking; while in this *Study* of Locke's the movement of thought is the other way around—from restrictions defined by practice to restrictions imposed on theory.

Accordingly, whereas Descartes sought truth wherever it was mathematically evident to him, and Bacon surveyed the "intellectual globe" with a view to "invasion and conquest", Locke the traveler undertakes to "marshal the parts of knowledge" largely with a view to "husbanding" man's precious little time for such matters. First in order of importance he puts "knowledge of heaven" as "our great business and interest".[18] This is proper, seemly, respectable, and all that. Then, immediately following: "The next thing to happiness in the other world, is a quiet prosperous passage through this, which requires a discreet conduct and management of ourselves in the several occurrences of our lives;" wherefore he assigns "the study of prudence" to "the second place in our thoughts and studies".[18] And finally: "If those who are left by their predecessors with a plentiful fortune are excused from having a particular calling, in order to their subsistence in this life, it is yet certain that, by the law of God, they are under an obligation of doing something," and "in these," he thinks, "it is incumbent to make the proper business of their calling the third place in their study"[19].

In short, as Locke delimits "the extent of knowledge" here, he confines it primarily to the domain of practice as determined by the most respectable standards of late seventeenth century, middleclass society. First and foremost he makes it an adjunct of a routine of industrious attention to business. And secondly he allows it to overflow a little as the kind of hobby which can lend respectability to life in such a society when the system of accumulation and inheritance makes industriousness not absolutely necessary in more obvious ways. After all, as Locke says, a man does have to do something! But even then, when inquiry is made a gentleman's indulgence, or possibly a *raison d'être* for a leisure class, it is still referred back to the callings which would have to be practiced did the labors of others not make that unnecessary. The whole undertaking is just as completely adjusted as in the first case to the exigencies of a *bourgeois* conception of "man's business". Without any of the involved argument or elaborate analytical paraphernalia of the other prefatory writings we have considered here, then, this early *Study* of Locke's gives an account of inquiry which we may now sum up by saying that it tends to—

1. Put inquiry in question *in terms of criteria of "practicality" in a limited business-class sense of the expression.*

2. To identify the agent of inquiry *as the "practical" type of substantial, industrious, Protestant business man who began to turn to intellectual and cultural matters in the latter 17th Century.*

3. To delimit the context of inquiry *as the sphere of this "practical" business man's "practical" interests.*

4. To single out the crucial problems of inquiry *as "practical" ones in the sense of relating to the difficulties which usually confront the business man.*

5. To interpret the issue of inquiry *to be advice as to the business man's immediate "practical" concerns.*

III: AGAINST THE DOCTRINE OF "INNATE IDEAS"

When we pick up the train of Locke's thoughts on the same matters more than a decade later in his *Essay Concerning Human Understanding*,[20] we again find him proposing to define "the extent of human knowledge" in order to forewarn the inquirer of its limits. "If, by this enquiry into the nature of the understanding, I can discover the powers thereof, how far they reach, to what things they are in any degree proportionate, and where they fail us," he writes in the first chapter, "I suppose it may be of use to prevail with the busy mind of man, to be more cautious in meddling with things exceeding its comprehension; to stop when it is at the utmost extent of its tether; and to sit down in a quiet ignorance of those things, which, upon examination, are found to be beyond the reach of our capacities."[21]

Locke's language here is perhaps less obviously colored with the ideology which gives his *Study* its characteristic tone; but it has much the same tenor, especially in his repeated insistence that our seeking faculties are fitted to give us guidance in our immediate *practical* affairs, rather than power or vision in any broader sense. It announces his conclusion that "the candle, that is set up in us, shines bright enough for all our purposes", not because of any newly found confidence on his part in the brilliance of our intellectual faculties, but simply because of the persistence of his belief that "our business here is not to know all things," and that "if we can find out those measures whereby a rational creature, put in that state which man is in this world, may, and ought to govern his opinions and actions depending thereon, we need not be troubled that some other things escape our knowledge" etc., etc.[22] It is quite unmistakable that Locke intended this treatise primarily as a more careful statement of the general interpretation made of inquiry in his *Study during a Journey*. But the *Essay's* lengthy account of "the understanding . . . set at a distance and made its own object" goes so far beyond the more obvious needs of such a purpose, that its origin in anything of the kind often seems lost to view even by Locke himself. It appears that in later life Locke somewhat outgrew his earlier hard-headed-undergraduate attitude. Or at least—and here both his own report and the record of history bear us out—the day came when he had more time and was free to see things from other points of view. Ill health and exile with the Earl of Shaftesbury forced him to neglect the business to which he had been concerned men should keep so strictly. And during this period he picked up from the currents of thought in his day a number of conceptions which carried him considerably further in the realm of speculation than he had previously allowed it wise for anyone to go, with the result that he then found very different ways of expressing the general convictions already sketched in the *Study*.

This development is apparent in the *Essay* from its very outset. At the beginning of *Book I*, Locke writes that it will "suffice" to his "present purposes" to "consider the discerning faculties of man, as they are employed about the objects, which they have to do with".[23] Construing this remark in the light of his earlier discussion of the same theme, one might well assume that he would then go on to consider how men deal with the various things which their business concerns. But as readers of the *Essay* soon find, he actually does something quite different. Before he is through with his introductory chapter, he adds a special section to apologize for his "frequent use of the word 'Idea' ", explaining that it is the term which he believes "serves best to stand for whatsoever is the object of the understanding, when a man thinks"[24]; and thenceforth it is "ideas" which he mainly discusses. Locke's first major departure in the *Essay*, from his earlier *Study*, is his assumption that, whatever business men may deal with, it is by "ideas" that they do so. Accordingly, whereas all the prefatory writings thus far examined here have begun with fairly direct criticisms of ways in which inquiry is sometimes approached, *Book I* of the *Essay* bottoms on a critique of a particular current doctrine of "ideas"—namely, that which asserted certain basically important ones to be "innate". Commenting on the intellectual temper of his age, Locke remarks that "There is nothing more commonly taken for granted, than that there are certain principles both speculative and practical . . . universally agreed upon; which therefore . . . must needs be constant impressions which the souls of men receive in their first beings, and which they bring into the world with them, as necessarily and really as they do any of their inherent faculties."[25] But he then proceeds systematically to marshal reasons against such a view, maintaining: that the "universal assent" commonly claimed for these "ideas" would be no proof of their "innateness" even if it were to be found; that consideration of many apparent contradictions among alleged "innate practical maxims", and of obvious widespread ignorance of alleged "innate theoretical maxims", reveals them not to be universally accepted anyway; and finally, that observation of children proves both to be of post-natal discovery even in those instances where they are encountered.[26]

It goes without saying, of course, that all this is most unlike the sort of critical observation which introduces the other prefatory writings thus far examined in *Part Two* of this study; and the consequences of that fact we shall presently consider in more detail. But first we should note that for all immediate purposes the main argument of *Book I* serves much the same ends. Locke's use of the word "idea" to "express whatever it is which the mind can be employed about in thinking"[27] is simply an adaptation of his language to the practice of his contemporaries.[28] More than anything else it is a sign of the influence which Descartes' prefatory writings had had on the thought of the seventeenth century. By turning from the academies and the world of affairs in the "fable" of his *Discourse,* and by invoking the "demon of doubt" to spirit away the whole universe of such things in his *Meditations,*

Descartes had confronted the thinking of the inquirer with a panorama of "ideas" presumed to constitute the stuff of his "beliefs", but alleged to be detached from any consideration of what they were beliefs about; and the resulting delineation of the agent and context of inquiry had so subtly insinuated itself into the thought of his readers that even those who, like Locke, attempted to challenge almost everything he wished to establish, tended to accept it as axiomatic in those very writings which they intended to be refutations of his. During the latter seventeenth century the doctrine of "innate ideas" was the form in which Descartes' "metaphysical" prolegomena found most popular expression; and consequently, Locke's attack on the doctrine is in effect an attack on a particular kind of approach which he found commonly made to inquiry in his day. For Descartes himself his "metaphysics" may have meant assurance, as against the claims of strongly intrenched traditional learning, that his mathematical physics and derived sciences had an independent claim to cultivation. But its later restatements in terms of the doctrines of "innate ideas" tended to mean assurance to others that further examination was not necessary for what they took to be the "first principles" of science, and that all subsequent research was simply a task of deducing the remoter implications of these "principles" or of interpreting in terms of them what new observations they could yet make. Although originally appealed to as a way of breaking down old restrictions and starting inquiry afresh, therefore, this "metaphysics" tended to develop into a way of confining inquiry within a new set of limitations after the fresh start for which it was appealed to had been made.

That, at least, is how it strikes Locke as a critic of the thinking of his contemporaries. His explanation of "whence the conviction of innate principles" reveals his whole attack upon them to be a protest against lazy un-inquisitiveness dominated by arbitrary dictatorship in matters of investigation.[29] After one has followed his arguments through to the end, the upshot of them all is that there is no easy short-cut to knowledge. The entire dialectical structure is "only by the by, to show how much our knowledge depends upon the right use of those powers nature hath bestowed upon us".[30] As Locke remarks himself in the abstract which he made of the *Essay* for *Le Clerc* to translate into French for the *Bibliothèque Universelle*, the purpose of its first book is "only to remove the prejudice that lies in some men's minds."[31] And he concludes it, under the caption "men must think for themselves", with the scorn-ful insistence that "the floating of other men's opinions in our brains, makes us not one jot the more knowing, though they happen to be true. What in them was science, is in us but opinionatry . . ." etc., etc.[32] And thus Locke's attack upon the doctrine of "innate ideas" develops to be simply an attempt, within the context of an essay prefatory to inquiry proper, to liberate the enterprise from its late liberators, by a critique of the very device through which its liberation had previously been attempted in a similar treatise. Part at least of the "rubbish" Locke wished to clear away from the feet of the "master builders" was the notion which seemed to him insinuated by Cartesian "metaphysics" that the foundations of learning, or the framework within which all further research was to be pursued, had already been construed for all time. And clearly, this is the sort of "under-labourer" work which needs most to be done in the most "knowing" ages.

But like the other introductory critiques we have observed here in prefatory writings, Locke's criticism of the doctrine of "innate ideas" also raises a fundamental question concerning the general project of inquiry—in this case, the question of its "origins". If we are asked to regard the immediate objects of our researches to be "ideas", and are next vigorously assured that these "ideas" are not "innate", we find our-selves naturally inclined to ask: *What are they then? If we have them now, but at one time did not, how did we since come by them?* And it is precisely this line of thought which Locke himself follows. Whereas in his *Study* he had suggested consideration of only the "extent and measure" of knowledge, at the outset of his *Essay* he proposes to in-vestigate its *"original,* certainty, and extent".[33] *Book II* of the latter treatise, furthermore, is devoted explicitly to showing "whence the understanding may get all the ideas it has, and by what ways and degrees they may come into the mind"[34]; from which we must conclude that Locke's presumption is that we can arrive at conclusions about the "extent and measure" of knowledge by examining how it is acquired. By raising the question of "origins", his attack on the doctrine of "in-nate ideas" calls attention to inquiry as a process which arrives where it does by starting from somewhere else, thus making consideration of its beginnings most relevant. And it is to Locke's treatment of this ques-tion of "sources" or "originals" that his introductory critique now com-pels us to turn.

IV: A COMMONSENSE APPEAL TO "EXPERIENCE"

As everyone who is even the least bit acquainted with the *Essay* knows, on raising the question of how the "understanding" comes by the "ideas" which he says constitute "all the materials of reason and knowledge", Locke's "answer in one word" is: "from experience." "In that all our knowledge is founded," he writes, "and from that it ultimately derives itself."[35] Accordingly, he makes the bulk of *Book II* an attempt to show in detail how all our various "ideas" may be traced to that origin, the bulk of *Book III* an attempt to show how the "words" which serve to communicate "ideas" may ultimately be traced to it too, and the bulk of *Book IV* an attempt to draw the implications for our knowledge and discourses of this common derivation of "ideas" and "words" from such a source. "Experience" is the second important conception which contributes to the argument of the *Essay*, causing it to depart from the language and form of the *Study*.

But what did Locke mean by the "experience" to which he thus attached so much importance? The notion was not new with him, and it has been invoked almost constantly since. Bacon's doctrine of "induction", for example, was certainly such an appeal by his own literal account of it; and we can hardly say that Descartes did not, in a sense, "experience" the amazing adventures reported in his *Metaphysical Meditations*. What is more, even Locke himself tends to write about "experience" in very different ways despite his concern to be circumspectly exact. As in the case of the comparable appeals considered in the preceding chapters, therefore, we must examine further the developments it has in the *Essay* before we can gather anything very instructive about it.

Doubtless the most commonplace meaning of the term "experience" is its simple reference in everyday discourse to *the happenings which befall one*. It is in this sense that we tell about *the experiences we have had*, that we call the worldly-wise *people of experience*, or that we regard the training we get from the jobs we have done to be *experience which qualifies* us for the jobs we should like yet to do. And it is in this sense, too, that Locke writes of it first and most obviously in his *Essay*. From the very beginning of *Book I*, his most telling arguments against the doctrine of "innate ideas" take the form of insistences that we have no knowledge of even the simplest things until we have met up with what they concern.[36] In *Book II* most of his accounts of the "origins" of our "ideas" trace them to their beginnings in our dealings with things as we come upon them in the regular course of our lives. And in both cases the process referred to is "experience" in the common, every-day sense of the chain of significant events which link one's present and future to one's past as far back as birth and the cradle. It is true that Locke does not in any one place make a very systematic attempt to fol-low up the total sequence of such events in strict chronological order. The plan of his analysis—starting from "simple ideas" of "one sense," "more than one sense", "reflection," and "sensation and reflection"; con-tinuing thence to "complex ideas" of "modes", "substances", and "re-lations"—not only does not require strict chronology, but actually cuts across it in a number of ways. Besides, he is not so simple-minded as to imagine that the matter is one which admits of very strict formulation of that kind, since he recognizes well enough that "the order wherein the several ideas come at first into the mind, is very various and uncer-tain also".[37] Yet it is clear enough, despite all this, that in most of what Locke says about the "origin of ideas", he assumes the "experi-ence" out of which he traces the growth of "understanding" to be the sum total of the events met with by the man who is said to have it. And throughout *Book II*, he constantly makes parenthetical remarks which suggest the general character of this assumed underlying process, even though he attempts for the most part to intersect it only at certain series of points which he regards to be particularly relevant to his analysis. The process begins, we may gather, with the first vague stirrings of life in the womb.[38] Then, as activity increases with general maturity, it broadens as a larger, more diversified range of material comes into ken[39]; and with that enlargement of the range of materials encountered comes an increasing ability to deal with them understandingly.[40] The process is simply that of the growth of a perceiving, thinking animal maturing in acquaintance with its environment, and becoming more competent to inhabit it intelligently.

Throughout *Book II* of the *Essay*, of course, the "experience" of which Locke writes is always a highly personal matter, since the "ideas" which he there traces to it are, for him, always an individual's private acquisitions—"all within his own breast, invisible, and hidden from others".[41] Consequently, on finding himself compelled by the implica-tions of his theme to consider, in *Book III*, the "words" which express "ideas",[42] the "experience" to which he there traces their "origin" is of a much more public character. Occasionally, in mentioning how indi-

viduals come by the use of language, he does refer again to the kind of
acquaintanceship with things which we must regard to be strictly that
of an individual.[43] But in most of *Book III* he is more concerned with
"speech" as "the great bond that holds society together, and the common
conduit whereby the improvements of knowledge are conveyed from
one man and one generation to another."[44] In taking up "words" in
relation to "understanding", he treats them primarily as instruments
of social intercourse; and so the background against which he reviews
them is naturally the social "experience" which men possess collectively.

Despite this broadening of the appeal, however, it has an even more
obviously commonplace, everyday meaning in its most immediate application. As in the case of the personal "experience" to which he traces
the origin of "ideas", Locke does not attempt to outline its process very
systematically in chronological order. The third book of the *Essay* is
patterned too closely on the plan of the second for that to be altogether
convenient. But here again frequent parenthetical remarks suggest the
general scheme of the process which Locke presumes his actual observations to intersect; and from these we gather that it is very much the social
equivalent of the process already described in his account of the genesis
of "ideas". Corresponding to the foetal or infant stage of the individual
when he begins to get impressions from his first surroundings, for example, there is an initial phase of communal life when men first strike
upon articulate sounds as the most convenient tokens by which to convey to each other their otherwise unapparent private thoughts.[45] And
then as society, like the individual, encounters more and more complicated issues, the structure of language grows in complexity to deal
with them adequately. In the broad sense in which Locke here writes
of the "experience" from which "words" derive, it may not even be
divisible into a large number of individual careers. It breaks down,
rather, only into the various collective careers of different cultural
groups whose joint dealings with things are sufficiently isolated from
each other to find expression in different tongues.[46] Nevertheless, it
relates just the same to the familiarity people acquire with things by
meeting with them in their daily lives—to "experience", that is to say,
in the most ordinary, everyday sense, whether it be that of a single individual or of a cultural group consisting of many millions of individuals.

To sum up this much, then, we may now state the outcome of Locke's
commonsense appeal to "experience" as we have thus far traced its role

in his prefatory account of the "ideas" and "words" which instrument inquiry. Clearly, it serves on the one hand to call the inquirer's attention to himself as one whose passage from womb to grave is one long, adventurous series of encounters with the things he would understand. It identifies the inquirer as a *man of experience* in exactly the same basic sense as the adventurer, the man of the world, and the man of broad business background; extending the same identification, of course, to traditions of inquiry, and calling them to awareness of possession of essentially similar careers only on a much larger scale. And on the other hand the appeal also serves to delimit the context of inquiry as the familiar world which is the locus of all such encounters—the commonplace, everyday world in which babes find for themselves that milk is white and sugar sweet, and in which hard-thinkers come to decide, singly or in synod, that God is great and just, or fictitious and absurd, depending on which conclusion the events of their pasts tend to point to.

V: THE PROBLEMS OF EVERYDAY "EXPERIENCE"

The *commonsense* account of "experience" just considered is of course not the only one which figures in the *Essay*. Locke interweaves his description of how men get understanding from the daily give-and-take of life with a more recondite account of the alleged circumstances under which the process takes place. But this latter development of the appeal will be considered in the next chapter where it may be given the more detailed discussion it warrants. Here we shall be concerned mainly with the implications of the first in those parts of the *Essay* where Locke draws most of his conclusions. The analysis is somewhat complicated by the fact that Locke himself was not very keenly aware of the ambiguity of this basic term in his book. But notwithstanding that complication, it appears that his account of how we come by our ideas and words through *everyday "experience"* tends in general to lead most directly to a consideration of the common misadventures with which such a way of encounter meets, and to suggestions as to what might be done about them.

In the last chapter of *Book II*, for example, Locke notes that, depending on how we meet with things, our "ideas" about them often tend to get linked together, or "associated", in ways which are highly adventitious. "Some of our ideas", he writes, "have a natural correspondence and connection with each other" which enables reason to "hold them together in that union and correspondence which is founded in their peculiar beings"; but "there is another connection . . . wholly owing to chance or custom", he adds, and "this strong combination of ideas, not allied by nature, the mind makes in itself either voluntarily or by chance, and hence it comes in different men to be very different, according to their different inclinations, education, interests, &c."[47] Some instances Locke gives of the tendency are as trivial as the fear of the dark which some people have because a foolish maid frightened them with stories of goblins and sprights when they were young[48]; but these serve merely to illustrate in an obvious, elementary way the strength and irrationality of the "association". Relating the point to graver matters, he goes on to observe that "intellectual habits and defects this way contracted are not less frequent and powerful, though less observed"[49]; and to "some such wrong and unnatural combinations of "ideas" he traces "the irreconcilable opposition between different sects of philosophy and religion." Since he does not believe that "interest, though it does a great deal in the case," can "be thought to work whole societies of men to so universal a perverseness," he concludes that "that which thus captivates their reasons, and leads men of sincerity blindfold from common sense, will, when examined, be found to be what we are speaking of: some independent ideas, of no alliance to one another, are by education, custom, and the constant din of their party, so coupled in their minds, that they always appear there together; and they can no more separate them in their thoughts, than if they were but one idea, and they operate as if they were so. This gives sense to jargon, demonstration to absurdities, and consistency to nonsense, and is the foundation of the greatest, I had almost said of all the errors in the world; or if it does not reach so far, it is at least the most dangerous one, since so far as it obtains, it hinders men from seeing and examining;" etc., etc.[50] What Locke points to here is what we might call today *ideological conditioning*; and we can hardly fail to agree with him that it is a kind of tampering with the process of free, unprejudiced "experience" which is among the more serious causes of stupid conflict in the world.

Similarly in *Book III*, in his chapters on the "imperfections" and "abuses" of language, Locke points out that the way in which we happen to come by the use of words often tends to defeat their end of communicating the lessons of "experience."[51] The critique is too long and involved to consider in detail, but an example or two will indicate its general drift. In its widest range it applies to the speech habits acquired by people of all sorts and callings, as where Locke remarks that much of the stupid jargon we hear people so commonly talking is due to the fact that they have picked up expressions in common use, and become facile in mouthing them, without ever having really examined what they are strictly intended to signify.[52] In such instances Locke assumes the resulting errors to be unwitting, since he attributes them to the failure of most people to realize with what care the use of language must be cultivated. But in the most important application of the critique he accuses the "sects of philosophy" of deliberately propagating "artificial ignorance and learned gibberish" by the systematic exploitation of this natural imperfection of language which deceives the ignorant; and he charges their "affected obscurity and wrong application of words" with the serious practical consequences of perplexing honest men's efforts to comprehend the law and religion they try to live by.[53]

Then finally, in *Book IV* Locke follows up these remarks with a number of observations on how men sometimes utterly disregard the manner in which we come to understand and communicate by encounter with things, and on how they are more often hindered from making what use they might of it. Recourse to "experience" is usually so laborious, and in the case of more extravagant beliefs often so impossible, he points out on the first score, that some men try to circumvent it altogether by persuading themselves that they enjoy "immediate revelation from God", which makes anything so mundane as experience unnecessary.[54] This, of course, is the most flagrant way of ignoring the lessons to be learned by the natural use of one's faculties; and it was common enough in Locke's age of latter-day prophets for him to devote a whole chapter to it under the name of *Enthusiasm*.

But whereas such fanaticism was somewhat exceptional, and at least half pathological, in the following chapter on *Wrong Assent or Error* he considers related problems of broader implication. That mistaken views are extremely widespread Locke takes to be evident from the fact that "there is nothing more common than contrariety of opinions" not all of which could possibly be correct[55]; and although he tends to explain this prevalence of error partly in terms of a frank recognition that many people are too stupid to be able to learn much anyway[56], he also calls attention to the restrictions imposed on what ability they have, by obstacles which prevent their making acquaintance with the things which might give them more adequate understanding. Among these, for example, are the difficulties faced by "the greatest part of mankind, who are given up to labour, and enslaved to the necessity of their mean conditions, whose lives are worn out only in the provision for living". "These men's opportunity of knowledge and enquiry are commonly as narrow as their fortunes," he observes realistically enough, "and their understandings are but little instructed, when all their whole time and pains is laid out to still the croaking of their own bellies, or the cries of their children."[57] But, "besides those, whose improvements and informations are straitened by the narrowness of their fortunes," he adds, "there are others whose largeness of fortune would plentifully enough supply books and other requirements for clearing of doubts, and discovering of truth: but they are cooped in close, by the laws of their countries, and the strict guards of those whose interest it is to keep them ignorant, lest, knowing more, they should believe the less in them." It is difficult not to conclude with Locke that: "These are so far, nay farther from the liberty and opportunities of a fair enquiry, than those poor and wretched labourers we before spoke of, and, however they may seem high and great, are confined to narrowness of thought, and enslaved in that which should be the freest part of man, their understandings."[58] Given an economic and political interpretation, the point admits of tremendous generalization for the contemporary scene in many places where the obstacles of poverty are alleged to be overcome or fast disappearing.

Lastly, even where Locke finds no fanatical impulse to fly in the face of all "experience", no lack of the ability to learn, and no obstacles of poverty or oppression to keep men from the free exploration of the world and its issues, he still finds that often they will not learn by it although they have every opportunity. Towards the very end of his long, earnest account of "human understanding", he cynically observes that most men are usually content to act without anything of the kind, for lack, perhaps, of the instinct or habit of intelligence. "Their hot pursuit of pleasure, or constant drudgery in business," he writes, "engages some men's thoughts elsewhere: laziness and obstinacy in general, or a particular aversion for books, study and meditation, keep others from any serious thoughts at all; and some out of fear, that an impartial inquiry would not favour these opinions which best suit their prejudices, lives, and designs, content themselves, without examination, to take upon trust what they find convenient and in fashion."[59] One thing Locke himself seems to have learned from his dealings with his fellows is how little most of them really learn from anything. "If any one should a little catechize the greatest part of the partizans of most of the sects in the world," we find him writing on one of the final pages of the *Essay*, "he would not find, concerning those matters, they are so zealous for, that they have any opinions of their own: much less would he have reason to think, that they took them upon the examination of arguments, and appearance of probability. They are resolved to stick to a party, that education or interest has engaged them in; and there, like the common soldiers of any army, show their courage and warmth as their leaders direct, without ever examining or so much as knowing the cause they contend for."[60]

Not to follow these observations further into their details, it is already clear that, having defined the inquirer as the familiar sort of fellow who gets on to things by coming into contact with them, and having delimited the context of inquiry as the familiar world in which this contact occurs, the whole train of thought turns quite naturally to a consideration of the circumstances and controls which affect the give-and-take between such a person and such a place. Application of Locke's appeal to "experience" in the *everyday* sense of the term makes the success of our "understanding" turn on the success of our efforts to enlarge and discipline our familiar day-to-day dealing with the matters which it concerns. Regardless of what may be said of other parts of the *Essay*, this strain of its argument singles out as the crucial problems of inquiry the kind of difficulties into which inquirers run because of restrictions placed on their opportunities for encounter with things, or because of failures to make the right use of them. Poverty, tyranny, and downright stupidity are typical of the former; mis-education, mis-use of language, fanaticism, and intellectual indifference are typical of the latter. Formally these may be said to be problems of acquiring "determinate ideas", or of making language "intelligible". But against the background of Locke's appeal to *everyday* "experience", they reduce to problems of thinking and speaking on the basis of broad first-hand observations, freely, but carefully, made. Unlike the difficulties which appear in the *Study*, they call for measures to cultivate natural curiosity rather than to confine it. They are challenges to action rather than warnings to inaction. As a result of his earlier sketch of the limitations of "human knowledge", Locke had found himself principally required to tell the inquirer how to avoid the "infinite windings, by-ways, and turnings" of research, lest they lead where man's "pilgrimage through this life" has no immediate practical concern.[61] But here he mentions "constant drudgery in business", along with "the hot pursuit of pleasure", and "laziness and obstinacy in general", as one of the more unfortunate obstacles to intellectual maturity. The difficulties which he finds confronting everyday "experience" lead up to the positive suggestions for the vigorous undertaking of research in such chapters of the *Essay* as those on *Remedies of the Imperfections and Abuses of Words* in *Book III*, and on *Probability* in *Book IV;* and they find further development in the constructive arguments of his later writings on *Education, Toleration,* and *The Conduct of the Understanding.* The whole line of thought becomes quite inevitably a demand for better training of the young, for freer governmental institutions, and for stricter self-discipline, because, as "understanding" is here portrayed, they are the sort of things which most vitally affect it.

VI: "EXPERIENCE" AS A DOCTRINE OF KNOWLEDGE

Thus, this development of Locke's *Essay* serves as a liberation from his narrow, earlier approach to inquiry, and it opens up the lines of thoughts which produced the most important of his later works. The point can perhaps be most interestingly illustrated in the treatise *Of the Conduct of the Understanding,* which one might well call *Locke's discourse on method.* Having observed that the growth of "understanding" through everyday "experience" depends largely on the range of the matters it encounters, and having pointed out the more common obstacles to this growth, Locke here advises inquirers against too little curiosity and too restricted a point of view. Those who "converse but with one sort of men, . . . read but one sort of books," and "will not come in the hearing but of one sort of notions," he writes, "canton out to themselves a little Goshen, in the intellectual world" within which they usually manage well enough, but outside of which they cannot even get their bearings, for sheer ignorance of what the rest of the "intellectual world" is like.[62] Hence, he warns his readers against the very kind of provincialism in matters intellectual that he had formerly advised them to cultivate in the interest of "husbanding" their time; and he appeals to men to exercise their understandings "in the full extent of things intelligible". Belittling the difficulties which keep one from being well informed, Locke writes of the man who would learn: "Let him exercise the freedom of his reason and understanding in such a latitude as this, and his mind will be strengthened, his capacity enlarged, his faculties improved; and the light, which the remote and scattered parts of truth will give to one another, will so assist his judgement, that he will seldom be widely out, or miss giving proof of a clear head, and a comprehensive knowledge."[62] Whereas Locke has begun his *Study* by insisting on the serious shortcomings of our minds, and the folly of presuming too much of them, here he proclaims that "we are born with faculties and powers capable almost of anything . . . but it is only the exercise of those powers, which gives us ability and skill in any thing, and leads us towards perfection."[63] And in a number of similar ways, the treatise *Of the Conduct of the Understanding*", like the other later writings of Locke mentioned above, follows up the problems of inquiry to which attention is directed by the *Essay* with positive suggestions as to how our "understanding" can be improved by broader, better disciplined, exploration of the world and its issues.

The development of Locke's appeal to *everyday* "experience" therefore, may be said to crystallize in a doctrine of knowledge in the positive sense of a theory of how knowledge is actually obtained. The most important single conclusion which emerges from the parts of the *Essay* in which this appeal occurs is that "understanding" is a competence which is got in the same busy, energetic way as any other competence, such as that of a craft for example; namely, by the sort of "experience" which is acquired through sound, active apprenticeship.

The prefatory writings of Bacon and Descartes are also, in their most important outcome, doctrines of knowledge in the same positive sense; but there is an important difference which should not be overlooked between them and this one of Locke's. In arriving at the conclusion that "knowledge is power", Bacon circumscribes it within quite definitely determined, if broad, limits. And the final outcome of Descartes' "metaphysical" account of knowledge is so much narrower a delimitation of its "extent," especially as regards the form which it can assume, that he remarks in the *Preface* to his *Principles*, in the manner of a man who feels he is making a considerable concession, that "it might be several centuries before all the truths which can be deduced from these principles have actually been found out".[64] But the definition of "the extent of human knowledge" at which Locke arrives by his primary account of how we come by our "ideas" and "words" is a challenge to any such attitude. Like the attack on the "doctrine of innate ideas" which introduces it, it is a denial that the exact form or extent of the findings of research can ever really be foretold in a profoundly instructive way; and at the same time, it is also an insistance that the contrary belief is more likely to be confusing than helpful.[65]

Here Locke's *empiricism*, if one wishes to call his attitude that, is *radical* in the sense that it bottoms on the simple view that inquiry finds what it finds—if equations, well and good; but if not, then something else the nature of which becomes apparent only when it has been approached closely enough to become so. "Things themselves", he writes in his treatise *Of the Conduct of the Understanding*, "are to be considered as they are in themselves, and then they will show us in what way they are to be understood. For to have right conceptions about them, we must bring our understanding to the inflexible natures and unalterable relations of things, and not endeavor to bring things to any preconceived notions of our own."[66] Perhaps we can find the "intellectual world" divisible into such "provinces" as "physics, practice, and semantics", Locke agrees[67]; but such lines of partition radiate from a common center without forming an outer boundary. All he implies about the latter sort of limits is that our knowledge of them goes no farther than our exploration; and that the danger is not that we shall rashly try to overstep them, but that we shall be stopped far short of them by obstacles grounded in our own habits or institutions, with the result that we shall either assume that what little understanding we have is all there is to be had, or else be satisfied to act without any at all.

Although it was doubtless directed most specifically at Descartes' efforts definitively to settle questions prior to the actual undertaking of inquiry, therefore, this account of "the extent of human knowledge" admits of considerable generalization. In its broadest application, it is a protest against all prolegomena to our inquisition of things which, in giving our researches an exclusive direction or emphasis, however valuable, tend to cut off other possible investigations which might also prove fruitful when actually tried. And it appears that its task of thus undoing what is most negative in previous prolegomena, is one that needs to be frequently undertaken anew, especially in a "knowing age" such as Locke was so modestly aware of addressing.

VII: NOTE IN TRANSITION

On the plan of procedure followed in the preceding chapters of *Part Two* of this study, we might now sum up in more general terms the immediate conclusions suggested by the foregoing analysis of Locke's history of understanding. The conclusions which can thus be reached, however, may be more instructively stated after comparable consideration has been given to the other strain of development in the *Essay* mentioned above. We interrupt this account of Locke's *commonsense* appeal to everyday "experience" as a doctrine of knowledge to take up, in the following chapter, his better known development of "experience" as a doctrine of ignorance.

LOCKE ON THE DOCTRINE OF EXPERIENCE

I: A "PHYSICAL" EXPLANATION OF "EXPERIENCE"

THE account of inquiry discussed in the preceding chapter is quite obviously a straightforward development of Locke's proposal at the outset of the *Essay* to "consider the discerning faculties of man, as they are employed about the objects which they have to do with," and not to "meddle with the physical consideration of the mind, or trouble . . . to examine, wherein its essence consists, or by what motions of our spirits, or alterations of our bodies, we come to have any sensation by our organs, or any ideas in our understandings; and whether these ideas do in their formation, any, or all of them, depend on matter, or no", etc.[1] The same account, moreover, is just as obviously the only one Locke intended to give in the *Essay*. "Physical considerations" of the kind enumerated he explicitly rules out as "speculations which, however curious and entertaining, I shall decline, as lying out of my way, in the design I am upon."[2]

Nevertheless, the reader who is familiar with the *Essay* only through secondary sources, or through edited selections from its pages, will not be likely to recognize it very readily by the analysis thus far made here. What has been summarized is the *natural history* which Locke gives of "understanding" to estimate its extent. But despite the obvious appropriateness of this account to the specific design he proposes for the work, it is not the only one he gives in the course of his argument, and it is most certainly not the one primarily associated with the reputation of the *Essay*. In the histories of philosophy, where the text has received most attention, it is most often discussed in terms of the alleged "physical" explanation of "experience" to which Locke tends to resort despite his clearly expressed determination to do nothing of the kind.

The departure from the original proposal starts in seemingly innocent metaphors. At the beginning of *Book II*, for example, Locke figuratively refers to the "understanding" as "white paper, void of all characters", and to "experience" as the process by which images are "painted" on it.[3] And farther on, in *Chapter xi* of the same *Book*, he likens the mind to a "dark room", and the senses to small "windows" through which, as sole entrances, "pictures" are received of the world without[4]. Such imagery as this serves an apparent rhetorical purpose which justifies it sufficiently not to require our placing any literal construction upon it. But there are other developments in the *Essay* which gradually compel us to take a differet view of this seemingly figurative language.

The crucial point of the transition is in *Chapter viii* of *Book II*, where it is argued that such "ideas" as those of heat and cold, light and darkness, are equally "positive" even though some theorists may say that one or the other is due to the presence or absence of the same "causes"—dark from the absence of light, cold from the absence of heat, etc. At first Locke is content to remark that a painter or dyer, who knows nothing of such controversies, usually has better "ideas" of black and white than "the philosopher who hath busied himself in considering their natures"; and this is quite in the spirit of his *everyday* account of "experience". But he adds, as though by irrepressible impulse: "*If it were* the design of my present undertaking, to enquire into the natural causes and manner of perception; I should offer this as a reason why a privative cause might, in some cases at least, produce a positive idea; viz. that all sensation being produced in us only by different degrees and modes of motion in our animal spirits, variously agitated by external objects, the abatement of any former motion must as necessarily produce a new sensation, as the variation or increase of it; and so introduce a new idea, which depends only on a different motion of the animal spirits in that organ". Then, having ventured thus much, he adds with unconscious humour: "But whether this be so or no I will not here determine, but appeal to every one's own experience," etc., etc.[5]

Obviously, at this point Locke just simply could not resist going beyond the simple encounter of white and black to tell how he would explain what underlies it, had he not previously said he was not going to do that sort of thing. And from there it is but a short and easy step for him to ignore his resolution altogether. His famous account of "primary and secondary qualities" and of the mechanism of "perception" begins but a paragraph later with the remark: "To discover the nature of our ideas the better, and to discourse of them intelligibly, it will be convenient to distinguish them as they are ideas of perceptions in our minds, and as they are modifications of matter in the bodies that cause such perceptions in us . . ."[6]; whereupon there follows an explanation: (1) that an "idea" is "whatsoever the mind perceives in itself, or is the immediate object of perception, thought, or understanding"; (2) that a "quality of a subject" is its "power to produce any idea in our mind"; (3) that the "primary qualities", namely "bulk, extension, figure, motion or rest, and number", may be called "real qualities" because they "really exist in . . . bodies"; (4) that "secondary qualities", such as "colours, sounds, tastes, etc." are "in truth . . . nothing in the objects themselves, but powers to produce various sensations in us"; and (5) that therefore all "ideas" of "bodies" must be produced in the mind "by the operation of insensible particles" which, "singly imperceptible", strike upon the "senses" and "thereby convey to the brain some motion, which produces these ideas which we have . . . in us"[7].

All of this implies such a totally different conception of "experience" than any thus far reviewed in the *Essay* that except for the inclusion of "bulk" among the "primary qualities" of things—an addition which is completely explained by the role of the conception of mass in Newtonian physics—its account of knower and known is almost identical to the one at which Descartes finally arrived in all the statements of his "metaphysical principles of knowledge". Its use of the terms "understanding" and "bulk", rather than Descartes' "thinking substance" and "pure extension", does not in the least affect its fundamentally similar outcome in an opposition between a focal point of "ideas", on the one hand, located in the "brain" and supplemented by a system of impulse-conveying nerves, and, on the other hand, a world of the pure subject matter of physical science, albeit one advanced by the theory of gravitational mass. Even Locke's introductory proposal to explain it all in the interest of discoursing "intelligibly" reminds one most forcibly of Descartes' first digression into such matters in order to "expound clearly" what he believed he had thus far set down "only in a confused and artless manner"[8].

But whereas Descartes' resort to description of the knowing situation in such a way is quite readily explained, if not justified, by the demands of the "intuitive and deductive" way of "certainty" to which he felt committed, Locke's is not a little difficult to comprehend in such terms, in as much as his original explanation of how we come by our "ideas" does not very obviously demand anything of the kind. His own repeated resolutions not to "meddle" with such matters is evidence enough that he himself recognized his account of the mechanics of perception to be a departure from his straightforward consideration of how the individual grows in command of the materials of understanding, and society grows in command of the means of discourse, as they encounter more and more of the familiar situations and issues which evoke ideas and words. Yet, the further he expounds these "physical considerations", the further he departs from the familiar domain of *everyday* "experience".

II: THE "REAL ESSENCES" OF "SUBSTANCES"

It is in the discussion of the "ideas" and "names" of "substances" that we find the greatest complication of this development of the *Essay*. "If anyone should be asked, what is the subject wherein colour or weight inheres," Locke writes in his chapter on the first of these, "he would have nothing to say, but the solid extended parts". This, of course, is consistent with the "physical explanation" just summarized. But then Locke adds that "if he were demanded, what is it that solidity and extension inhere in, he would not be in much better case than the Indian . . . , who, saying that the world was supported by a great elephant, was asked what the elephant rested on; to which his answer was, A great tortoise. But being again pressed to know what gave support to the broad-backed tortoise, replied, Something, he knew not what."[9] Despite the obvious absurdity of his Indian's predicament, Locke seems to regard the question addressed to him as a legitimate one. In our "fashions of speaking" of this or that thing without any direct reference to its manifest characteristics, he finds an implied reference to a "substratum" supposed to be "always something besides the extension, figure, solidity, motion, thinking, or any other observable ideas"[10]. And this "substratum" or "real essence" he defines as "the real constitution of any thing, which is the foundation of all those properties that are combined in, and are constantly found to coexist with the nominal essence; that particular constitution which everything has within itself, without relation to any thing without it."[11]

In first explaining how we come by our "ideas of substances", Locke had remarked merely that: "The mind being . . . furnished with a great number of the simple ideas, . . . takes notice also that a certain number of these simple ideas go constantly together; which being presumed to belong to one thing, and words being suited to common apprehensions, and made use of for quick dispatch, are called, so united in one subject, by one name"[12]; and these "bundles of ideas", he had observed, serve in a rough, but usually satisfactory way, to organize our thinking about our countless impressions for most ordinary practical purposes. But when he now considers these same "ideas" over and against the "internal constitutions" of what he presumes to be their underlying "archetypes", he naturally finds them quite "inadequate"[13]. And likewise, in his discussion of the names of "substances", he can find their signification only in the same "inadequate complex ideas", which he there calls their "nominal essences" as distinguished from the "real essences" of their "archetypes" in the real scheme of things. Thus Locke arrives at the conclusion that neither the "ideas" which constitute the matter of our thinking, nor the words which implement our discourse, are really relevant to the sources in natural existence from which they ultimately derive[14]. In bottoming his "physical" explanation of "experience" on a still more basic explanation of the "real essences" of "substances", he construes both the inquiring mind and the ultimate objects of its inquiry to be undiscoverable somethings, we know not what. In this second, more recondite account of "experience", it finally becomes a relation between terms thoroughly inaccessible to the kind of familiar process implied by his appeals to it in the *everyday* sense previously examined here. If what we considered in the last chapter is a *natural history* of understanding, we are dealing here with a kind of *un-natural history* of the same process—*un-natural* at least in so far as the potentialities of men are concerned.

III: "EXPERIENCE" AS A DOCTRINE OF IGNORANCE

Against this background, the main technical argument of *Book IV* of the *Essay* is a mere formality. Its *discovery* that we can have no "science of nature" is plainly inevitable. On the one hand, "knowledge" is defined from the point of view of "higher spirits" who "see and know the nature and inward constitution of things" by "a direct grasp" of their "real essences"[15]. And on the other hand, the thought and discourse of men is represented as confined to "ideas" and "words" intrinsically unequal to the comprehension or expression of anything of the kind. We need only inspect these premises to deduce with Locke that, however much we may strive for it, "scientific knowledge" will always be "out of our reach; because we want perfect and adequate ideas of those very bodies which are nearest to us, and most under our command"[16].

In the second sense in which Locke appeals to it in the *Essay*, "experience" tends to become *mere experience*. Indeed, at times it is almost a term of contempt. Throughout the crucial chapters in *Book IV*, such as those on *The Extent of Human Knowledge, The Reality of Knowledge, and Universal Propositions*, wherever Locke finds lines of inquiry dependent on it, the result is immediately to deprecate their promise[17]. The difficulty is that, in bottoming his *everyday* account of "experience" with his *recondite* account of the underlying "substrata" of its ultimate terms of seeker and sought, Locke is led to interpret the only possible knowledge-relationship between these terms in such a way as to make its occurrence impossible in the course of our familiar acquaintanceship with things as we ordinarily meet with them. Our dependence on our usual ways of getting on to the hang of things, by observation, experiment, and the like, becomes a barrier, rather than a means to "knowledge", because "knowledge" is conceived from a point of view quite external to any such method of approach. "Could we begin at the other end", Locke writes, "and discover what it was, wherein that colour consisted, what made a body lighter or heavier, what texture of parts made it malleable, fusible, and fixed, and fit to be dissolved in this sort of liquor, and not in another; if (I say) we had such an idea as this of bodies and could perceive wherein all sensible qualities originally consist, and how they are produced; we might frame such ideas of them, as would furnish us with matter of more general knowledge, and enable us to make universal propositions, that should carry general truth and certainty with them. But whilst our complex ideas of the sorts of substances are so remote from that internal real constitution, on which their sensible qualities depend, and are made up of nothing but an imperfect collection of those apparent qualities our senses can discover; there can be few general propositions concerning substances, of whose real truth we can be certainly assured: since there are but few simple ideas, of whose connection and necessary co-existence we can have certain and undoubted knowledge." etc., etc.[18]

In other words, it is as though, toward the end of his prefatory writings, Bacon had been forced by some side-development of his procedure to conclude that knowledge must be of such a nature as to be ultimately inaccessible by the operations of social institutions and technological processes; or as though, at a similar point and for comparable reasons, Descartes had been forced to conclude that its form must be ultimately unexpressible by algebraic equations or geometrical diagrams. Locke had good reason to be reluctant to make the digression in which this comes about.

The problems of inquiry on which attention is focussed by Locke's second delineation of its basic set-up, then, do not in the least concern such matters as the discipline of observation and speech, or the liberalization of social, political, and economic institutions. Sanity, commonsense, diligence, and tolerance, contribute nothing to their solution, because they cannot be affected by any possible extension or clarification of our familiar acquaintance with the world of our daily living. They are strictly confined to certain theoretical doubts as to whether "experience", although the only means we have of knowing, can, under any circumstances consistent with the basic nature of man and his world, bring things *really* into ken.

Consequently, the outcome of their discussion is a doctrine of knowledge only in a most negative sense. Its development leaves man in secure enough possession of such information as that the sun will very likely rise tomorrow, that the "idea" of red is the "idea" of red and not the "idea" of blue, that the sum of the angles of a triangle is equal to two right angles, and perhaps even that to steal or murder is unjust. The first is admitted, however, only as a matter of mere "probability" which is said to fall short of "knowledge"; and the others are admitted only because their relevance is regarded to concern only mere "ideas" of things, rather than their intrinsic natures. But as regards "certainty" concerning the "real" scheme of existence, the whole line of thought points only to "an huge abyss of ignorance"[19]. It forces a view of man as "in all probability . . . one of the lowest of all intellectual beings"[20].

Whatever it may imply as to the competence of "the Divine Mind", or of "detached spirits", as it affects inquirers of *everyday* "experience", this development of the *Essay* might well be said to constitute a *doctrine of ignorance* rather than of knowledge. Indeed, were it the only outcome of the treatise, its text might have been more appropriately titled; *An Essay Concerning Human Mis-understanding.* The great irony is that, whereas Bacon and Descartes, in an age whose ignorance they deplored, had sought in their respective ways to "bring to light the full richness of our minds"[21], Locke, in an age whose knowingness he humbly admits, takes pains to expose at great length our profound intellectual poverty. And it is this development of the *Essay* which we previously said was of the greatest historical consequence.

IV: ANOTHER "TRANSFORMATION OF COÖRDINATES"

Locke, of course, did not end his *Essay* at this point of its argument; and we shall consider the conclusion he himself gave it in the next section of this chapter. But since this is the point at which many of his readers left off following him with due care, and also the point of the greatest divergence between the two main tendencies of his thinking in the *Essay*, it is a convenient place to summarize its development thus far.

We may gather from *Chapter VI* above that by his natural history of "understanding" Locke tends to:

1. Put inquiry in question *in terms of criteria of sound footing in everyday "experience"*.

2. Identify the agents of inquiry *as men of "experience" in the sense of men of broad working familiarity with the world and its issues.*

3. Delimit the context of inquiry *as the context of "experience" in the sense of the whole unpredictable range of things which men can encounter by first hand contact and observation.*

4. Single out the crucial problems of inquiry *as those of broadening and disciplining "experience" by such means as education, the liberalization of governmental institutions, and the exercise of sound judgment in the making of observations and the use of language.*

5. Interpret the outcome of inquiry *as "understanding" which may be generally characterized as the sort of working familiarity with things that derives from this sort of "experience", but which is otherwise quite unpredictable until actually achieved.*

It may be gathered from the analysis thus far developed in this chapter, however, that by his more recondite explanations of the circumstances presumed to underlie "experience", Locke modifies this most obvious delineation of the general project of inquiry. Although still formally addressing the question of the "original" of our "ideas", by his "physical explanation" of the process he tends to:

2. Identify the agent of inquiry *as the "mind" in the sense of a locus of "ideas" seated at the terminus of the sensory system, presumably somewhere in the human cranium, and receiving images from the world without much as a blank tablet might receive inscriptions from a stylus or dark room might receive pictures through a window.*

3. Delimit the context of inquiry as *ultimately the "primary qualities" of things such as their "bulk, extension, motion, and number"; that is to say, the system of gravitational masses which figure in Newtonian physics.*

4. Single out the crucial problems of inquiry as *those of reducing the "secondary" and "tertiary" qualities of things, such as their color, feeling, sound, odor, and various qualitative effects on each other, to their "causes" in terms of the above mentioned "primary qualities".*

5. Interpret the outcome of inquiry as *knowledge which lends itself to formulation in terms of the basic concepts and equations of Newtonian physics.*

Then, by his further bottoming of "mind" and "mass" on an account of the "real essences" of "substances", Locke tends finally to:

2. Identify the agents of inquiry as *"spiritual substance" whose "secret nature" somehow combines such "powers" as reasoning, doubting, believing, and perceiving, in a single inscrutable "substratum".*

3. Delimit the context of inquiry as *most immediately the "ideas" available to this "spiritual substance", but as ultimately the "real essences" from which these "ideas" derive, but which are themselves incomparably different from anything of the kind and radically inaccessible to comprehension by any such means.*

4. Single out the crucial problems of experience as *most immediately the perhaps solvable problems of comparing and relating "ideas" among themselves, but as ultimately the humanly unsolvable problems of discerning the adequacy or inadequacy of these "ideas" to their "archetypes in real existence".*

5. Interpret the outcome of inquiry *to be limited discernment of the relationships of some ideas among each other, as contrasted to the truly "scientific knowledge" which "God and higher spirits" may have of the necessary connections of all ideas through direct perception of their dependance on the "internal constitutions" of the "real essences" of the "substances" from which they derive.*

The effect of this last delineation of the general project of inquiry, of course, is to remove "understanding" as it is eventually defined entirely from the range of the "experience" appealed to for its definition, and to make it something which could possibly be achieved only by a circumvention of the whole system of nature confronted by man. We may note, however, that the sequence of delineations by which this is effected suggest the same sort of reversal of perspective, or re-orientation of total attitude, which is characterized in *Section vi* of *Chapter V* above as a kind of *transformation* of the *coordinates* with respect to which all thinking operates. Locke's own repeated insistances that our "ideas" and the very meaning of our words "derive from experience" are vigorous reminders that the intelligibility of discourse depends very largely, if not altogether, on its reference to the domain of familiar everyday existence which sustains our thinking and communication with each other. But just as Descartes does in his account of the "first things of knowledge", Locke here dismisses the whole scene of man's day-to-day living among things of colour and feeling, odor, and sound, as a systematic illusion which would melt away had he but the "faculties" to penetrate the veil it suspends between his intellect and what things really and truly are. Only, there is an important difference between what Descartes and Locke gained thereby. Descartes, we have noted at length, was reinforced by the shift, in his conviction that the "certain" mathematical way of inquiry he advocated was the true way to sound the very depths of reality and thus bring the quest of knowledge to its greatest achievement, most glorious fulfillment. And Locke, at an intermediate point, appears to do something very similar for the methods of Newtonian mechanics. But later he is forced to the conclusion that the way of "experience", which he argues to be the only possible human way to knowledge, is in truth but a confinement to "invincible ignorance". Unlike Descartes, he does not undertake his first characterization of inquiry for the purpose of later dismissing it. He holds to his original rejection of "innate ideas" and his original appeal to everyday "experience" to the very end. When compelled by his later convictions to choose between his first observations and an optimistic view of man's competence in knowledge, it is the latter which he surrenders. Locke is eventually pushed by his line of reasoning to the conclusion that, although "ideas", as he has so painstakingly shown, are not "innate", they really ought to be. In this one respect at least, *Book IV* of the *Essay* is a kind of lament on having to follow *Book I*; but it does follow *Book I* nevertheless.

The insinuation of a radically shifted perspective on the very grounds of intelligibility, then, is by no means accidental in Descartes' writings.

prefatory to inquiry. It reappears just as strongly in Locke's *Essay*; and apparently it does so despite Locke's wishes. This fact invites comment on the general nature of the preface to inquiry, but first it should receive a little additional clarification in terms of its specific provocation in the *Essay*.

V: ANOTHER NOTE ON CONTROLS

More than most writers who attempt such themes, Locke was conscious of the extent to which his *Essay Concerning Human Understanding* was a fated enterprise. In his *Epistle to the Reader* he characterizes himself as "one of those who let loose their own thoughts, and follow them in writing"; and at the end of *Book I* he announces his intention "in the future part of this discourse" to "raise an edifice uniform and consistent with itself", and to "endeavor it shall be all of a piece and hang together".[22] The analysis just completed, however, is a strong indication that the thoughts which Locke lets loose are not all of the kind which can be consistently followed up in one and the same piece of writing. The suspicion is that they do not "hang together" as do Bacon's institutional and technological notions concerning the enterprise of learning, or Descartes' notions of the special significance of mathematical technique and of the facts of mind and structure. It is particularly instructive, therefore, to consider just what Locke's basic ideas were, how they variously controlled his attempt to define the limits of "understanding", and how, by coming into conflict with each other, they involved it in the kind of conflicting tendencies just reviewed.

In his very similar undertaking, it will be recalled, Descartes had conceived of "philosophy" as primarily a structure; and consequently, he believed he could best define its nature and limits in his "metaphysical first principles of knowledge" by exhibiting its structural "foundation", thus indicating what kind, and how much, super-structure they could sustain. But Locke's most fundamental idea in the *Essay* appears to be the conception of "understanding" as a kind of historical process. It is not merely the burden of explanation with which he is left on denying that "ideas" are "innate" which induces him to explain their "origin" himself.[23] On first proposing, at the very outset of *Book I*, to "consider the discerning faculties of a man as they are employed about the objects which they have to do with", he describes the procedure he will attempt to follow as a *"historical*, plain method" by which he hopes to give an account of "the ways whereby our understandings *come to attain* those notions of things we have".[24] At the end of his long attack on "innate ideas", he proclaims that had the champions of the doctrine "examined *the ways whereby men came* to the knowledge of many universal truths, they would have found them to result in the minds of men from the being of things themselves, when duly considered; and that they were discovered by the application of those faculties that were fitted by nature to receive and judge of them when duly employed about them", whereupon he announces that "to show how the understanding *proceeds* herein is the design of the following discourse".[25] And constantly throughout most of the rest of the work, his efforts are those of "one who would acquaint himself thoroughly with the *progress* of the mind in its apprehension and knowledge of things."[26] It appears, therefore, that in writing the *Essay* Locke thought of "understanding" most generally as a happening, or coming-about, with a chronological sequence to its phases. Conceiving it as a temporal process with a beginning, a middle, and an end, his inevitable assumption was that its possibilities could best be indicated by an exhibition of the succession of its phases. His confidence was that the most relevant information about something which happens is information as to *how* it happens. The specific appeal to everyday "experience" in the *Essay* is simply a recognition of how things generally happen to men. Its natural history of "understanding" is an acknowledgement of the kind of succession of events by which individuals and cultural traditions progress from immaturity to maturity .

At the crucial point where Locke introduces "physical considerations" concerning the circumstances of "understanding", however, he departs from his able, straightforward narrative of its happening to construe the fact of its happening in terms other than those of its happening. Instead of trying to interpret the Newtonian conception of the world against the background of its origin in man's "experience", he suddenly tries to construe man's "experience" against the background of the Newtonian conception of the world. And the very fact that he presumes this reversal of procedure to aid him in discoursing "more intelligibly" is evidence that the ideology of the great *Principia* of his day here takes precedence as a control of his thinking.

But when Locke next undertakes to explain what he means by the "substances" or "real essences" the "ideas" and "names" of which he still seeks to trace to the events of everyday living, these conceptions are in turn supplanted by an essentially Cartesian ideal of what knowledge should be quite aside from any consideration of how it may be arrived at. Despite his lengthy attack on the doctrine of "innate ideas" associated so largely with the popularization of Cartesian metaphysics, many long passages, particularly in the latter part of his *Essay*, might well be mistaken for excerpts from the writings of Descartes. Locke's accommodation of his thinking to Cartesian terminology by his use of the word "idea" has already been noted in the preceding chapter.[27] But his *Essay* may be shown to have much more than this in common with the Cartesian tradition. *Book IV* almost paraphrases Descartes' *Rules* in its explanation of "intuition", and "demonstration" by "steps" which "must have intuitive evidence", as the only "degree of knowledge",[28] and also in its argument for the possibility of a "rational morality".[29] And it appears that the reason for this is an equally strong dependence on mathematics as the conspicuous example of the form knowledge should take. At bottom it is the example of mathematical science as a rigorous deductive system which suggests to Locke the very notion of "real essences" in things, inaccessible to us through our ways of dealing with them by our natural means. For example, in arguing in *Book II* that our "complex idea of a substance" can include at most "but some few of those properties which flow from its real essence and constitution," Locke reasons: "The essence of a triangle lies in a very little compas, consists in a very few ideas,—three lines including a space makes up that essence,—but the properties that flow from this essence are more than can be easily known or enumerated. So I imagine it is in substances, their real essences lie in a little compas, though the properties flowing from that internal constitution are endless."[30] A "complex idea" such as we can have, he also argues here, "cannot be the real essence of any substance; for then the properties we discover in that body would depend on that complex idea, and be deducible from it, and their necessary connexion with it be known: as all properties of a triangle depend on, and as far as they are discoverable, are deducible from the complex idea of three lines including a space."[31] And to reinforce the point, he adds that "mathematical figures" would be equally "imperfect and inadequate", if "we were to have our complex ideas of them only by collecting their properties in reference to other figures. How uncertain and imperfect would our ideas be of an ellipsis, if we had no other idea of it but some few of its properties? Whereas having in our plain idea the whole essence of that figure, we from thence discover those properties, and demonstratively see how they flow, and are inseparable from it."[32]

Consequently, Locke's remark in *Book IV* that we could have a true "science" if we could only "begin at the other end", amounts substantially to the statement that all our "ideas" would produce "knowledge" if they were only all basically similar to our mathematical ideas. The passage containing this bit of wishful thinking, quoted in the preceding section of this chapter, continues further along with the clarification: "Could any one discover a necessary connection between malleableness, and the colour or weight of gold, or any other part of the complex idea signified by that name, he might make a certain, universal proposition concerning gold in this respect; and the real truth of this proposition, "that all gold is malleable", would be as certain as this, the three angles of all right lined triangles are equal to two right ones."[33] It appears that the higher spiritual quality of the information which Locke allows only to the "higher spirits" from whose point of view he ultimately defines knowledge, consists simply in its mathematical-like form. By "higher spirits" Locke means ultra-super-mathematicians. "It may not be doubted," he writes, "that spirits" of a higher rank than those immersed in flesh may have as clear ideas of the radical constitution of substances, as we have of a triangle, and so perceive how all their properties and operations flow from thence: but the manner how they come by that knowledge exceeds our conceptions."[34] The *Essay*, therefore, is as strongly imbued as any writing of the seventeenth century with what Pascal so aptly called *l'esprit géométrique*.

Despite his firm determination to keep his feet on the solid ground of experience, Locke was as profoundly influenced as any modern by the Renaissance revival of the Pythagorean tradition. And the result is that, telling how understanding actually happens to men, he contrasts what is thus achieved to what might be supposed to spring into being in the mind of a mathematical deity. His account of "experience" tends eventually to become a doctrine of ignorance because, while following its course with keen realistic discernment of how it develops in its own terms, he keeps in the back of his mind a mathematical conception of what its fulfillment should be ideally. His *Essay* begets scepticism because its delineations of the general character of inquiry combines an account of means comparable to Bacon's with an expectation of ends comparable to Descartes'.

It is well to note, however, that Locke himself seems to have had little notion that readers would make what they did of the *Essay*'s more negative conclusions. In the total argument of *Book IV*, their principal consequence is not the posing of a proposition for academic debate, but a return to the argument of his early *Study during a Journey*. In his own thinking, the scepticism suggested by the *Essay* had a directly practical, rather than academic implication, because the ultimate control by which its argument is finally resolved is the same as that which brings Descartes at length to a recognition of what is most sound in Bacon's prefatory writings—namely, the common domain in which institutions, machines, mathematical techniques, mind, structure, everyday living, mechanics, and geometric ideals are all relevant to man's exploration of his world. "Had we senses acute enough to discern the minute particles of bodies and the real constitution on which their sensible qualities depend," Locke writes at one point, "I doubt not but they would produce quite different ideas in us; and that which is now the yellow colour of gold would then disappear, and instead of it we should see an admirable texture of parts of a certain size and figure", etc. etc. But such an improvement of faculties, he hastens to add, would embarrass a man more than it would edify him, since it would place him in so different a world from his fellows' that he would lack even a common basis of communication with them. By the help of "microscopical eyes", for example, "a man could penetrate farther than ordinary into the secret composition and radical texture of bodies"; but "he would not make any great advantage by the change, if such an acute sight would not serve to conduct him to the market and exchange; if he could not see things he was to avoid, at a convenient distance, nor distinguish things he had to do with, by those sensible qualities others do".[35] Locke finally concludes that, however ill fitted men's faculties may be for ideally "adequate knowledge", they are excellently fitted to "the conveniences of life, and the business we have to do here." He insists that all the important problems of men's living are well enough defined without strict scientific certainty such as they cannot have anyway.[36]

Consequently, the eventual outcome of Locke's exposition of "experience" as a doctrine of human ignorance, is to restate his exposition of it as a doctrine of human knowledge, but in such terms as relate it back to his original insistence that the proper domain of inquiry is that of the practical interests of man's business in the world. The remarks just quoted repeat the thesis of his early *Study*. Only, as a consequence of the long life *journey* which actually intervened between that early sketch and this lengthy, complicated development, it has a more mature, liberal tone. On next proceeding in the *Essay* to the question of *The*

Improvement of our Knowledge, Locke takes care to remark that he does not mean by the foregoing argument to dismiss the inquisition of nature as futile, but intends, rather, to urge care and moderation in its pursuit.[37] And from there on, he continues with all the appeals to sanity, discipline, and tolerance, already discussed in *Section v* of the preceding chapter. As a post-graduate in the school of experience, Locke returned to the view he had entertained as an undergraduate, but without his former sophomoric narrowness. After all, the call to "experience" may have both a ring of challenge and an undertone of warning, and Locke was acute enough to realize this as he sounded it.

VI: "EXPERIENCE" AND "UNDERSTANDING"

Although the *Essay* as thus finally worked out was sufficiently consistent with itself to allow Locke to feel that it all contributed to a common set of conclusions, its divergent strains of development received very different consideration from readers who felt provoked to follow them up in their own thinking. The historical influence which the book exerted has followed the lines of argument separately traced in these last two chapters. And this fact gives point to our distinguishing quite sharply between its two principal strains while now discussing its relation to the critique of propaedeutic prolegomena to inquiry in the first chapter of this study.

Locke's account of "understanding" as a gradual gleaning of information from the trials of everyday "experience" is quite clearly an interpretation of inquiry which returns the attention of the inquirer back to his regular business of research with a heightened sense of its character as a general undertaking and possibly with a firmer determination to keep his feet on the ground. The inquirer, in considering his "discerning faculties . . . as they are employed about the objects which they have to do with," is not required to employ these "faculties" in any fundamentally different way than he always does. All he is required to do is to take a more detached and comprehensive view of his usual procedures; and such a view invites nothing so much as a return to their undertaking. But Locke's more recondite explanations of the "experience" which constitutes these procedures assumes a kind of divine perspective of inquiry which admittedly has nothing in common with the ordinary pursuit of "understanding" to which man is committed by his human nature. It requires a confessedly impossible detachment, and hence a complete break with the natural continuity of the actual undertaking of inquiry. To the extent that an attempt is made to follow it up, therefore, no relevance can be claimed to the undertaking as a human enterprise. The resulting speculation must make the impossible claim of "higher spiritual" significance. And thus an endless sidetracking is invited.

To put the same point a little differently: the first account addresses the question of the genesis of "understanding" in the processes of its pursuit, and consequently calls for a line of investigation which illustrates these processes; but the latter account raises the question of the relationship of what is thus arrived at to what is said to be impossible to arrive at by such means, and so calls for either the transcendence of the whole scheme of nature or the commission of an absurdity. Attention is drawn from the possible understanding of nature to the impossible nature of "understanding". Quite inevitably the interest of those who ordinarily pursue inquiry is lost, and the theme is left open to those who specialize in miracles and nonsense.

This development, of course, marks a critical point in the history of literature prefatory to inquiry. It is not too extravagant to suggest that, had Locke's *Essay* not taken such a twist, it is just possible that the approach to knowledge as a problematic matter might never have split into two radically separate traditions—on the one hand, that of the reflective inquirer's clarification of his day to day work of actually getting knowledge; and on the other hand, that of the academic epistemologist's comparatively remote dialectical elaboration of notions introduced to this end, with little attention to the actual course of research, except perhaps occasionally to draw on its newer vocabulary or to exploit its more spectacular successes as occasions for sidelights of slight relevance. For all we know, had Locke not given his influential history of understanding such an alternative statement, the rivalry between philosophical *empiricism* and *rationalism,* to mention only one case of subsequent debate, might have been expressed in a contest between advocates of the corresponding rival conceptions of inquiry in revealing broader aspects of their respective techniques or in bringing about more brilliant achievements by their application in practice.

Be that as it may, however, the fact is that by the particular kind of sidetracking to which Locke's recondite account of "experience" led, a line of controversial reconsideration of his argument was provoked which encouraged interpretation of the fact of understanding as a topic for metaphysical debate. There is a characteristic irony in this, in that the *Essay Concerning Human Understanding,* like all the other writings considered in *Part Two* of this study is an attempt to dispose of controversy. On elaborating his explanation of the "occasion" of the work, in the first chapter of *Book I,* Locke exclaims that "men, extending their inquiries beyond their capacities, and letting their thoughts wander into those depths where they can find no sure footing, it is no wonder that they raise questions, and multiply disputes, which, never coming to any clear resolution, are proper only to increase their doubts," etc. But, "were the capacities of our understandings well considered," he adds, "the extent of our knowledge once discovered, and the horizon found, which sets the bounds between the enlightened and dark parts of things, between what is and what is not comprehensible by us; men would, perhaps, with less scruple acquiesce in the avowed ignorance of the one, and employ their thoughts and discourse with more advantage and satisfaction in the other."[38] His confidence, we may gather here, is that in "searching out the bounds of knowledge" he is dividing all issues into two kinds: the knowable which it were futile to dispute because better explored, and the unknowable which it were equally futile to dispute because incapable of determination anyway.

It must be granted, moreover, that the *Essay's* commonsense account of "experience" had tremendous possibilities as a means for avoiding the more pointless kind of contention. "Perhaps it is the affectation of knowing beyond what we perceive, that makes so much useless dispute and noise in the world," Locke aptly observes at its outset;[39] and his pertinent observations as to the way in which experience begets understanding are genuinely strong incentives to men to "regulate their assent" and "moderate their persuasions", and meanwhile to exercise their faculties as best they can about the matters they have to do with, rather than consult the conflicting oracles of their own imaginations or predispositions. His thesis that "all those sublime thoughts which tower above the clouds, and reach as high as heaven itself, take their rise and footing" in "experience", rather than in some "innate" source in the "mind, is a fruitful suggestion that the active exploration of the world and its issues is the only possible arbitrator of learned contention.[40] And his thesis that the meanings of the "words" which instrument discourse have a similar origin, is an equally fruitful suggestion that language be disciplined accordingly, rather than exploited for the multiplication of arguments. Despite the naive opinion of some of our contemporaries that semantic analysis is a twentieth century discovery, *Book III* of Locke's *Essay* is as keen and competent a discussion of its characteristic problems as has ever been written.[41]

But in his attempt to underpin his historical account of how men may avoid useless quibbling, with a final explanation of why some matters may be profitably considered and others not, Locke ignored his own advice and took a highly controversial stand. In undertaking to explain why the "dark parts of things" were not "enlightened", he overstepped the boundaries which he himself drew between "what is and what is not comprehensible"; and thus he made "experience" a problem to be "solved by arguments rather than a means of resolving arguments, for it was precisely on this step that he was most seriously challenged by men like Leibniz, Berkeley, and Kant, who gave his remarks the kind of dialectical development which eventually led to the purely academic isolation of the *problem of knowledge* from the problems of getting knowledge. By its different delineations of the project of inquiry, the *Essay* illustrates how, between a single pair of covers, the prefatory consideration of inquiry can both avoid and incur the kind of criticism which has provoked the contemporary reaction against the propaedeutic tendency in such literature, and sometimes, through a confusion of the propaedeutic tendency with the central effort, indiscriminately against all attempts at the epistemological clarification of inquiry.

Despite all these complications and the many grounds on which Locke's *Essay* may be severely criticised, however, the book still remains an unforgettable expression of the character of inquiry as, not only a social, technological, and structural matter, but also a genetic process of becoming subject to all the controls by which men, individually and collectively, mature. Whatever other questions may be asked concerning inquiry, it is most certainly relevant to ask how it comes about in that process of intimate intercourse with things men call their experience. Whatever other more special characters inquirers and nature may exhibit, they are conspicuously the agents and context between which this intercourse takes place. And whatever more special constructions may be placed on the problems and outcome of inquiry, they are also the difficulties which make this process the adventurous one it is for inquisitive living, and which enrich it with what understanding such a process can result in. Inquiry is experience; and the chief power of the *Essay Concerning Human Understanding* is the force with which, even by caricature, it expresses that fact.

PART THREE

CONCLUSION

8

THE QUEST AND THE THEORY OF KNOWLEDGE

In the preceding chapters the epistemological writings of Bacon, Descartes, and Locke have been carefully distinguished from their other works in order to focus attention the more sharply on the contributions made by these men to the literature here in question. The distinction, however, cut across strong bonds of internal unity. It was forced by the analytic requirements of this twentieth century study, rather than by any pronounced line of cleavage in the seventeenth century materials dealt with. As has already been indicated, Bacon, Descartes, and Locke, like most early modern thinkers, were more inclined to think of inquiry in terms of the inter-relatedness of all its phases and the unity of its whole undertaking, than in terms of such differences as that between its straightforward pursuit and its reflective elucidation. For these men there was no radical dichotomy between the quest and the theory of knowledge; both were cultivated by them as parts of a larger enterprise comprehending all inquisitive activities.

In his *Great Instauration*, for example, Francis Bacon was concerned with "the entire fabric of human reason". If in what he actually accomplished of its ambitious project he tended to emphasize "the proper foundations", that was not because he did not intend to raise upon them "a total reconstruction of sciences, arts, and all human knowledge." *The Advancement* and *The New Organon* dealt with only the first two phases of his larger program which he fondly hoped would achieve "no mere felicity of speculation, but the real business and fortunes of the human race, and all power of operation".[1] In his attempts to "furnish a nuptial couch for the mind and the universe," therefore, Bacon would never have thought of divorcing the theory from the practice of inquiry. Similarly in the case of Descartes, notwithstanding the very different historical developments his epistemological and scientific writings have had, they were intimately interrelated as he himself presented them. His *Metaphysical Meditations* does center somewhat exclusively about the themes of the former. But as has already been pointed out, his *Rules* actually develops into a mathematical treatise; the first edition of his *Discourse on Method* appears in the same volume as his

Geometry, Dioptrics, and *Meteors,* which it serves to introduce; and his restatement of the *Meditations,* as "principles of knowledge" in *Book I* of his *Principles of Philosophy,* is accompanied by three longer *Books* on physics, astronomy, physiology, and related sciences for which such "principles" ostensibly prepare the way. Despite the incomparability of the problems which men later found suggested by each of these two groups of writings, Descartes himself appears to have dedicated both to the same general undertaking. For him, we must remember, the findings of both were comprehended in "philosophy" as a single, unified body of the sum total of *all* man's wisdom, which could aptly be likened to a growing tree. In the thought of John Locke also there was comparable, if not quite so striking, universality of interest. His epistemological *Essay Concerning Human Understanding* is the longest, and certainly the most ambitious, book he published. Yet, in his collected works it is more than counterbalanced by many others reporting explorations, according to its recommendations, into such fields as economics, government, and agriculture, which fact is evidence that he too was most seriously concerned with the whole of the general undertaking which Francis Bacon had popularized as the enterprise of learning. And perhaps much the same can be said for Leibniz and for a number of other men of his century and of the century which followed.

But after these men left the scene, there tended to be a parting of ways between followers who cultivated one or the other of the two chief interests which were thus so thoroughly blended. As the new learning grew in total bulk and intricacy of detail, a higher degree of specialization within its minor departments became necessary. Even workers in closely related technical fields of research began to lose track of all of each other's activities; and the divergence of interest was nowhere so great as between those who tended to follow the suggestions of the literature here examined on the level of inquiry proper and those who tended to pursue further the themes it invoked on the level of prefatory consideration. In the case of these two main groups there was more than the limitation of specialized interest to draw them apart. During a long period—roughly two centuries—there was, on the one hand, a tendency among those engaged primarily in the quest of knowledge to ignore the speculation of those engaged primarily in the theory of knowledge, because they had comparatively little further need of it in their own work; and on the other hand, there was a corresponding tendency among theorists concerning knowledge to concede the independence of the quest of knowledge and to confine themselves more and more to the dialectical elaboration of such lines of thought as we have already seen in the writings of Descartes and Locke to have little bearing on man's actual probing of his world.

II: SPECIALIZATION IN THE QUEST OF KNOWLEDGE

The modern tradition of scientific inquiry, despite the fact that it derived much of its impulse from the concern of those who cultivated it to follow its own leads in their own special terms, must also have derived considerable impetus and conscious direction from the great prefatory essays of men like Bacon, Descartes, and Locke. Organizers of learned societies, laboratory technicians, mathematicians, and explorers into all the nooks and crannies of nature must have found in such writings challenges to promote the enterprise of learning along the lines of their recommendations. The specific directions actual researches took may have been determined by the specific clues similar researches previously turned up—by the same sort of clues, indeed, which originally suggested the grand prolegomena themselves—but investigators were helped to find these clues significant in the ways they did largely because of the meanings which the great inquiries concerning inquiry had revealed to be latent in them. The hints nature gave men for the achievements of modern science had been staring them in the face for as long as they had been on hand or at leisure to take notice. But the illumination of the grand prolegomena, in combination with the historical forces which suggested them, transformed mere hints into positive suggestions for programs of action by which nature might be probed, comprehended, and in a measure controlled. When Bacon, Descartes, and Locke flourished, after all, institutionalized learning in the modern sense was nothing but a Utopian dream, technological and mathematical methods were still mere promises, and the discoveries possible by experience were as yet only dimly surmised. The prefatory essays of these men were as much proclamations of faith as they were expressions of insight. And so the whole tradition of modern science may be regarded as a movement which not only derived much important suggestion from these writings, but which was also largely sustained by the confidence they voiced in the early days before it so brilliantly justified itself by its own fruits.

The main influence of epistemology on the modern scientific tradition, however, was exerted principally through the general attitudes and challenges of the total arguments of works like those considered here, rather than through any particular details of their dialectic or subsequent elaboration. Until quite recently, at any rate, modern scientific workers confined themselves mainly to the progressive development of the procedures broadly suggested in the seventeenth century. As the writers of the original grand prolegomena naively intended all men should do, mathematicians, biologists, physicists, economists, and their fellow workers concentrated throughout this period on the straightforward examination of their respective subject matters along general lines already suggested, without bothering constantly to reconsider the fact of their doing so. Viewing the nature of their work as already well enough understood for their main purposes, these men focussed their attention on its details; and they turned to prefatory considerations, if at all, only as a kind of diversion or hobby in which they indulged much as they might in sport or art. As has been remarked by Sir Arthur Eddington, a member of the scientific tradition in his own right: until about twenty years ago "traffic with philosophy had been a luxury for those scientists whose disposition happened to turn that way. . . . To advance science and to philosophise were essentially distinct activities."[2] Quite naturally, therefore, scientists tended in the main to be indifferent, if not actually contemptuous, concerning whatever new thoughts others had on matters prefatory to inquiry. And they were confirmed in the belief in the soundness of this insular attitude by the remarkably constant progress they made in practically all branches of scientific investigation.

The clarifications of prefatory essayists like Bacon, Descartes, and Locke, having become integral parts of the scientific tradition, stood other research workers in good stead so far as making basic issues understood was concerned; so these men had good reason to feel free to devote their best efforts to overcoming the particular technical difficulties presented by their respective subject matters.[3] And they were left unchallenged by new *philosophical* Baconians, Cartesians, and Lockians, largely because the latter found themselves confronted with an ever more imposing mass of substantial achievement in science which they had greater and greater difficulty even in comprehending, let alone helpfully criticizing. There could be no question of "new instaurations" to propose, because scientific edifices were standing only too obviously well on their own foundations.

III: SPECIALIZATION IN THE THEORY OF KNOWLEDGE

Meanwhile those men who have been most responsible for what has been called in *Chapter I* the "sidetracking" of the grand prolegomena, took as the point of departure for their development of these writings the conceptions which had first been employed in them only instrumentally for the purpose of explaining or demonstrating their conclusions concerning how inquiry into other matters should be undertaken. In the preceding chapters much attention has been paid to the *natural origins* of the early modern prefaces to inquiry there considered at length. Despite the obviously great indebtedness of such epistemologists as Bacon, Descartes, and Locke to their Renaissance predecessors, to the mediaevals, and even to the ancients for many of their ideas and for the very language they employed, there is an important sense in which their prefatory essays were originally inspired, freshly conceived. But once these writings became established literature their dialectic itself became an object of investigation and further development by some, either for its own sake as a matter of intrinsic technical interest in its own right, or else for some purpose secondary to that of the promotion of inquiry proper along sounder lines.

David Hume, in expanding on the sceptical strain in Locke's thought, to chasten the inquiry of his day of some of its persistent extravagance, may have remained fairly faithful to the general intent of the text from which he borrowed. But in this he was quite exceptional. Malebranche restated Descartes' "principles of knowledge" almost *in toto* chiefly for the purpose of Christian apologetics. Lebniz countered Locke's *Essay* with *New Essays* primarily to give what he believed to be a sounder account of such matters as "understanding", "ideas", and "experience", which it discussed. And whereas even Locke introduced his *Essay* with a critique of the Cartesian doctrine of "innate ideas" rather than with direct criticism of the approach to inquiry which it represented, thus focussing attention as much on his means as on his ends, Berkeley in turn introduced his *Treatise Concerning the Principles of Human Knowledge* with a critique of the Lockian doctrine of "abstract ideas."[4]

George Berkeley, indeed, presented this chief epistemological work of his primarily as an examination, not of the manner in which inquiry proper was being pursued in his day, but of the epistemological construction that was being placed upon it, notably by developments of the part of Locke's account of experience referred to in the preceding

chapter as a doctrine of human ignorance. "Upon the whole," he
writes in its *Introduction*, "I am inclined to think that the far greater
part, if not all, of those difficulties which have hitherto amused philosophers, and blocked up the way to knowledge, are entirely owing to
ourselves—that we have first raised a dust and then complained we cannot see."[5] Deploring the "forlorn Scepticism" which he found to derive
from the Lockian insistence that "the faculties we have are few, and
those designed by nature for the support and comfort of life, and not to
penetrate into the inward essence and constitution of things," etc.[6], he
explained his own purpose to be to try if he could "discover what those
Principles are which have introduced all that doubtfulness and uncertainty into the several sects of philosophy; insomuch that the wisest men
have thought our ignorance incurable, conceiving it to arise from
the natural dullness and limitation of our faculties."[5] He justified his
effort "to make a strict inquiry concerning the First Principles of Human Knowledge, to sift and examine them on all sides," on the grounds
of a suspicion that "those lets and difficulties, which stay and embarrass
the mind in its search after truth, do not spring from any darkness and
intricacy in the objects, or natural defect in the understanding, so much
as from false Principles which have been insisted on, and might have
been avoided."[5] Consequently, except for occasional expressions of
pious hope that his arguments would bring men to "the consideration
of God and our Duty" in "the first place in our studies",[7] and a few attempts to explain why the brilliantly competent mathematicians of his
day should have derived their equations differently than they did,[8] his
dialectical treatment of Locke's epistemological notions were confined to technicalities which little affected the researches which scientific
men were undertaking. Just as Samuel Johnson's kicking a rock had no
real relevance to Berkeley's essential conclusions concerning the "ideal"
nature of the objects of thought, these conclusions in turn had no real
relevance to the inquisitive exploration of the natural world as it was
actually under way. In becoming secure, they also became remote. If
Locke confined himself to "under-laborer work" on behalf of the
"master builders", Berkeley chose to remain a by-stander who com-
mented on all their labors safely, but quite unheeded, from the sidelines.

Kant's *Critique of Pure Reason*, the most monumental treatise in the
entire literature of epistemology, moreover, was a dialectical development of the conceptions of previous prefatory accounts, which restricted

the field of its own relevance to inquiry even more explicitly. In so far as Kant attempted by this work to facilitate "metaphysical" investigation through prior scrutiny of "pure reason", it was a fresh attempt at epistemological clarification of a field of research. But from its very first sentence, "That all our knowledge begins with experience there can be no doubt" etc., the entire treatise was also a commentary on the epistemological schools of *rationalism* and *empiricism*.[9] What is more, it was a commentary on the doctrines of these schools which left completely untouched the practical conclusions concerning the pursuit of inquiry reached by the great treatises which defined their modern formulations.

It is instructive to note that in the very same contexts in which Kant deplored the utter chaos of "metaphysical science" as attempted "pure, *a priori*, philosophical cognition," he freely commended "mathematics, physical science, etc.", as resting "upon a secure foundation", and declared that they not only maintained their "ancient fame", but, in the case of the latter, even greatly surpassed it.[10] Far from addressing his preliminary investigation to the going concern by which they were derived, he actually drew upon their more spectacular achievements for inspiration and suggestion. In the *Preface to the Second Edition* of the *Critique of Pure Reason* he remarked, for example, that after a long period of crude, unscientific calculation by the ancient Egyptians, mathematics finally got on the "royal road" of real science by an "intellectual revolution" among "that wonderful people of the Greeks"; and that physics in turn "entered on the highway of science" when "the ingenious proposal of Bacon" helped to bring about a comparable "rapid intellectual revolution" in modern times.[11] It was with these accomplishments in view, as admittedly brilliant successes in inquiry, that he offered his own novel approach to the restricted field of "metaphysics", suggesting, indeed, that his idea in doing so was much like that of Copernicus "who, not being able to get on in the explanation of the movements of the heavenly bodies as long as he assumed that all the stars turned round the spectator, tried whether he could not succeed better by assuming the spectator to be turning round, and the stars to be at rest", etc.[12] Kant's confidence was that in examining how the "objects of metaphysics" conform to "our mode of cognition", rather than trying to explore them directly, he was reproducing for their study "the essential element" in the "intellectual revolutions" which he believed had already done so much for other branches of inquiry.[13] And so, respectfully assuming the competence of those who were doing most of the work of the enterprise of learning, he limited the final relevance of his great *Critique* to the use of reason in dealing with the remoter issues of "God, freedom (of will), and immortality", as distinguished from its use by most reasonable men in investigating the broad wide world of "phenomena."

Later, therefore, it was perfectly possible for a man like Schopenhauer to accept the dialectic of the *Critique of Pure Reason* in its entirety, detach from it the "practical" appendage of Kant's "Categorical imperative", replace it with the pang of pain which served him in lieu of sense of obligation to obey the Golden Rule, and thus completely negate every conclusion Kant finally reached by it without in the least affecting the bustle of activity that was becoming ever greater in the workshops and expeditions of science. Like the *Critique* from which it borrowed so much, Schopenhauer's *World as Will and Idea* may have profoundly affected the moral tone and attitude of millions of people, but it hardly affected them at all in most of their essential relations to the world as an object of specific inquisitions. The epistemological labors which Kant so painstakingly undertook, and then exploited to confirm his pious convictions in the face of rational difficulties, Schopenhauer simply pirated in the night of nineteenth century *Weltschmerz* to confirm his equally impious convictions in the face of similar rational difficulties; but the main part of the enterprise of learning went its way unperturbed.

A great many other examples, important and unimportant, might be given of the same tendencies within the *philosophical,* as opposed to the *scientific,* movements stemming from the great prefaces to inquiry in the modern period. But that would involve an un-called for survey of the vast bulk of *modern philosophy.* Enough has already been said here to indicate that what even the originally inspired thinkers within the main tradition, such as Locke and Kant, tended to do to some extent, was carried much further by men such as Malebranche, Berkeley, and Schopenhauer. In proportion as the conceptions and dialectic of previous prefatory essays were accepted as points of departure rather than fresh observations of the actual pursuit of inquiry which might afford fresh insight into it, and in proportion as there was a corresponding narrowing or attenuation of the field immediately considered, the whole tradition tended to become farther and farther removed from the research activities which Bacon, Descartes, and Locke had mainly attempted to get under way. In the course of time, books dedicated to the theory of knowledge, tended to have less and less relevance to the immediate concerns of most people who were devoting their lives to the acquisition of knowledge.

This fact, of course, does not in itself reflect discredit on the tradition. However far they may have wandered from the intent of the originators of the dialectic they exploited, many of these men did remarkable things with it. To review only a few, of whom particular mention has been made here, Malebranche was, after all, a man of intense spirituality and religious fervor, Berkeley was a most astute and provocative dialectician, Kant was perhaps the most phenomenal *pure reasoner* of all time, and Schopenhauer was a man of the finest aesthetic sensitivity and social sympathy. In making use of epistemological considerations as vehicles for the exposition of their schemes of total reflective thought, men like these did much of philosophical significance, regardless of whether they meanwhile engaged the professional interest of other investigators. Wisdom, if not science, was wooed thereby.

It happens, however, that minds of this order are as rare in philosophy as in other fields of intellectual endeavor; and the consequence has been that, particularly in academic quarters, the tradition of the dialectical development of epistemological conceptions long tended to be taken as presumptive evidence that knowledge is somehow a puzzle. to be solved or a mystery to be explained. The history of the movement, with all its fussing about "idealism" and "realism", "objectivism" and "subjectivism", "matter" and "consciousness", "scepticism" and "solipsism", were dreary to relate, and as infinitely far removed from the vital concern of philosophy as from the vital concerns of anything else. This last sterile offspring of the tradition of prefaces to inquiry has had such a musty odor about it that it could hardly help provoking widespread indifference or contempt for anything smacking of epistemology among inquirers in other fields, and arousing vigorous repudiation among the quick within the field of philosophy itself.

In view of the analyses of the preceding chapters, this process of degeneration would seem to a certain extent inevitable. The themes and rhetorical catch-phrases of the great original prefaces to inquiry were as provocatively arresting as they were persuasively effective. Even men of the stature of Locke, Leibniz, and Kant were given considerable pause by them; so, it required only a little unimaginative scholarship—a most available commodity—to perpetuate their endless review and revision in the most pointless terms. However, the misfortune has been that, partly for this very reason, the rejection of the movement has mistakenly tended to run it back to its sources. The contempt justly incurred by the pretentious, but visionless, elaboration of artificial problems of knowledge has been wrongly extended to include the great attempts to deal with the real problems of knowledge out of which they once arose. Consequently, even were there no important new incentives to the clarification of inquiry into inquiry—that is to say, even were the enterprise of learning still in the same kind of position as toward the end of the last century—it would still be worthwhile now to try applying the analysis made here to a more general discrimination of what is sound and unsound, relevant and irrelevant, in such attempts. But as the present general situation in learning gives additional point to the task, some attention should be paid it first.

IV: PRESENT-DAY RAPPROCHEMENTS

Although the divergence between the quest and the theory of knowledge became gradually greater for some two centuries after the publication of Locke's *Essay*, more and more exclusive specialization in two such activities could not continue indefinitely if there were any point at all in their original union. And the fact of the matter is that with the beginning of our, contemporary, age some of the circumstances which encouraged the tendency were quite abruptly changed.

First of all, the experimental data which later led to relativity and quantum theory suddenly confronted physicists with situations that could not even be intelligibly approached, let alone competently handled, in terms of traditional methods of investigation, thus compelling the more alert fundamentally to reconsider the nature of their undertaking whether they wished to or not. As has now become common knowledge, a general uneasiness developed at the turn of the last century concerning the very meaning of many physical conceptions which had been accepted unquestioningly for hundreds of years. And when the original apprehensions proved to be well founded, inquirers in other departments, jolted by what they saw happening where basic assumptions had seemed most securely established, began to scrutinize theirs more suspiciously and to give more heed to misgivings of their own which they had hitherto tended to dismiss rather lightly. The spirit of critical reconsideration began to spread, and a new drive developed toward a unification of inquiry proper and its epistemological clarification such as had been taken for granted by the early moderns. This is hardly the place for a survey which could claim to be the least bit comprehensive of the entire movement which then arose, but a sampling of a few of its more representative expressions will serve to indicate its main characteristics.

Fairly close to its main line of development, for example, we may consider Professor P. W. Bridgman's *Logic of Modern Physics*, admittedly "an excursion into the field of fundamental criticism by one whose activities have hitherto been confined almost entirely to experiment."[14] This book is written in full awareness of a "growing reaction favoring a better understanding of the interpretive fundamentals of physics", which, Bridgman observes, "is not a pendulum swing of the fashion of thought toward metaphysics, . . . or anything of the sort, but is a reaction absolutely forced upon us by a rapidly increasing array of cold experimental fact."[15] Specifically in view of the data which suggested relativity and quantum theory, this *logic* is addressed to "our problem" as "the double one of understanding what we are trying to do and what our ideals should be in physics, and of understanding the nature of the structure of physics as it now exists."[16] Consequently, it assumes the form of an essay toward "a systematic philosophy of all physics" to replace the "hand-to-mouth philosophy which is now (in 1927) growing up to meet special emergencies."[17]

A very similar discussion of "scientific epistemology" by another practicing physicist is Sir Arthur Eddington's *Philosophy of Physical Science*, which is represented as "epistemological" in the strict sense that it "takes knowledge as the starting point rather than an existent entity of which we have somehow to obtain knowledge."[18] That the theme with which this book deals is "an integral part of philosophy", Eddington himself acknowledges, adding that "those whose work lies in the epistemological development of modern physics must therefore be counted as specialists in one of the departments into which philosophy is divided—a department not far from the heart of the subject."[19] He justifies his own venture into the field, however, not only on the ground that "a definite epistemological outlook has become a necessity" for reinterpreting physical research in the light of recent experimental findings, which is Bridgman's main explanation of his *Logic*, but also on the ground that for the working out of present day theories of matter and radiation it is "the direct source of the most far-reaching scientific advances." Like Bridgman, of course, Eddington observes that:

"Most of us, as plain men of science, begin with an aversion to the philosophic type of inquiry into the nature of things. Whether we are persuaded that the nature of physical objects is obvious to commonsense, or whether we are persuaded that it is inscrutable beyond human understanding, we are inclined to dismiss the inquiry as unpractical and futile."[20] But in view of what he construes their work to be, he finds that: "Theoretical physicists, through the inescapable demands of their own subject, have been forced to become epistemologists, just as mathematicians have been forced to become logicians."[20] Indeed, he interprets the most important basic principles of relativity and quantum theory to be essentially "epistemological" in character, rather than "physical" in the sense of relating directly to the properties of natural things. "In raising the question: 'What is it we really observe?' ", he writes, "relativity theory summoned epistemology to the aid of science."[21] The unobservability of distant simultaneity he reduces to "a purely epistemological conclusion."[22] And he takes the introduction of probability in wave mechanics after Heisenberg to emphasize "the fact that it is knowledge that is being treated", rather than its object, since "probability is an attribute of our knowledge of an event" and "does not belong to the event itself, which must certainly occur or not occur."[23] Consequently, he construes the "epistemological" turn of contemporary physical theory, as he understands it, to be its most typical feature and the one which primarily distinguishes it from the physical theory of preceding ages; and he explicitly characterizes the physics of today as "epistemological physics" which "directly investigates *knowledge*", in contrast to "classical physics" which "investigated or endeavored to investigate an *entity* (the external world) which the knowledge is said to describe."[24]

Thus the essential unity between prefatory and post-prefatory investigation is asserted in this work as emphatically as it ever has been. "Formally we may still recognize a distinction between science, as treating the *content* of knowledge, and scientific epistemology, as treating the *nature* of knowledge of the physical universe," Eddington writes. "But it is no longer a practical partition; and to conform to the present situation scientific epistemology should be included in science. We do not dispute that it must also be included in philosophy. It is a field in which philosophy and physics overlap".[25] Moreover, Eddington's claims for what comes of such unification are, if anything, even more striking. Although he insists that he did not set out with any preconceived idea of the scope of the epistemological method", he declares himself to have been driven by following it to the conclusion that "not only the laws of nature (i.e. 'all the laws of nature usually classed as fundamental') but all the constants of nature (e.g. 'the *cosmical number*', the total number of particles in the universe, etc.) can be deduced from epistemological considerations."[26] It is doubtful whether any professional metaphysician, however zealous, has ever made stronger claims for the cogency of his epistemological findings.

The present day return to prefatory consideration of inquiry thus originating in physics, however, has naturally spread to other fields. Even the physicists most responsible for it have felt the temptation to follow its implication beyond the border of their own special domain. Quite early in his account of the "operational point of view" in his *Logic of Modern Physics*, Bridgman makes bold to suggest that "many questions asked about social and philosophical subjects will be found to be meaningless" when examined in terms of it.[27] And Eddington does not hesitate to predict in his *Philosophy of Physical Science* that, just as the mathematician's invasion of logic contributed to its advancement, the physicist's invasion of epistemology has "a wider bearing" than "the restricted field of scientific epistemology" and offers "an effective contribution to the philosophical outlook as a whole."[28] But the movement has also been extended in ways more indirect and, perhaps to some extent, independent.

Among the more general symptoms of the tendency of our time to fundamental reconsideration of the *how*'s and *why*'s of inquiry, for example, is the current revival of interest in "semantics", which has found popular expression in such best sellers as Stuart Chase's *Tyranny of Words*, but which traces back in its more scholarly development to *The Meaning of Meaning* by C. K. Ogden and I. A. Richards. This treatise, mentioning "the recent revolution in physics" only as quite incidental illustrations of what advantages are to be obtained from the kind of analysis it proposes,[29] is formally described by its authors as an essay in "the science of Symbolism" which arose "out of an attempt to deal directly with difficulties raised by the influence of Language upon Thought."[30] Deploring the obstructions and confusions which, not only in physics, but in all departments of human interest, have been caused by superstitious linguistic attitudes, they describe this science as one which "singles out for special inquiry the ways in which symbols help us and hinder us in reflecting on things."[31] But this is essentially an instance of the kind of undertaking characteristic of what we have here called prefaces to inquiry. That is clear from specific references Ogden and Richards make to it, as well as from the general introduction which they give it. At different places throughout their text they refer alternatively to their "problem of meaning" as "this central problem of knowing"[32], to their "theory of reference" as "a theory of knowing"[33], and to their fundamental account of "signs in perception" as "a highly probable step in the most plausible systematic account of 'knowing' which can be given," or as "the material for an account of knowing itself."[34] It appears, therefore, that the "meaning" which Ogden and Richards *mean* is defined by a theory of knowledge. Their attempt is at bottom the universal epistemological attempt "to set out from the known facts as to how we acquire knowledge" on the expectation that, with the construction they place upon it, "the way is open to the systematization of all that is known and further of all that will ever come to be known."[35]

Similarly, a great multitude of other recent books and articles could be pointed out in which the main attempt is, not to elaborate on the technicalities of some particular branch of inquiry, but to direct attention back to reflection on broader questions as to what is involved in such research. To discuss them adequately would be to review the greater part of the more fundamental critical literature in almost every field of research today where we encounter such titles as *Economic Thought and Language, The Mind and Society, The Philosophy of Mathematics, Knowledge for What?, Approaches to History* and the like. But here we may mention only that it is works such as these which constitute the greater part of the significant literature prefatory to inquiry now being written, and that the widespread interest they have aroused is the strongest evidence that ours is an age intellectually not a little like the seventeenth century in so much as it is one in which the need for critical awareness of what is involved in the pursuit of knowledge is felt with particular urgency by an exceptionally large number of people. The total enterprise may have grown too vast and too complex for universal interest to make possible a well nigh universal competence such as a man like Descartes had some reasonable expectation of achieving in his day; but present indications are that such specialization as has become inevitable in learning is now tending to be less restricted in perspective, less exclusive in development.

V: REMAINING DIFFICULTIES

Notwithstanding the encouragement which may be derived from such observations, however, it must be noted that the present-day rapprochement between the scientific quest of knowledge and the philosophical theory of knowledge has been not a little embarrassed by their long estrangement, and not a little inconvenienced by a lack of easy mutual acquaintance between them. Particularly in the case of those current epistemological ventures which claim exceptionally broad relevance, one may find a striking tendency toward the propaedeutic twist of some of the great early modern prefatory essays discussed in the foregoing chapters; and one may find equally striking evidence of unawareness, on the part of those who write them, of what the history of the attempt has been—unawareness usually due, of course, to lack of interest in, or disrespect for, the degenerate end of the tradition of its cultivation. The texts already taken for purposes of illustration are quite typical in this respect.

Despite what has here been pointed out about *The Meaning of Meaning*, Ogden and Richards show in this work an unmistakably hostile attitude toward the entire philosophical tradition to which they seem to be trying to return. Despite the fact that their "science of Symbolism" is an attempt to probe anew the central issue of epistemological speculation, their prompt announcement at the outset that they will be much concerned with "the errors and omissions of metaphysicians"[36] is obviously a reference to their eighth chapter in which they give a most unflattering discussion of *The Meaning of Philosophers*. Later in the course of their argument they take the trouble to comment on common metaphysics as "a (sterile) hybrid of science and poetry", adding that "the proper separation of these ill-assorted mates" is "one of the most important consequences of the investigation into symbolism."[37] And they point to "the theory of knowledge" they have previously been acquainted with as precisely the field in which "confusion and obstruction," due to "shorthand expressions" they would amend, is "especially" great, because "no problem is so infected with so called metaphysical difficulties."[38] Moreover, in diagnosing these "metaphysical difficulties" to be "due here, as always, to an approach to a question through symbols without an initial investigation of their functions",[38] they offer their "science of Symbolism" as "a new avenue of approach to traditional problems hitherto regarded as reserved for the philosopher and metaphysician," claiming that "such an investigation of these problems is in accordance with the methods of the special sciences whose contributions have enabled the new study to be differentiated from vaguer speculations with which it might appear to be associated."[39]

Thus Ogden and Richards take the stand of men confronting the entire epistemological tradition with a competing doctrine which both shames and replaces it—a stand which is quite easily understood in terms of how the main line of the tradition has degenerated, but which is not likely to enable them to learn much from its hard earned experience. And consequently they tend to risk the sad fate with which their many predecessors have met, partly in this very treatise at their own hands. Perhaps it is still too early to shout alarm. Possibly the *Meaning of Meaning* will never have enough historical development to have an unfortunate development. But since it has already attracted enough attention to run through five editions, we should note that it tends, with apparent unawareness of what awaits such intrepidity, to suggest the naive propaedeutic twist of the more confused grand prolegomena to inquiry. Early in its argument, Ogden and Richards refer to their "account of the simplest kind of Sign-situations" as an *"essential preliminary"* to the disposal of problems raised by language difficulties, describing it, incidentally, as an *"essential preliminary"* which *"will enable us to understand how we come to 'know' or 'think' at all."*[40] And at the back of their book where they undertake a *Summary* of what they believe they have established, they feel justified in concluding that in its tenth chapter "the first stage of the development of Symbolism as a Science is thus complete, and it is seen to be *the essential preliminary to all other sciences."*[41] At the present state of this study, we hardly need expand on the dangers which beset such confident assumptions; the important point to be made is that the possible sources of warning have been rejected.

Equally indicative of the lack of intimate relationship between the present day quest of knowledge and the traditions of the theory of knowledge is Professor Bridgman's only too apparent haste in assuring his reader that the project of his *Logic* is not "evidence of senile decay" on the part of a laboratory experimenter.[42] He is obviously anxious to lose no time in acknowledging that: "The average physicist is likely to depreciate his own concern with such questions, and is inclined to dismiss the speculations of fellow physicists with the epithet 'metaphysical',"—an attitude which he himself finds to have "a certain justification in the utter unintelligibility to the physicist of many metaphysical speculations and the sterility of such speculations in yielding physical results."[43] We need not doubt that he has shared the "suspicion or even sometimes contempt" with which he says all such attempts have been regarded until recently. On settling down to the body of his own argument with a discussion of the impact of Einstein's work on theoretical physics, however, Professor Bridgman insists that: "Reflection on the situation after the event shows that it should not have needed the new experimental facts which led to relativity to convince us of the inadequacy of our concepts, but that *a sufficiently shrewd analysis should have prepared us* for at least the possibility of what Einstein did." "Looking now to the future," he adds, "our ideas of what external nature is will always be subject to change as we gain new experimental knowledge, but *there is a part of our attitude to nature which should not be subject to future change, namely that part which rests on the permanent basis of the character of our minds.* It is precisely here, in an improved understanding of *our mental relations to nature*, that the permanent contribution of relativity is to be found. *We should now make it our business to understand so thoroughly the character of our permanent relations to nature that another change in our attitude, such as that due to Einstein, shall be forever impossible.*"[44] This, if we may be guided by the foregoing chapters, is a specific proposal to recommence the task of preliminary clarification of inquiry close to where Descartes began to work on it. We may well ask, therefore, whether it does not also invite the same kind of historical fate as Descartes' prefatory writings, should it ever receive comparable attention, unless its subsequent development is controlled by more critical awareness of what is involved in all such undertakings.

But it is Sir Arthur Eddington's *Philosophy of Physical Science* which best expresses the problems inherent in the current reawakening of scientific interest in broader epistemological questions. Eddington himself calls attention to the most essential features of the historical background of the renaissance by justifying his venture into "scientific epistemology" partly on the grounds that physics was "not so very long ago" the "natural" part of philosophy (i.e. *natural philosophy*), later becoming regarded as a distinct discipline only because of its specialization "in a particular direction"[45]; and it is against this background that he acknowledges two main sources of resistance to his book as an essay in the *philosophy* of physical science rather than in physical science *pure and simple*: On the part of fellow physicists he anticipates mere "grudging acceptance" of his approach, an unwillingness to go the whole way in being guided by epistemological elucidations of their work;[46] and on the part of philosophers, he anticipates a certain amount of aloofness, a manner implying that the physicist taking to any phase of philosophy is out of his element, if not actually intruding.[47] But in appealing against these attitudes, that both physics and philosophy might profit through more intimate mutual intercourse, he tends to assume a bias in favor of his own major associations. "Scientific epistemology has always been part of the domain of physics,"[48] he rightly maintains, and "between science and scientific epistemology there has been a give and take by which both have greatly profited."[49] Whereas he simply calls on his fellows in the field of physics to be less conservative and more consistent in order to accept these conclusions, however, he is more provocative as regards the philosophers. Remarking that "the nature of physical knowledge . . . has long been a battleground for rival schools of philosophers," he first protests that "physicists can scarcely be denied a hearing on a subject which concerns them so intimately"—a stand soundly justified on the ground that "a student of physical science should be in a position to throw some light on the nature of the knowledge obtainable by the methods which he practices."[50] But shortly afterwards he gives the same point a somewhat different twist by suggesting that "it seems . . . unreasonable to maintain that the working out of these wider implications of the new conception of the physical universe should be left entirely to those who do not understand it." By far the greater contribution, he implies, can be made by physics to philosophy. With all too much truth he points out that "in practice, if not in theory, academic philosophy has also become specialized and is no longer co-extensive with the system of thought and knowledge by which we orient ourselves towards our moral and material environment." Confident, therefore, that "the great change in theoretical physics which began in the early years of the present century" is one which "must affect the general current of human thought, as at earlier times the Copernican and Newtonian systems have done," he claims that "in the last twenty years it has been the turn of physics to reassert itself as natural philosophy".[51] Thus, despite many proposals for amicable conferences and exchanges of view, Eddington tends somewhat to assume the role of daring physicist invader—with a just claim, to be sure, such as invaders always have—into the philo-

sophical field of epistemology. He does call to his scientific compatriots
to join in the movement, chiding them when they fail to rally, promis-
ing them spoils, and proclaiming that both parties will be benefitted
thereby, but he tends to assume withal, in the manner of invaders, that
it is the invaded rather than the invaders who will receive the greater
enlightenment.

Yet, it is Eddington's *Philosophy of Physical Science* which, of all
the contemporary works considered here, most strongly suggests the
strict propaedeutic twist which has caused so much trouble in the interpretation of the grand prolegomena to inquiry. "We may distinguish
knowlege of the physical universe derived by study of the results of
observation as *a posteriori* knowledge," he explicitly states, "and knowledge derived by epistemological study of the procedure of observation
as *a priori* knowledge."[52] Consequently, his claim that "the whole system of fundamental hypotheses (in physics) can be replaced by epistemological principles" is "put equivalently" as the claim that "all the
laws of nature which are usually classed as fundamental *can be fore-
seen wholly from epistemological consideration*" and therefore "correspond to *a priori* knowledge."[53] Eddington is most careful to avoid
the "disreputable associations" which he recognizes the term *a priori*
to have, giving such explanations as that he means by it knowledge
which is "prior to the carrying out of the observations, but not prior
to the development of a plan of observations," etc.[54] But at the same
time, his subsequent development of the epistemologically *a priori*
tends to follow fairly traditional lines. His reduction of "fundamental
physical hypotheses" to "epistemological principles" in turn becomes
a reduction of them to a *"wholly subjective status"*.[53] His consideration
of their *"subjective pattern"* in turn leads to a consideration of the
"predetermined form or frame of thought" into which "the knowledge
we acquire observationally is fitted,"[55] and of which, Eddington is inclined to believe, "the ultimate root is *definitely mental*—a predisposi-
tion inseparable from consciousness."[56] We need not be surprised, therefore, to find Eddington making statements such as that, in considering
"the common root from which scientific and all other knowledge must
rise, . . . the only subject presented to me for study is *my consciousness* . . ."[57]—which might well be mistaken for an excerpt from a late
seventeenth century Cartesian. Nor need we be surprised to find him
making such generalizations as: "We reach then the position of *idealist*
as opposed to *materialist*, philosophy. *The purely objective world is the*

spiritual world; and *the material world is subjective* in the sense of *selective subjectivism,*"[58]—which might well be mistaken for an excerpt from a disciple of Kant who had accepted his master's essential conclusions but tampered a little with his terminology. Ironically enough, although he declines to accept the Kantian "label" on the grounds that "it would make the scientist a party to controversies in which he has no interest even though he does not condemn them as altogether meaningless," Eddington concedes that "as a matter of acknowledgement, it is right to say that Kant anticipated to a remarkable extent the ideas to which we are now being impelled by the modern development of physics."[59] Viewing this conclusion the other way around, may we not take it as evidence that Eddington's particular expression of the return to epistemological considerations by scientific men goes back to the phase of development which the specialized epistemological tradition had reached at the time of Kant's contributions to it? And may we not take it as grounds for believing that contemporary essays like *The Philosophy of Physical Science* unless generally construed in terms of a broader awareness of what is involved in such ventures, are likely to receive developments which will take the "irrelevant" and "sterile" forms against which they so strongly protest in that part of the epistemological heritage they have soundly rejected for their immediate present purposes?

The current reawakening of interest in the reflective clarification of inquiry, then, although it reflects a broad concern with the whole of man's inquisition into the *how's* and *why's* of things such as has not prevailed since the early days of the modern period, is seriously handicapped by the gulf which grew between the quest and the theory of knowledge in the intervening time. Most particularly, those scientific research workers who have been prompted to take the initiative in the movement, by crises developing from their purely scientific labors, have had difficulty in making contact with the epistemological tradition which has tended to concentrate on projects remote from their interest, with the result that they have been able to get little instruction from its hard-earned experience. Despite much chiding by both sides of the limitations of the other, therefore, it would seem that what is seriously needed today is a broader understanding of the issues of common interest to both. As remarked at the end of the preceding section of this chapter, specialization will doubtless have to continue in both the quest and the theory of knowledge; but if this inevitable specialization can be made an emphasis of attention by a larger number of competent men, rather than an exclusive pre-occupation, we should be able to expect much of their joint efforts. The following chapter, which concludes this study, is an attempt to contribute to that end by a summing up of the entire foregoing analysis in terms of its bearing on the general significance of the preface to inquiry.

9
PREFACES TO INQUIRY

I: A NOTE IN APPRECIATION

FIRST a few words concerning the more general cultural significance of the texts examined in *Part Two* of this study. . .

All of these works, and especially those considered in *Chapters V* and *VII*, have been criticized for extravagance in their treatments of the themes they develop. But this very fact about them enhances as well as detracts from their interest. It is plain in the foregoing discussion that all these texts give exceptionally vigorous, if somewhat exclusive articulation to the views they express. *The Advancement of Learning, The New Organon,* the *Discourse on Method,* the *Metaphysical Meditations,* and the *Essay Concerning Human Understanding,* in making too much of their respective themes of institutional organization, technological instrumentation, reason, and experience, also enunciate them in unforgettable terms. Consequently, since the themes themselves are of great historical importance in our intellectual tradition, these ultra-enthusiastic assertions of them assume the character of signally instructive specimens of the flora and fauna of the intellectual world, as relevant to the understanding of *the life of reason* as are the comparable flora and fauna of the earth to the understanding of organic life.

That does not mean that these writings escape technical criticisms only in so far as they are in some respects philosophic monstrosities inviting clinical study as perturbations in *the life of reason.* In view of what has been pointed out about them in the foregoing chapters, it appears that they rise above mere technical issues in much more important ways. Bacon's accounts of the enterprise of learning suggest an elaborate plan for the ideal learned society conceived on a Utopian scale. His accounts of the technology of research suggest the detail of this plan for "Solomon's House" as the crowning institution of that society and the radiant source of its power, through knowledge, over the whole "dominion of man". Descartes' accounts of the way of certainty and of the first things of knowledge are conducted excursions through this world of abundant perplexity and error to a panoramic vision of its total structure all harmony and number *sub speciae aeternitatis.* And Locke's accounts of the genesis of understanding and misunderstanding are elaborate tales of experience with a common moral as to man's proper place in the scheme of things. Sound or unsound on technical scores, therefore, all are telling parables of aspects of life thoughtfully lived, reflectively pondered. Logically consistent or inconsistent they give cogent expression to aspirations which come of philosophic meditation. Like many of the other great philosophic essays which later stemmed from them, they are ventures in philosophy in the broader sense of the wooing of wisdom.

Consequently, these writings are largely significant in world literature as odysseys of the spirit, as adventures in the realm of mind heroically conceived and almost as heroically undertaken. Quite aside from any epistemological soundness they may or may not have, they are epics of reflective thought possessing all the power and fascination of epic art in other fields. It is these qualities of representative significance and epic greatness which, notwithstanding the best founded criticisms of logicians and metaphysicians, sustain interest in the grand prolegomena by students of the history of ideas, lovers of wisdom, and readers of great literature.

II: THE STRUCTURE OF PREFACES TO INQUIRY

Returning to more technical matters, however, we may begin by considering more generally what has been remarked in *Part Two* of this study concerning the pattern to which all the writings there examined in detail have been found to conform. In each case it has been shown through examination of specific texts that the prefatory accounts of inquiry under consideration tended to—

1. Put inquiry as a general undertaking in question *in terms of some particular criteria of criticism for its thorough reconsideration.*

2. Identify the agents of inquiry *in such terms as to emphasize their special competence for its undertaking in view of the requirements of such criteria.*

3. Delimit the context of inquiry *in such terms as to give special prominence to that aspect of things most appropriate to exploration in accordance with these criteria.*

4. Single out the crucial problems of inquiry *as those basic difficulties of working contact between agent and context on which our attention is thus focussed.*

5. Interpret the outcome of inquiry *as primarily the kind of result most particularly obtainable by the solution of these difficulties and hence best satisfying the original demands.*

Perhaps the first point of this general pattern is the one which is most likely to be questioned in retrospect, since more recent academic contributions to the themes of prefatory literature tend to contain little which might be interpreted as an expression of it. Beginning with the tacit assumption that "the problem of knowledge", "the epistemological problem", or some other such unique "problem", is already fully familiar to the philosophical reader, they seem to take it for granted that their remarks are addressed to difficulties clamoring for solution, rather than requiring formulation. As we have pointed out in *Section iii* of the preceding chapter, however, the authors of such writings tend to take as their point of departure a tradition of dialectic already established. They endeavor to carry on where others have left off. But in the treatises which have here been considered in most detail we find the more primitive beginnings of such essays so far, at least, as they may be traced in the modern age. And one may well ask how these could begin otherwise than in terms of such critiques. As Locke says of "understanding", in particular—"like the eye, whilst it makes us see, and perceive all other things", it "takes no notice of itself; and it requires art and pains to set it at a distance, and make it its own object. . . ."[1] The same holds for all our seeking activities, however construed. They pry readily enough into other things, but only art and pains direct them back upon themselves. Inquirers probe the nucleus of the atom and the breadth of the universe without hesitation. But as is witnessed by their long disregard of reflective prefatory consideration, discussed in the preceding chapter, something must go wrong with this sort of quest before they will stop to consider what is fundamentally involved in it. Then, of course, it is largely in terms of what has gone wrong that they do so. The introductory critique states the very *raison d'être* of the preface to inquiry, the specific criteria which it suggests merely expressing a particular writer's particular view as to the root of the trouble. In terms of Dewey's analysis of "reflective thinking", this phase of epistemological inquiry is that of the "intellectualization of felt difficulties". It is the deliberate address of intelligence to problems which confuse the quest of knowledge. If it is absent, that is merely a sign that the undertaking has been formalized for academic treatment, and is removed from its vital provocations in the going concern of straightforward research.

But when grounds for pause have thus brought men to reconsider inquiry as a general project, how else can they proceed except by consideration of who undertakes the work and under what circumstances? To belabor the obvious, *investigation*, after all, is carried on by *investigators* in a domain which is *investigated*. Inquiry is a relationship, however, close and indissoluble, between seeker and sought. Discussion of it, therefore, especially when aimed at clarification or improvement, tends quite inevitably to crystallize in conclusions as to the strict identity of the one and special character of the other. In being asked to take thought about what he does, the inquirer is asked to take thought about himself as the party implicated, and about nature as the place of his implication. Such blunt appeals to doctrines of knower and known as that in the digression of Descartes' *Rules* underline this fact so as to make it inescapable. But it should not be concealed by the organization of prefatory writings around such themes as those of "induction", "idols", "deduction", "reason", "ideas", "understanding", "experience", "pure reason", "logic", etc. All these terms serve primarily to call attention to some particular phase or aspect of the give-and-take between investigator and investigated; so that the discussion of them leads implicitly, if not explicitly, to the same kind of conclusions. Regardless of variations in different approaches, the fundamental obligation remains the same: namely, that of calling the inquirer to more critical awareness of his own role in his undertaking and of sharpening his discernment of its control by the circumstances under which it proceeds. This is the whole point of the traditional *subject-object* distinction.

The procedure having begun with a scrutiny of inquiry as a problematic matter, moreover, the resultant new identification of its agent and delineation of its context serves chiefly to revise our views of the crux of the relationship between them and of what can derive from it. A different or more sharply focussed view of the inquirer and of the context of his operation provides a different slant on what is crucially problematic in his work and on what can be accomplished by it. These fourth and fifth steps serve mainly to apply the findings of the second and third to the difficulty which gives occasion to the first.

We need not imply, of course, that the pattern described here in its most general form is strictly chronological or is followed in exactly the same way in all instances. On the contrary, it may be very differently illustrated in different specific cases. Depending upon the rhetorical plan, or the special interest expressed by any particular treatise of the kind, the sequence may be varied in the order of exposition, or one or more parts may be emphasized to the comparative neglect of others. In his concentration on a survey of the acts and works of learning, for example, Bacon tends to emphasize the third in the *Advancement*; and in his lengthy treatment of "perfect and imperfect questions", Descartes tends to emphasize the fourth in his *Rules*. In every case considered, however, all receive at least implicit development. These special instances are merely variations which serve better to illustrate the importance of different phases of the same general procedure. And the likelihood is that, if other prefatory writings neglect any altogether, they are to that extent very seriously incomplete.

III: DERIVATIVE CRITERIA OF CRITICISM

What, now, is the relevance of this analysis? Most important is the fact that it suggests a number of criteria for the criticism of literature prefatory to inquiry which help us better to understand the critique of propaedeutic prolegomena in *Chapter I* above.

The most vitally important thing about prefatory accounts of inquiry, as we shall presently attempt to show, is their positive revelation of what is significant in the quest of knowledge. Consequently their chief requisite is original discernment, which is subject to no formal precepts. No rules that might have been laid down could ever have led to a recognition of the possibilities of inquiry as an institutional enterprise, as a technological project, as a mindful, mathematical analysis of structure, or as an apprenticeship in experience. Insights such as these are unpremeditated acts of observation, almost spontaneous responses of intelligence to the provocations of the materials upon which it operates; and so, the only criteria in terms of which they can soundly be criticized, are the obvious ones of *aptness, acuteness,* or *importance,* which it were pointless to formulate in canonical terms. But the manner in which such insights are developed and expressed is another matter. Their formulations admit of appropriate comparative study and critical elaboration. Since they follow a fairly uniform pattern of questioning, identifying, delimiting, circumscribing, and interpreting, it is relevant to ask *how* they do so. *Do their procedures follow the controls of their common subject matter? Are they consistent with their own conclusions?* Questions such as these, obviously important to ordinary investigations, are particularly important to those which concern the fact of investigation itself.

In the case of the procedures found in *Part Two* above to be unaffected by the critique in *Chapter One*—in the case, that is to say, of Bacon's accounts of the enterprise of learning and the technology of research, Descartes' account of mathematical way of certainty, Locke's account of everyday experience, and the more tentative sketches given in the beginning of Descartes' *Discourse* and in the notes of Locke's *Study During a Journey*—it was observed that no violence was done to the patent facts of inquiry. Man's inquisitive probing of the entire domain of his habitation was found to be illuminated by pertinent remarks without being construed as an unintelligible miracle or a cosmic hoax, because no attempt was made to underpin the fact of his probing with a presumed explanation of what it *really* is somehow apart from what it can be discovered to be by examination as it is under way. The explorable characteristics of inquiring man and the context of his inquiring remained in control of the whole proceeding. Moreover, since the identifications and delimitations that were thus made of the agent and context of inquiry were such as the familiar traits of man and nature actually sustain, the problems to which attention was drawn were genuinely problems confronted by investigators in their actual workaday tasks, and the corresponding interpretations which were placed on successful dealings with these problems were such as contribute to our appreciation of knowledge actually had or to be had. Having the common control of a common identifiable subject-matter, these delineations of inquiry supplemented each other in revealing aspects of the infinitely complex fact of seeking and finding knowledge. Each may have had somewhat different emphases in its total delineation of this fact; and these different emphases may have had practical implications which were different in important ways for the daily routine of research. But such differences as thus arose were not incompatibilities. They were initial, rather than final; and they were ultimately reconcilable by means of the same common subject matter which originally evoked their conception and subsequently controlled their formulation.

But in the case of those writings found in *Part Two* to be seriously affected by the critique of *Chapter I* so far at least as they received literal interpretation—in the case, namely, of Descartes' accounts of the first things of knowledge and Locke's more recondite account of experience—it was noted that the entire procedure was not so controlled. These latter lent themselves to interpretation as ostensible propaedeutic prolegomena to inquiry because a presumed special, and final, revelation of the ultimate nature of the circumstances enveloping inquiry was at one point interposed to abbreviate, or exclude, more detailed consideration of its actual processes. The devices by which this was done were many, ranging from the naive to the ingenious and back again: in the argument of the *Rules*, a digression to explain a "useful hypothesis" alleged to "facilitate" exposition; in the fable of the *Discourse*, a *deus ex machina* rescue of a fabulous seeker after certainty about to be fabulously overwhelmed by fabulous doubts; in the *Metaphysical Meditations* and *Book One* of the *Principles*, an irrational faith in God's exclusively mathematical rationality, intermediated by "metaphysical" symbols; in the *Demonstrations in Geometric Order*, a blunt "postulation" of the essence of the conclusions to be "demonstrated"; and in the *Essay Concerning Human Understanding*, a gradually more literal construction of figurative expressions, eventuating in an irresistible recourse to "physical considerations", reluctantly yet irrevocably admitted. But in all these instances, the processes of identification of agent and delimitation of context of inquiry—unless viewed merely as hyperbolic restatements of more literally construable procedures, for which they were doubtless intended—eventually suggested problems of the relationship between agent and context, seeker and sought, which provoked doubt as to whether inquiry were really possible at all, as to whether anything which could come of it deserved the dignity of being called knowledge. And thus encouraging an epistemological tradition which ignores the problems of knowledge which its seekers actually confront, these developments recall to the contemporary nothing so much as the long "pitting of nature and human nature over against each other—man and nature with knowledge a possible link between them; I the knower here, and yonder the to-be-known, and the wonder how I can go to it or it can come to me; soul and body, mind and the world order, subject and object and the former trying to know the latter; knowledge set at a distance and nature set at a distance, with a knowledge called upon to shorten the distance."[2]

Summing up this much in schematic form, then, we may say on the one hand that those essays prefatory to inquiry which are not adversely affected by the critique in *Chapter I* above, tend most generally to—

1. Put inquiry in question *in terms of criteria relevant to its actual, or possible, character as the questing familiar to our everyday life.*
2. Identify the agents of inquiry *in corresponding ways consistent with the equipment to which men are discernibly committed in the undertaking of this quest.*
3. Delimit the context of inquiry *in corresponding ways consistent with the character nature exhibits as confronted by this quest.*
4. Single out the crucial problems of inquiry as *problems on which attention is thus focussed as the basic difficulties men actually, or possibly may, meet with in confronting nature accordingly.*
5. Interpret the issue of inquiry *as the outcome at which this quest actually does, or possibly may, arrive by the ways thus indicated for dealing with such difficulties.*

But we must add that, on the other hand, those essays adversely affected by this critique have been found open to interpretation as tending to do one or more of these things in some radically different way by the surreptitious insinuation of a point of view somehow wholly external to the explorable character of inquiry as a discernible exercise of man's discernible natural capabilities.

Procedures such as these latter tend particularly to be sidetracked from their proclaimed original purposes because, failing to eventuate in genuinely relevant observations concerning the quest of knowledge, they naturally arrest much of the attention they receive at their crucial points of departure from it. When men first read books like Bacon's *Advancement of Learning* and *New Organon* and Descartes *Rules for the Direction of the Mind,* they were stimulated to thinking mainly about such projects as the British Royal Society and about the possibilities of instrumental and mathematical techniques in research. Some may have paused to reconsider further details of the social, technological, and mathematical characteristics of the agents and context of inquiry; but they were not pressed to do so with particular urgency. The relevance of these books was immediately practical and foreward looking, and such can doubtless be said too of many of the alleged prolegomena, in so far as they were intended and accepted as hyperbolic expressions of similar procedures. But when, with the passing of time and the occurrence of conducive circumstances, they and other writings which they provoked came to be more literally construed, it was their seemingly arbitrary identification of the agents of inquiry and delimitations of its contexts which drew most attention. Despite the implicit presumption of the more pretentious prolegomena that their central propaedeutic doctrines stand somehow apart from the regular course of inquiry, the characteristics of man and of nature on which they attempt to pass arbitrarily, or sometimes unwittingly, invite indefinite reconsideration; and this fact explains the tendency of such writings to suggest sidelines of investigation rather than finally to settle ultimate questions concerning all investigation.

As to the particular viciousness of the kind of controversy which is thus promoted rather than disposed of, its inevitability is clear from the fact that the characteristic turn of these writings amounts to an abandonment of the only controls by which practical working agreement is possible. None of the non-propaedeutic texts we have examined contains any conclusions which are wholly beyond differences of opinion. But they do contain many suggestions for resort to some kind of exploration of subject matters differed upon, rather than to mere contention concerning them; and they themselves invite reconsideration by the very same means. The others, however, by their implied claims to finality and special unchallengeable status, tend to deny the relevance to themselves of any such investigations. As allegedly ultimate ways of construing all dealings with all subject matters, they presume to be untouched by what comes of such dealings, and so remain unreconcilable by what comes of them. When claims are made to the discernment of what inquiry is by circumvention of what it is, every man is at liberty to be his own seer and to brook no contradiction. The resulting *-isms* become controversial *-isms* because they admit of no other kind of development; and the otherwise unintelligible absurdities of *absolute solipsism* and *absolute scepticism* become perfectly possible as conclusions of their reasoning. While dismissing lightly the going concern of the quest of knowledge, the abstracted pseudo-epistemologist has no special difficulty in egocentrically defining himself as the only agent of inquiry, nor has he any difficulty in so defining its agents and delimiting its context as to represent them in a manner which makes them mutually inaccessible to each other. In metaphysical fairyland, as in more charming and interesting fairylands, fancy knows no bounds.

The important thing to note here, however, is the way in which these difficulties are brought about. They derive, we must most particularly realize, from variations of a general pattern of procedure which has produced results of demonstrated value and soundness—the pattern, namely, which is pointed out in the preceding section of this chapter to be quite inevitable in all reflective considerations of the fact of inquiry. Consequently, such difficulties as thus arise cannot legitimately be regarded to reflect either on the general attempt of this kind of reflective consideration of the fact of inquiry, or on the general pattern of procedure to which it conforms. They rightly incur the contempt and the repudiation with which they have lately met on all sides; but the entire literature from which they originate should not be ignored for that reason.

In other words, the central attempt of the epistemological theory of knowledge should not be ignored or abandoned in this day when its services are so badly needed just because after performing its great services at the beginning of the modern era it later fell into such idle ways. The current reaction against what has so long been mistakenly taken as essential in dealing with problems of knowledge should result rather in a return to a sounder way of dealing with what is most vitally problematic in knowledge. This return, moreover, should be one chastened by past misadventures and aided by a broad understanding of the background against which it now operates. And in particular, the upshot of the foregoing analysis should be its implied warnings—that the procedure of such attempts must be regarded as an expression of the same inquisitive activity which it examines; that no uniqueness of perspective, no special finality of result, is obtainable by its means; that the considerations by which it is supported must satisfy the conclusions at which it arrives; and that it must eventually square with all other sound results arrived at in the same way.

Perhaps all this advice sounds a bit obvious and a little too elementary for so elaborate a substantiation. But if the past experience from which it is derived is any guide, there will nevertheless be many failures to observe it by subtle, perhaps unintended, insinuations between the lines of carefully written treatises . . . treatises which may very well be read later more in terms of what they thus imply than in terms of the many things they so explicitly state. In this field, more almost than in any other, the simplest, most apparent precepts are the easiest to transgress with the most momentous consequences; so they cannot be too painstakingly stated.

IV: THE PROBLEM OF KNOWLEDGE

Another important implication to be drawn from the foregoing analysis concerns the interpretation of the *problem of knowledge* traditionally associated with the theory of knowledge.

Perhaps the most prevalent conception of the central problem of epistemology is still largely dominated by the late preoccupation of its academic cultivators with such questions as *whether a mind's cognitive states can relate to anything beyond the immediacy of its own consciousness,* or *whether sense data are directly relevant to the nature of Reality,* etc. The common assumption of these is that knowledge is somehow a mystery to be explained or a puzzle to be solved by the dialectic of *metaphysical* verbalism. The difficulty they address is that of certifying or discrediting all man's inquisition of his explorable environment, whatever its outcome in its own terms, against the measure of some presumed all-embracing cosmic principle external to it. And when the main point of epistemology is thus taken to be its suggestion of ingeniously conceived perplexities, the entire modern literature of the subject is placed in rather strange perspective. The writings of Francis Bacon to which two whole chapters are here devoted, for example, then appear merely *to prepare the way* for discussion of *the problem of knowledge* without actually evidencing any understanding of it or attempt to solve it; and the related writings of Descartes and Locke, to which even more attention has been given here, appear to be significant mainly in so far as they serve better to enunciate this difficulty, again without satisfactorily contributing to its actual solution.[3] But although the formal treatment of such queries has had quite a respectable development in more secluded departments of philosophy in our colleges and universities, it should be clear from the analysis made here that only the long parting of ways between the quest and the theory of knowledge has made anything of the kind possible.

As we are helped to realize by the difficulties confronting present-day rapprochements between workers in these two fields, the modern tradition of reflective consideration of the fact of inquiry originated in hesitations of a very different kind. It is of course perfectly correct that Francis Bacon had little prophetic foresight of the ways in which academic metaphysics was going to become entangled in the confusions of its own dialectic. But that is not a real criticism, either of his uncanny knack of predicting the shape of things to come far better than he knew, or of his very sharp, if incomplete, insight into what is genuinely problematic in the quest of knowledge. His prefaces to inquiry, and the other great early modern essays of their kind, were better focussed on the common problems of inquiry—the problem of getting and assimilating knowledge—than the vast majority of writings which later appeared under the specific title of epistemology. Like the freshly inspired prefatory essays that are being written again in our day, their purpose was not to ferret out additional, quite gratuitous, difficulties by which to add to the inquirer's usual perplexity. It was rather to enhance his comprehension of what he is about, thus to bring to the project of inquiry itself some measure of the illumination which it tries to bring to everything else. The primary problem of knowledge raised by this literature, therefore, is a phase of the most general problem of getting and understanding knowledge—that phase, namely, which is concerned with the intelligent comprehension of what is basically involved in the attempt to know as it is daily undertaken by scholars and research workers in laboratories, libraries, and studies, on great expeditions, and in the daily routine of everyday life.

In view of the general pattern to which we have seen attempts to undertake this conform, we can well understand how this original problem could come to be differently conceived. As is pointed out in the preceding section of this chapter, once accounts of the identity of the agent involved in inquiry and of the nature of the context addressed have been minutely elaborated in technical terms not directly relevant to their functional character in the going concern of inquiry, they may be considered in detachment from the reasons for their being investigated in the first place, whereupon they readily provoke other lines of thought. In the direction of broader development, the results arrived at may well suggest generalizations concerning man's whole spiritual being and his total spiritual relationship to all things. Man has so frequently been defined as a rational animal that it is easy to take an account of his rationality as a statement, or at least a hint, of the ultimate things which can be said about him. This is the kind of tangential departure which we have mentioned in the preceding chapter in the cases of Descartes and Malebranche and of Kant and Schopenhauer. Then, in the direction of narrower development, the same results may also suggest more and more minute scrutiny of the dialectic involved. Identification of the agent of inquiry and delimitation of its context, as has also been pointed out in the preceding section of this chapter, may be artificially construed to raise the absurd question of whether knowledge—including such knowledge as has been appealed to in the very process of identification and delimitation—is indeed knowledge, regardless of how fruitful may be the exploration of the world of our familiar dwelling from which it derives. In this case, *step four* of the general pattern interrupts the whole procedure to recommence it again in terms of criteria of *absolute validity* or *reality* as demands for . . . we know not what. And this second kind of departure from the main task is the one which has here been blamed for the more sterile, unintelligible sort of epistemology which has lately given a distorted impression of the whole tradition.

But as the central undertaking from which both of these diverge, we must keep in mind the original approach to the specific, but endlessly complex problem of making better understood man's essential relationship to the world as its inquisitor, interpreter, and knower. That is the main problem of knowledge with which we have here found prefaces to inquiry to be concerned, and which we are here compelled to regard as the only problem of knowledge with vital epistemological significance.

V: THE FUNCTION OF PREFACES TO INQUIRY

Since the function of the theory of knowledge is admittedly to treat of the epistemological problem of knowledge, then, we may conclude that its task is primarily that of clarifying the quest of knowledge so that it may be more intelligently pursued and communicated.

At times the attempt to fulfill this obligation may tend to take a critical turn in the interest of liberating the quest of knowledge from attitudes which might obstruct it. We may recall, for example, Bacon's "Great Instauration" and Descartes' *one-man-instauration* as critical attacks on Scholastic and Renaissance ideas of learning, by which they attempted basically to re-orientate the labours of investigators. Such ambitiously destructive efforts as theirs, it is pointed out in the preceding chapter, have been called for less and less as the super-structure of learning has towered more impressively and its foundations have been sunk more deeply. But even John Locke, for all his admiration of the "master builders", still felt called upon to undertake somewhat the same kind of critical activity, even if only as an "underlabourer" unpretentiously clearing the "rubbish" from around their feet; Kant undertook to define the limits of "pure reason" largely to warn presumptuous contemporaries against creating confusion by rashly overstepping these limits; and to a certain extent, a similar concern to liberate constructive inquiry from the obstructions which *hinder* its *progress*, as progress is from time to time redefined, persists through most related undertakings.

Even the strictest expressions of this *negative* function of the literature, however, are accompanied by more *positive*, constructive suggestions. Situations in which abused, or basically opposed, traditions of scholarship find themselves in confusion are but special instances of the kind of circumstances in which inquirers have reason to be in doubt as to the course they should follow, the manner in which they should conceive their tasks; and in all such cases the appeal to the special instructiveness of prefaces to inquiry is particularly strong. Their illumination might also be invited, for example, by growing awareness of techniques with unexplored possibilities, as in the case of the technological devices which influenced Bacon so profoundly and the analytic geometry which suggested to Descartes the idea, first of a universal mathematics, and then of a generalized methodology of all inquiry. Or it might be invited by growing awareness of insufficiently exploited conditions of the pursuit of inquiry, as in the case of Bacon's appeal to the institutional organization of the enterprise of learning, and Locke's appeal to its better control by the experience out of which it arises. In such cases, the underlying purpose of prefatory clarification is largely to call attention to, and in some measure anticipate, the range of new possibilities.

In performing both these functions prefatory essays almost invariably have an immediate historical application which restricts the form of their expression and confines their immediate conclusions. But regardless of such limitations, their most important outcomes usually admit of considerable generalization. Regardless of how dated they may be by being addressed to the occasions which immediately provoke them, if they are truly significant they have a certain residual relevance to the general undertaking of inquiry even after those occasions are quite obliterated by the sweep of historical events. What Bacon, Descartes, and Locke wrote concerning the institutional, technological, mathematical, and experiential possibilities of the quest of knowledge was unmistakably conditioned by the state of that quest as they knew it in the seventeenth century and as it tended possibly to persist into the eighteenth century. But what they pointed out about its essential relation to the facts of society, machinery, equations, mind, structure, and the genetic process of becoming may readily be construed in terms of the state of knowledge at any other time. The aspects of inquiry to which they called special attention may be viewed in changing perspective against the background of changed historical conditions; but these aspects remain nevertheless unforgettably prominent so long as the cultural tradition enriched by this literature endures.

To put the same point somewhat differently, writers of the more significant sort of prefaces to inquiry discuss its undertaking as it is actually under way for their consideration. Their treatises are prefaces to future inquiry, but they are postscripts to such past inquiry as they have made their observations from. What light they have to shed on the undertaking, therefore, may illumine all the way ahead, but its source remains fixed. Like the light of evident nature, it gives most illumination at points nearest its source, and least at points farthest away. Moreover, it cannot bend around sharp corners or disclose the far side of remote obstacles. Only when points farther along the path have actually been reached can its light be reflected in such directions or its source be rekindled there. But to the extent that the inquiry to which such writings are most immediately addressed is representative—to the extent, that is to say, that it has prominent features which are typical or recurrent—they have some bearing on all man's probing of his world at any time or at any place, and need only to be re-interpreted to be found instructive.

VI: FUTURE PREFACES TO INQUIRY

The limitations of this essay as a study of prefaces to inquiry cannot be too strongly emphasized here in its closing paragraphs. A further consideration of their very extensive literature has been foregone for the sake of a more intensive analysis of a few of the more monumental works which appeared at the beginning of the modern period. Only the briefest mention has been made of the many significant discussions being given today to the more special problems of knowledge in the various special fields of inquiry. And most notably, only incidental reference has been made in the first chapter to the most important contribution to prefatory literature in our day, John Dewey's *Logic—The*

Theory of Inquiry, and none at all to the late Professor Woodbridge's most significant *Essay on Nature.*

These last two works were published after the plan of this essay was fully worked out and most of its chapters had been set down in a fairly final form. But they illustrate, more aptly than any others here mentioned, the kind of approach to the theory of knowledge pleaded for. This fact may possibly be obscured a little by the attention given in Dewey's book to the problem of "the ultimate subject matter of Logic", and by the emphasis in Woodbridge's on "the theory of nature". As is indicated by the sub-title of the former, however, what Dewey means by logic is "the theory of inquiry" which is exactly what is here construed to be the real concern of epistemological prefaces to inquiry.[4] Dewey's address to the more technical problem of logic, therefore, does not in the least preclude his founding the entire work on broad discussions of such matters as the "biological and cultural matrices of inquiry".[5] Likewise, although Professor Woodbridge gives his book the emphasis it has, explicitly to distinguish it from those responsible for "the long subjection of theories of nature to an initial criticism of knowledge", his purpose in doing so is to advocate a theory of knowledge more like that recommended here. "It is only when the attempt is made to set knowledge at a distance from life and make it its own object", he writes in its earlier published prospectus, "that theories of knowledge become theories of nothing at all." But "a theory of nature and a theory of knowledge may well go hand in hand, for the employment of life for enlarged and more penetrating views of that with which life is employed is an exercise of life's possibilities under conditions which control that exercise." "Throwing initial emphasis on life," therefore seems to him "to have the promise of keeping the theory of knowledge and the theory of nature together," with the only difference between them "not a difference in subject-matter, but a difference in attention."[6] Consequently, since both these books give positive development to such criteria of sound procedure as are here suggested in critical terms, they illustrate better than any mere canonical formulation their constructive implications.

The purpose of this preface to prefaces to inquiry, however, has not been to be exhaustive or encyclopaedic. Rather, it has been, by means of a few provocative and intrinsically interesting examples, to call attention to the theory of knowledge, not as a fussing with irrelevancies, but as a means of deepening our appreciation of the intellectual life on all its levels, from the puzzled querying of the child as to the simple *what*'s and *why*'s of household gadgets and neighborhood commonplaces to the same sublime impertinence of scientist and philosopher throughout all the realm which sustains their questioning. As long as men may still pause from fretful war and often more fretful peace, some will yet be seized with the ancient wonder in which Aristotle tells us the love of wisdom began, and try to comprehend the fact, as well as the objects, of their perplexity. And thus long, there will be a recurrent need for further clarification of the fact of man as, not only an acquisitive, fighting animal, but an inquisitive, knowing one as well.

Just what specific directions future prefaces to inquiry may take were rash to predict. But surely it is naive to assume that all the possibilities of things as explorable or expressible have been fully surmised, even if not actually exhausted, and that man has come to full realization, if not final fulfillment, of all the implications of his role as prober and interpreter of the realm of his habitation. As our inquiries become more sharply focussed from time to time in one direction or another, it is more likely than not that specialists in these fields will find it necessary to reconsider their relation to subject matters in its more minute, special details. And as our culture changes—*changes*, we may well say, lest it were too optimistic to presuppose it will *evolve* or *mature*—it is more likely than not that man will continually find himself called upon to reconsider his total relation as knower to all he finds himself called upon to know. Unless we wish to conclude, after the manner of the simple minded in all ages, that with our appearance on the scene the history of such efforts has come to a definite close, we must expect that in these processes, along with much re-discovery of old insights re-expressed in new terms, there will be much that is genuinely new as a revelation of the nature and obligation of man's inquisition of his world. The task of this continual re-clarification is that of future prefaces to inquiry.

REFERENCES

NOTES FOR CHAPTER I

1. Almost all the histories of philosophy bear out this point by the very divisions under which they expound the philosophical doctrines of each period, considering its *epistemology* along with its ethics, ontology, etc.

   It may be objected that some of these distinctions, and particularly the last mentioned, are of essentially modern origin. The implication then is that they are artifically superimposed upon the philosophical materials of other ages, with the result that they falsify history rather than illustrate any universality of its categories. Doubtless, there is much to such protests in cases where the distinctions in question are given highly restricted meanings which they have acquired only in the contexts of recent technical discussions. It would be artificial, for example, to treat any part of Aristotle's writings as *epistemological* in the sense of centering about an attempt to determine somehow *a priori* whether knowledge is *real*. It is only too obvious that, beginning with the observation of his *Metaphysics* that, "All men by nature desire to know," his writings proceed mainly to develop the implications of knowledge as a natural fact. But this does not mean that much of Aristotle's *Metaphysica* and *Organon* are not comments on the assumed natural fact of knowledge which are epistemological in the broader sense defined in the text above. Critically used, the distinction is fully as sound as it is commonplace.

2. Professor Richard McKeon, we may note, devotes his two volumes of *Selections from Mediaeval Philosophers* (Scribners, N. Y., 1929) to texts dealing with such speculations, for the avowed reason, op. cit. pp. x-xi:

   . . . The problem of knowledge has been inquired into, with different emphases and different consequences, throughout not only the mediaeval period but through the whole age of western philosophy. The significant characteristics of the philosophy, no less than the further problems to which attention was turned, has been determined in large part by the answer which has been given in each case to the problem of how we know . . . etc.

3. *Logic—The Theory of Inquiry*, Holt, N. Y., 1939, p. 102.

4. I.e. that period roughly designated as having anticipations in the sixteenth and preceding centuries, getting well under way in the seventeenth century, and continuing to, but not including, the *contemporary* age.

5. Adam & Tannery, *Oeuvres de Descartes*. Cerf, Paris, 1908, Vol. VI, p. 17. The translation of this passage, and of all others from Descartes, is by the writer. The italics are editorial.

6. *Principles of Philosophy, Preface*, Ibid, Vol. IX, pp. 13-4.

7. Ibid, p. 2.

8. "Tout de bon", ibid, p. 14.

9. *Meditations*, ibid, p. 4.
10. *Principles of Philosophy*, ibid, p. 14.
11. Ibid.
12. Op. cit., I, 1, i.
13. The italics here are editorial.
14. *Chapter VII* below.
15. E.g. *Prolegomena to Any Future Metaphysic, Preamble*, § 1.
16. E.g. *Immanuel Kant's Critique of Pure Reason, translated into English by F. Max Müller*, London, 1881, Vol. I, p. 369.
17. Ibid, Vol. II, p. 4.
18. Ibid, p. xxi.
19. Ibid, p. 3.
20. Ibid, p. xxii.
21. Ibid, p. 10.
22. Op. cit. Vol. II, p. 32, English edition, Scribners, N. Y., 1887. The italics are editorial.
23. *The Importance of Living*, John Day, New York, 1937, p. 202.
24. *The Logical Syntax of Language*, Harcourt Brace & Co., New York, p. 279. The italics are Carnap's.
25. Ibid, p. 332.
26. Russell's book, titled *Philosophy* (W. W. Norton & Co., N. Y., 1927) in the American edition, and *An Outline of Philosophy* in the British edition, begins on page one with the remark:

> . . . The definition of "philosophy" will vary according to the philosophy we adopt; all that we can say to begin with is that there are certain problems, which certain people find interesting, and which do not, at least at present, belong to any of the special sciences. These problems are all such as to raise doubts concerning what commonly passes for knowledge; and if the doubts are to be answered it can only be by means of a special study, to which we give the name "philosophy". etc., etc.

27. Ibid, p. 15.
28. For its wary circumspectness of this point, the paragraph from which these lines are cited warrants attention in its entirety. It appears on pp. 70-1 of the text cited.
29. Published in Muirhead's *Contemporary British Philosophy*.
30. Ibid, p. 359.
31. *Reconstruction in Philosophy*, Henry Holt & Co., New York, 1920, p. 21. Other summary statements of the general point occur on pp. 49 & 70, to mention only two.
32. It should be mentioned, of course, that in Dewey's usage, *epistemology* and its derivatives are usually *nasty words*. But this should not obscure the fact that his *Logic* is exactly what is here meant by *epistemology*—namely,

"inquiry into inquiry" (e.g. p. 4). Dewey usually uses the term *epistemology* in a very narrow sense to designate only the matter of controversy between *phenomenalists, absolute idealists, solipsists,* and other such philosophical eccentrics who grapple in the backwash of the main streams of philosophical thought. However, he himself recognizes the broader sense of the term in his remark on p. 65, that a particular problem which he is discussing is "not epistemological (save only as that word means the *logical*)"—i.e. *related to the theory of inquiry.*

33. *Logic—The Theory of Inquiry,* Henry Holt & Co., New York, 1939, p. 20.
34. Ibid, p. 21.
35. For example, see F. J. E. Woodbridge on *The Promise of Pragmatism* in his *Nature and Mind,* Columbia, 1937, pp. 215-29.
36. For example, we find on p. 230 of *The New Rationalism,* Henry Holt & Co., 1918, with Prof. Spaulding's own italics:

    As is well known, much, and perhaps most modern philosophy centers around the epistemological problem. . . . For especially since Kant, but also since Descartes, Locke, Berkeley, and Hume, most philosophers have deemed it necessary to solve *the problem of knowledge,* in order subsequently to define the status of that which is known. In other words, philosophers have set out to discover the facts, or the *status of affairs* concerning knowing and the relation of knowing to the object known, *as a prerequisite* for solving the other problems of philosophy and as a result, they have issued with these definite solutions which have received such names as Phenomenalism, Subjective Idealism, Positivism, Pragmatism, and even Materialism.

    Again, on p. 43, with Prof. Spaulding's own italics:

    It is characteristic of the majority of the philosophical systems of at least the last century and a half that they have deemed it necessary to solve the problem of *how* we know before they have endeavoured to solve other problems. The *epistemological* problem has thus had a *temporal* priority over other problems . . . etc.

37. Ibid, p. 87. The italics are Spaulding's.
38. Ibid, p. 53.
39. Ibid, p. 431-2.
40. Ibid, p. 232.
41. Ibid, p. 364-430.
42. *Enquiry Concerning the Principles of Natural Knowledge,* Cambridge, 1919, p. vii.
43. *The Concept of Nature,* Cambridge, 1920, p. 28.
44. Ibid, p. 30.
45. Science and the Modern World, Macmillan, N. Y., 1925, p. xi.
46. *Process and Reality,* Macmillan, N. Y., 1929, pp. 4-14.
47. Ibid, p. 12.

48. *The Realm of Mind,* Columbia, 1926, pp. 54 & 55.
49. Ibid, The passage continues:

> . . . It helps us not to claim that the facts of logic and psychology are more intimately associated with the process of knowing than are any other facts, for this is not true. Without other facts there could be neither psychology or logic. The "knowledge of knowledges" or the "science of sciences" may please us as pretty phrases, but we cannot discreetly claim for them a higher value. The piling of one act of knowledge on another leaves knowledge precisely where it was in the beginning with no super-science as the result. This is what makes examinations of knowledge so often wear that strained and troubled look. . . .

50. F. J. E. Woodbridge; *Journal of Philosophy,* Vol. xxxi, No. 1, p. 18.
51. This is the case, for example, in F. J. E. Woodbridge's *Realm of Mind,* quoted above.

NOTES FOR CHAPTER II

1. Ellis and Spedding, *The Works of Francis Bacon,* London, 1858-9, Vol. IV, pp. 7-8. Hereafter this edition is designated as *E. & S.*
2. Ibid, pp. 22-3.
3. Ibid, pp. 24-29.
4. Ibid, pp. 29-30.
5. Ibid, p. 31
6. Ibid, p. 32.
7. Chapter I, Sections iii & iv, above.
8. E. & S., Vol. IV, p. 14.
9. Ibid, Vol. III, p. 264:

> . . . That Knowledge is of those things which are to be accepted of with great limitation and caution; that the aspiration to over much Knowledge was the original temptation and sin whereupon ensued the fall of man; that Knowledge hath in it somewhat of the serpent, and therefore where it entereth into a man it makes him swell; *scientia inflat."* etc., etc.

10. Ibid, Vol. VI, p. 497.
11. Ibid, Vol. III, p. 294.
12. E.g. *The Advancement,* Everyman Edition, pp. ix to xii.
13. E. & S., Vol. III, pp. 263-4.
14. Ibid, p. 322.
15. Ibid, p. 323.
16. Ibid, pp. 322-8.
17. Ibid, p.328.
18. For example, in the last paragraph of the *Preface* to the *Great Instauration,* Ibid, Vol. IV, p. 8.

19. Ibid, Vol. III, p. 373.
20. Ibid, Vol. IV, p. 389.
21. Adam & Tannery, *Oeuvres de Descartes*, Vol. I, pp. 105-6.
22. E. & S. Vol. III, p. 328.
23. For documentation of this point, see T. Fowler, *Bacon's Novum Organum*, Oxford, 1889, *Int., Section 14.*
24. E. & S., Vol. III, p. 295.
25. This interpretation is ably summed up in *The Making of the Modern Mind* (Houghton Mifflin, Boston, 1926) by J. H. Randall, Jr., *Book I, Chapters II, III, & V.*
26. E. & S., Vol. IV, p. 24.
27. Ibid, Vol. III, p. 327.
28. E.g. *Reconstruction in Philosophy*, pp. 28-34.

NOTES FOR CHAPTER III

1. E. & S. Vol. IV, p. 52.
2. The first characterization appears throughout the *New Organon* itself; the second appears in its prospectus in *The Advancement*, e.g. E. & S. Vol. III, pp. 383-4.
3. Chapter Two above, Section iv.
4. Ibid, Sections v & vi.
5. E. & S., Vol. IV, p. 72.
6. Ibid, p. 73.
7. Ibid, p. 39.
8. *Aphorism I, lxx,* Ibid, pp. 70-1. The explanation is—
   . . . the manner of making experiments which men now use is blind and stupid. And therefore, wandering and straying as they do with no settled course, and taking counsel only from things as they fall out, they fetch a wide circuit and meet with many matters, but make little progress; . . . etc., etc.
9. Ibid, p. 80.
10. *Aphorism I, xii,* Ibid, p. 48.
11. Ibid, *Aphorism I, viii.*
12. Ibid, p. 74.
13. *Aphorisms II, xi to xx.*
14. Suggested in "instances" 5 and 6 under *Aphorism II, xxviii.*
15. As suggested in practically all the "perogative instances".
16. As suggested in the "instances of the lamp", *Aphorisms II, xxxviii to xlii.*
17. As suggested in the "instances of the course" and "of quantity". *Aphorisms II, xlvi and xlvii.*
18. As suggested in the "instances of power", *Aphorism II, xxxi.*

19. E. & S., Vol. IV, p. 21.
20. Ibid, p. 42.
21. Ibid, p. 49.
22. Ibid, p. 48.
23. As is common knowledge, these "idols" are divided into four groups: those "of the Tribe", which "have their foundation in human nature itself" (*Aphorism I, xli*); those "of the Cave", which affect "the individual man" (*I, xlii*); those "of the Market-place" which are "formed by the intercourse and association of men with each other" (*I, xliii*); and those "of the Theatre" which "have immigrated into men's minds from the various dogmas of philosophies, and also from wrong laws of demonstration" (*I, xliv*).
24. Ibid, p. 26.
25. Ibid, p. 27.
26. Concerning this point Bacon explicitly states in *Aphorism I, xxxvii*, Ibid, p. 53:

    The doctrine of those who have denied that certainty could be attained at all, has some agreement with my way of proceeding at the first setting out; but they end in being infinitely separated and opposed. For the holders of the doctrine assert simply that nothing can be known; I also assert that not much can be known in nature by that which is now in use. But then they go on to destroy the authority of the senses and understanding; whereas I proceed to devise and supply helps for the same, etc.

27. Ibid, p. 26.
28. Ibid.
29. Ibid, p. 69.
30. E.g. Ibid, p. 28:

    Those . . . who aspire not to guess and divine, but to discover and know; who propose not to devise mimic and fabulous worlds of their own, but to examine and dissect the nature of this very world itself; must go to facts themselves for everything.

31. Ibid, p. 32.
32. Ibid, p. 25.
33. Ibid, p. 137.
34. Ibid, p. 58.
35. Ibid, p. 120.
36. Ibid, p. 110.
37. As in the "polychrest instances" of *Aphorism II, l*, and in a proposed, but unwritten, additional section to treat of "Applications to Practice and Modes of Experimenting", Ibid, p. 233.
38. Ibid, pp. 237-41.
39. Ibid, pp. 233-7.

40. Ibid, p. 121.

41. Ibid, p. 122.

42. *Aphorism II, xxxi*, Ibid, p. 170.

43. Ibid, Vol. III, p. 384. The italics are editorial.

44. Ibid, Vol. IV, p. 47. The italics are editorial. Compare Ibid, *Aphorism I, lxi*, pp. 62-3.

45. Ibid, p. 40. The italics are editorial.

46. For a more detailed account of this interpretation see *The Making of the Modern Mind* by J. H. Randall, Jr., *Book I, Chapters II, III & V.*

47. E. & S. Vol. IV, p. 70.

48. Ibid, Vol. III, pp. 156-164.

49. Ibid, p. 145.

50. Ibid, p. 146.

51. Ibid, p. 147.

52. Ibid, Vol. IV, p. 424.

53. Ibid, Vol. III, p. 384.

54. Ibid, p. 389.

55. Compare, Ibid, Vol. IV, p. 70.

NOTES FOR CHAPTER IV

1. It may possibly seem to some that the *Rules* is not sufficiently important to be given very detailed consideration. Critics may protest, for instance, that it is only a fragment, that Descartes himself never even published it, and that it is obviously an early draft of ideas which he later saw fit to re-work in quite different form. But such objections do not warrant our lightly dismissing this work. Even though the *Rules* is incomplete, the essential structure of what is missing is fairly apparent from what we have of it. Then too, although Descartes himself did not give it to the press, it has appeared in many editions since 1701 when it was first published in a volume of posthumata, and long before then it passed quite freely from hand to hand, in manuscript form, among quite a number of important thinkers of Descartes' own century (for an account of which see A. & T. Vol. X, pp. 351-7).

2. Adam & Tannery, *Oeuvres Complètes de Descartes*, Cerf, Paris, 1908, Vol. X, p. 359. The translation and italics are the writer's. Hereafter this edition will be referred to as "A. & T."

3. Ibid, p. 361.

4. Ibid, p. 374.

5. Ibid, p. 360.

6. E. & S., Vol. IV, p. 62, *Aphorism II, ix*.

7. A. & T., Vol. VI, p. 2.

8. Ibid, Vol. X, p. 371.

9. Ibid, p. 372.

10. Ibid.

11. In his explanation of *Rule iii*, for instance, he writes, Ibid, pp. 366-7,

> . . . Authors are naturally inclined, each time they allow themselves, out of some blind credulity, to maintain some controversial opinion, always to want to lead us to their conclusion by the most subtle arguments; whereas on the contrary, each time that they have the good fortune to strike on something certain and evident, they never explain it save in an ambiguous manner, be it whether they fear that simple proofs might take away credit from the discovery, or whether they begrudge us the bare truth.

12. Ibid, *Rule ii*, pp. 365-6.

13. Ibid, *Rule iii*, pp. 367-8.

14. Ibid, p. 362.

15. Ibid, p. 356.

16. Ibid, p. 363.

17. Ibid, p. 368.

18. Ibid, p. 368.

19. Ibid, pp. 368-9.

20. Ibid, p. 428.

21. Ibid, p. 429.

22. Ibid, p. 430.

23. Ibid, p. 431.

24. Ibid, p. 440.

25. Ibid:

> It must be noted . . . that comparisons are not called simple and clear except when the thing sought and the thing given participate equally in a certain nature, that all other comparisons on the contrary, must be prepared only because this common nature is not found in the same quantity in the two terms, but only according to certain other relations or proportions in which it is involved; and that the principal part of human industry consists only in reducing these proportions so that the equality between what is sought and something known is clearly seen.

26. This fact Descartes announces himself further on in his explanation of *Rule xiv*, Ibid, p. 441, where he writes:

> . . . It is certain and assured, then, that perfectly determined questions contain scarcely any other difficulty save that which consists in discovering the proportional measure of inequality, and that all matters in which one finds precisely this difficulty easily can, and ought to be, separated from all other considerations, and then related to extension

and figures, concerning which, for this reason, we shall treat exclusively from this point up to the twenty fifth rule.

27. Ibid, p. 438.
28. Ibid, p. 453.
29. Ibid, p. 461.
30. Ibid, p. 442.
31. In explaining the order in which he proposes to take up these "questions" Descartes tells his reader, Ibid, p. 429:

> . . . This division has been made advisedly, as much in order not to say anything which presupposes the knowledge of what follows, as to teach first that to which we judge one ought to apply oneself first in order to cultivate the mind.

Furthermore, at the end of his explanation of *Rule xvi*, Ibid, p. 459, Descartes writes of further applications to be made of *Rules xiii* to *xvi* in the last section of the treatise which deals with "imperfect questions".

32. Ibid, p. 438.
33. Ibid, p. 439.
34. Ibid, pp. 447-9.
35. Ibid, p. 431.
36. Ibid, p. 374.
37. Ibid, p. 375.
38. Ibid, p. 376.
39. Ibid, pp. 377, 8.
40. Letter to M. de Beaune, Feb. 20, 1639; Ibid, Vol. II, p. 511 et seq.
41. Ibid, Vol. VI, p. 371.
42. Ibid, pp. 369-76.
43. Ibid, p. 376.
44. Ibid, p. 485.
45. Ibid, p. 376.
46. Ibid, Vol. X p. 363.
47. Ibid, p. 406.
48. Ibid, p. 430.
49. Ibid, p. 460.

NOTES FOR CHAPTER V

1. A. & T., Vol. X, p. 425.
2. Ibid, p. 411.
3. Ibid, p. 412.
4. Ibid, p. 417.
5. Ibid, Vol. IX, *Meditations*, p. 13.
6. This last work was never published by Descartes himself, but appeared for the first time in the volume of posthumous works in which the *Rules* was first printed in 1701.

7. A. & T., Vol. IX, *Meditations*, p. 13.
8. Ibid, *Principles*, p. 25.
9. Ibid, *Meditations*, p. 125.
10. Ibid, Vol. X, p. 508.
11. Ibid, Vol. IX, *Meditations*, pp. 17-8.
12. Ibid, p. 13.
13. Ibid, p. 18.
14. Ibid, p. 64.
15. Ibid, pp. 109-10.
16. E.g., Ibid, p. 68.
17. Ibid, p. 63.
18. Ibid, Vol. X, pp. 410-1.
19. Ibid, p. 373.
20. Ibid, Vol. I, p. 339.
21. Ibid, Vol. X, p. 496.
22. Ibid, Vol. IX, *Principles*, pp. 3-4.
23. Ibid, Vol. VI, p. 19.
24. Ibid, Vol. IX, *Principles*, p. 18.

NOTES FOR CHAPTER VI

1. A. & T. Vol. X, p. 396.
2. Ibid, p. 398.
3. Chapter I, Section ii, above.
4. John Locke, *An Essay Concerning Human Understanding*, London, 1690, I, i, 7. All references to this work are by Locke's own convenient book, chapter, and section numbers which are uniform in all editions.
5. Ibid, *Epistle to the Reader.*
6. Descartes' *Rules* perhaps comes closest to being an exception to this generalization.
7. *The Life and Letters of John Locke*, Lord King, Bohn, London, 1858, p. 93.
8. Ibid, p. 94.
9. Ibid, p. 95.
10. Ibid, p. 96.
11. Ibid, p. 88.
12. Ibid, p. 94.
13. Ibid, p. 95.
14. Ibid, p. 94.
15. Ibid, p. 106.
16. Ibid, p. 89.
17. The quoted passage continues, for example, (with editorial italics):
    . . . Why should we think ourselves hardly dealt with, that we are not

furnished with compass nor plummet to sail and fathom that restless, unnavigable ocean, of the universal matter, motion and space? Since there be shores to bound our voyage and travels, *there are at least no commodities to be brought from thence serviceable to our use, nor that will better our condition;* and we need not be displeased that we have not knowledge enough to discover whether we have any neighbors or not in those large bulks of matter we see floating in the abyss, or what kind they are, since *we can never have any communication with them that might turn to our advantage.* Etc., etc.

18. Ibid, p. 97.
19. Ibid, p. 98.
20. See note 4 above.
21. *Essay I, i, 4.*
22. *I, i, 5 & 6.*
23. *I, i, 2.*
24. *I, i, 8.*
25. *I, ii, 2.*
26. *I, ii, iii, & iv. Chapters ii* and *iii* are worked out largely in terms of "principles" or "maxims" alleged to be "innate", but in *Chapter iv,* Locke reduces these to the constituent "ideas" of which he finds them compounded.
27. *I, i, 8.*
28. Malebranche, for example, writes in his *Search for Truth, II, 1, i,* (the translation is editorial):

I believe that everyone agrees that we do not perceive objects which are outside of us in themselves. We see the sun, the stars, and an infinity of objects without us; and it is not likely that the soul leaves the body and that it goes, so to speak, to walk the skies in order to contemplate all these objects. It does not see them, then, in themselves; and the immediate object of our mind, when it sees the sun, for example, is not the sun, but something which is intimately united to our soul, and that is what I call *idea.* Thus, by the word *idea,* I understand nothing other here than what is the immediate object, or the closest thing to the mind, when it perceives some object.

29. *Essay, I, iv, 24:*

When men have found some general propositions, that could not be doubted of as soon as understood, it was, I know, a short and easy way to conclude them innate. This being once received, it eased the lazy from the pains of search, and stopped the inquiry of the doubtful concerning all that was stiled innate. . . . Nor is it a small power it gives one man over another, to have the authority to be the dictator of principles, and teacher of unquestionable truths; and to make a man swallow that for an innate principle, which may serve to his purposes who teacheth them.

30. *I, iv, 22.*

31. *The Life and Letters of John Locke,* Lord King, p. 365.

32. *Essay, I, iv, 23.*

33. *II, i, 2.* The italics are editorial.

34. *II, i, 1.*

35. *II, i, 2.*

36. A simple instance of this is Locke's observation, in *I, ii, 16:* that:

> A child knows not that three and four are equal to seven till he comes
> to be able to count seven, and has got the name and idea of equality:
> and then, upon explaining those words, he presently assents to, or
> rather perceives the truth of that proposition . . . etc.

The argument here is that even so elementary a matter as *one, two, three*
. . . is something we must somehow encounter before we can be knowing
about it—a point which Locke easily generalizes to imply that, without "experience" made up of many such encounters, we should know absolutely
nothing of the many "theoretical maxims" which we so readily believe ourselves always to have known once we have comprehended them. See also
I, iii, 22-7 on this point.

37. *II, ix, 7.*

38. *II, ix, 5:*

> . . . I doubt not but children, by the exercise of their sense about ob-
> jects that affect them in the womb, receive some few ideas before they
> are born; as the unavoidable effects, either of the bodies that environ
> them, or else of those wants or diseases they suffer: etc.

39. *II, i, 6-7:*

> He that attentively considers the state of a child, at his first coming
> into the world, will have little reason to think him stored with plenty
> of ideas that are to be the matter of his future knowledge: It is by de-
> grees he comes to be furnished with them. And though the ideas of ob-
> vious and familiar qualities imprint themselves before the memory be-
> gins to keep a register of time or order, yet it is often so late before some
> unusual qualities come in the way, that there are few men that cannot
> recollect the beginning of their acquaintance with them. . . . But all
> that are born into the world being surrounded with bodies that per-
> petually and diversely affect them; variety of ideas, whether care be
> taken of it or no, are imprinted on the minds of children. Light and
> colours are busy at hand everywhere, when the eye is but open; sounds,
> and some tangible qualities fail not to solicit their proper senses, and
> force an entrance to the mind. . . .
>
> Men then come to be furnished with few or more simple ideas from
> without, according as the objects they converse with, afford greater or
> less variety; and from the operations of their minds within, according as
> they more or less reflect on them. . . .

40. *II, i, 22:*

> Follow a child from its birth, and observe the alterations that time makes, and you shall find, as the mind by the senses comes more and more to be furnished with ideas, it comes to be more and more awake; thinks more, the more, it has matter to think on . . . etc.

41. *III, ii, 1.*

42. In *II, xxxiii, 19,* Locke tells his reader that he had at first believed he needed consider only "ideas" in order to "proceed to show what use the understanding makes of them, and what knowledge we have by them"; but that he found, "on nearer approach", that "there is so close a connection between ideas and words", that he had to devote a whole additional book to the discussion of the latter as well.

43. E.g., *III, iii, 7.*

44. *III, xi, 1.*

45. *III, ii, 1:*

> . . . The comfort and advantage of society not being to be had without communication of thoughts, it was necessary that man should find out some external sensible signs, whereof those invisible ideas, which his thoughts are made up of, might be made known to others. For this purpose nothing was so fit, either for plenty or quickness, as those articulate sounds which with so much ease and variety he found himself able to make. Thus we may conceive how words, which were by nature so well adapted to that purpose, came to be made use of by men, as signs of their ideas . . . etc.

46. Locke points this out a little indirectly in the following passage in *III, v, 8,* while still elaborating the point of the quotation in the preceding note:

> A moderate skill in different languages will easily satisfy one of the truth of this; it being so obvious to observe great store of words in one language, which have not any that answer them in another. Which plainly shows, that those of one country, by their customs and manner of life, have found occasion to make several complex ideas, and give names to them, which others never collected into specific ideas. . . . The terms of our law, which are not empty sounds, will hardly find words that answer them in the Spanish or Italian, no scanty languages; much less, I think, could any one translate them into the Caribbee or Westoe tongues: and the Versura of the Romans, or Corban of the Jews, have no words in other languages to answer them; the reason whereof is plain, from what has been said.

47. *II, xxxiii, 5 & 6.*

48. *II, xxxiii, 10-2.*

49. *II, xxxiii, 17.*

50. *II, xxxiii, 18.*

51. *III, ix & x.*

52. *III, x, 4:*

> Men having been accustomed from their cradles to learn words, which are easily got and retained, before they knew, or had framed the complex ideas to which they were annexed, or which were to be found in the things they were thought to stand for; they usually continue to do so all their lives; and without taking the pains necessary to settle in their minds determined ideas, they use their words for such unsteady and confused notions as they have, contenting themselves with the same words other people use: as if their very sound necessarily carried with it constantly the same meaning, etc.

53. *III, x, 12.*
54. *IV, xix, 5, 6, & 9.*
55. *IV, xx, 1.*
56. *IV, xx, 5.*
57. *IV, xx, 2.*
58. *IV, xx, 4.*
59. *IV, xx, 6.*
60. *IV, xx, 18.*
61. Section ii of this chapter.
62. *Of the Conduct of the Understanding, Section 3.*
63. Ibid, *Section 4.*
64. A. & T. Vol. IX, *Principles,* p. 20.
65. For example, Locke comments in *section 24* of the *Treatise on the Conduct of the Understanding:*

> . . . Some men have so used their heads to mathematical figures, that, giving a preference to the methods of that science, they introduce lines and diagrams into their study of divinity, or politic inquiries, as if nothing could be known without them; and others, accustomed to retired speculations, run natural philosophy into metaphysical notions, and abstract generalities of logic; and how often may one meet with religion and morality treated of in the terms of the laboratory, and thought to be improved by the methods and notions of chemistry? But he that will take care of the conduct of his understanding, to direct it right to the knowledge of things, must avoid those undue mixtures, and not, by a fondness for what he has found useful and necessary in one, transfer it to another science, where it serves only to perplex and confound the understanding. . . .

66. Ibid.
67. *Essay, IV, xxi.*

NOTES FOR CHAPTER VII

1. *Essay, I, i, 2.*
2. *I, i, 2.* As far along in the course of his argument as *II, xxi, 73,* Locke repeats the same insistence.

3. *II, i, 2.*

4. *II, xi, 17.*

5. *II, viii, 4-5.* The italics are editorial.

6. *II, viii, 7.*

7. *II, viii, 7-26.*

8. Sections i and iv of Chapter V, above.

9. *Essay, II, xxiii, 2.*

10. *II, xxiii, 3.*

11. *III, vi, 6.* By the "nominal essence." Locke means simply the common referent in discourse.

12. *II, xxiii, 1.*

13. *II, xxxi, 6.*

14. *III, vi, 9.*

15. *IV, iii, 6.*

16. *IV, iii, 26:*

> . . . Those which we have ranked into classes under names, and we think ourselves best acquainted with, we have but very imperfect and incompleat ideas of. Distinct ideas of the several sorts of bodies that fall under the examination of our senses, perhaps we have: but adequate ideas, I suspect, we have not of any one amongst them. And though the former of these will serve us for common use and discourse, yet whilst we want the matter, we are not capable of scientifical knowledge; nor shall ever be able to discover general, instructive, unquestionable truths concerning them. Certainty and demonstration are things we must not, in these matters pretend to.

17. Consider, for example, the general implication of the following typical remark quoted from *IV, iii, 23* (with editorial italics):

> . . . all the simple ideas we have, *are confined to* those we receive from corporeal objects by sensation, and from the operations of our own minds as the objects of reflection. But how much these *few and narrow inlets* are *disproportionate* to the vast whole extent of all beings, will not be hard to persuade those, who are not so foolish as to think their span the measure of all things. . . .

18. *IV, vi, 10.*

19. *IV, iii, 24.*

20. *IV, iii, 23.*

21. The phrase is Descartes' from the *Preface* of the dialogue on *The Search for Truth.*

22. *I, iv, 25.*

23. Chapter VI, Section iv, above.

24. *I, i, 2.* The italics are editorial.

25. *I, iv, 24-5.* The italics are editorial.

26. E.g. *II, xxix, 1.* The italics are editorial.

27. Chapter VI, Section iii, above.

28. *IX, ii, 1-7.*

29. E.g. *IV, iii, 20:*

> . . . Confident I am, that if men would in the same method, and with the same indifferency, search after morals, as they do mathematical truths, they would find them to have a stronger connexion one with another and a more necessary consequence from our clear and distinct ideas, and to come nearer perfect demonstration than is commonly imagined, etc.

30. *II, xxvii, 24.*

31. *II, xxxi, 6.*

32. *II, xxxi, ii.*

33. *IV, vi, 10.*

34. *III, xi, 23.* The italics are editorial.

35. *II, xxiii, 12.*

36. For an amusing reply to the objections which a Cartesian might make to such a commonsense attitude, see especially *IV, xi, 8.*

37. *IV, xii, 12:*

> I would not . . . be thought to dis-esteem, or dissuade the study of nature. I readily agree the contemplation of his works gives us occasion to admire, revere, and glorify their author: and if rightly directed, may be of greater benefit to mankind, than the monuments of exemplary charity. . . . All that I would say, is, that we should not be too forwardly possessed with the opinion, or expectation of knowledge, where it is not to be had; or by ways that will not attain to it: that we should not take doubtful systems for compleat sciences, nor unintelligible notions for scientifical demonstrations. In the knowledge of bodies, we must be content to glean what we can from particular experiments: . . . experience, observation, and natural history must give us by our senses, and by retail, an insight into corporeal substances. . . .

38. *I, i, 7.*

39. *II, i, 19.*

40. *II, i, 24.*

41. Consider, for example, the very keen awareness of the significance of semantic considerations in controversy shown in *III, ix, 9 & 21; x, 22; & xi, 6.*

NOTES FOR CHAPTER VIII

1. *Distribution of the Work, E. & S.,* Vol. IV p. 32.

2. *The Philosophy of Physical Science,* Macmillan, N. Y., 1939, pp. 4-5.

3. To quote again from Sir Arthur Eddington's *Philosophy of Physical Science,* p. 52:

From the time of Newton until recently the epistemology of science was stationary; for two hundred years the extension and ordering of our knowledge of the physical universe continued without modifying it. We have seen that the physicist is by origin a philosopher who has specialized in a particular direction; but for him epistemology had become ancient history, and he had long ceased to concern himself with it. Generally he prided himself on being a plain matter-of-fact person—which was his way of describing a man who accepted the naive realism of Newtonian epistemology. If he indulged in philosophy at all, it was as a hobby kept apart from the serious occupation of advancing science, etc.

4. *The Works of George Berkeley*, Bohn Library Edition edited by George Sampson, London, 1898, Vol. I, pp. 163-177.

5. Ibid, p. 162.

6. Ibid, p. 161.

7. Ibid, p. 252.

8. E.g. in *The Analyst* and *A Defense of Free Thinking in Mathematics*, Ibid, Vol. III, pp. 1-96.

9. See Chapter I, Section ii, above.

10. *Critique of Pure Reason, Preface to the First Edition*, F. Max Müller Translation, Macmillan, London, 1881, Vol. II, p. xii, footnote.

11. Ibid, Vol. I, pp. 366-7.

12. Ibid, pp. 370-1.

13. Ibid, p. 370.

14. Op. cit., Macmillan, N. Y., 1927, *Preface*, p. v.

15. Ibid, *Introduction*, pp. vii-viii.

16. Ibid, p. x.

17. Ibid, p. ix.

18. Op. cit. p. 3.

19. Ibid, p. 9.

20. Ibid, p. 6.

21. Ibid, p. 32.

22. Ibid, p. 38.

23. Ibid, p. 50. The preceding passage runs:
The mathematical symbolism (of wave mechanics) describes our knowledge, and the mathematical equations trace the change of this knowledge with time. Our knowledge of physical quantities is always more or less inexact; but the theory of probability enables us to give an exact specification of inexact knowledge, including a specification of its inexactitude. . . .
Compare p. 51:
The statement often made, that in modern theory the electron is not a particle but a wave, is misleading. The "wave" represents our knowledge of the electron. The statement is, however, an inexact way of emphasiz-

ing that the knowledge, not the entity itself, is the direct object of our study, etc.

24. Ibid, p. 49. The italics and parentheses are Eddington's. The passage continues:

> . . . Accordingly the modern physicist has devised a technique appropriate to the investigation of knowledge of the kind investigated in physics; whereas the classical physicist devised a technique appropriate to the investigation of an entity such as he conceived the external world to be.

25. Ibid, p. 7. The italics are Eddington's.
26. Ibid, pp. 57-8. The parenthetical insertions are editorial.
27. Op. cit. p. 30.
28. Op. cit. p. 7.
29. Op. cit. 5th ed., Harcourt, Brace and Co., N. Y., 1938, p. 13.
30. Ibid, *Preface to the First Edition,* p. v.
31. Ibid, p. 9.
32. Ibid, p. 13.
33. Ibid, p. 15.
34. Ibid, p. 81.
35. Ibid, p. 82.
36. Ibid, p. 2.
37. Ibid, p. 82, footnote.
38. Ibid, p. 14.
39. Ibid, *Preface to the First Edition,* pp. v-vi. Compare Ibid, p. 249, *Summary of Chapter 10* on *Symbol Situations:*

> . . . Together with such portions of grammar and logic as it ("the science of Symbolism") does not render superfluous it must provide both what has been covered by the title Philosophy of Mathematics, and what has hitherto been regarded as *Metaphysics*—supplementing the work of the scientist at either end of his inquiry.

40. Ibid, p. 47.
41. Ibid, p. 249.
42. *The Logic of Modern Physics, Preface,* p. v.
43. Ibid, *Introduction,* p. vii.
44. Ibid, pp. 1-2.
45. Op. cit. p. 8.
46. Ibid, p. 53.

> The question may be raised, How far does general opinion among leading physicists today recognize this reunion? It is difficult to ascertain. My impression is that the general attitude might be described as *grudging acceptance* . . . , etc.

47. Ibid, p. 4.

> One often finds an impression that it is an innovation for scientists to indulge in philosophy. . . .

Ibid, p. 52.

. . . The physicist had left it (scientific epistemology) so long unculti-
vated that, when at last he turned attention to it, his right-of-way was
questioned . . . , etc.

48. Ibid, p. 52.
49. Ibid, p. 5.
50. Ibid, p. 4.
51. Ibid, p. 8.
52. Ibid, p. 24.
53. Ibid, p. 57.
54. Ibid, p. 24.
55. Ibid, p. 115.
56. Ibid, p. 132.
57. Ibid, p. 195.
58. Ibid, p. 69.
59. Ibid, pp. 188-9.

NOTES FOR CHAPTER IX

1. *Essay, I, i, 1.*
2. F. J. E. Woodbridge, *Nature and Mind,* Columbia, 1937, p. 278.
3. Thomas Fowler, editor of the Clarendon Press edition of Bacon's *Novum
   Organum* (Oxford, 1884), for example, remarks in his introductory essay
   on *Bacon's General Philosophical Opinions,* p. 15, that:
   . . . On the standing feud between what are, somewhat uncouthly,
   called the Idealists, the Materialists, and the Dualists, there is, so far as
   I am aware, no formal discussion in Bacon's writings. . . .
   Explaining that "the genius of Descartes" had not yet "impressed" these
   "metaphysical discussions" on the public, Fowler dismisses Bacon's contributions to the entire field of speculation by remarking, p. 16, that:
   . . . Bacon assumes the ordinary distinction of mind and matter, an
   universe of objects to be known and a thinking subject capable, with due
   care and discipline, of attaining to a knowledge of them, without apparently troubling himself as to the ulterior questions, what is knowledge,
   how can I become conscious of that which is not myself, and what are
   the ultimate meaning and relation of the two terms in this comparison,
   etc.
4. E.g., op. cit., pp. 3-4.
5. Ibid, *Chapters II* and *III.*
6. F. J. E. Woodbridge, *The Theory of Nature,* contained in *Nature and
   Mind,* pp. 277-8. The passage continues:
   . . . The exhibition of the principles which govern the understanding
   in attempting to gain a comprehensive view of nature would be a theory

of knowledge. It would also be a theory of nature because those principles would exhibit characters of nature by which the understanding is governed and without which the attempt to understand would not itself be understood. Understanding, being as natural a performance as any other, would derive its comprehensiveness from those features of nature which are comprehensive, like space, time, and communication. In this respect a theory of nature and a theory of knowledge would be well-nigh indistinguishable. A theory of this kind would be an initial discipline which might hold our wayward speculations in wholesome check, and enable us to distinguish between vision and the visionary.

ACKNOWLEDGMENT OF SPECIAL PERMISSIONS

Quotations made in this essay from the following treatises are by special permission of the following publishers:

By special permission of the John Day Company, New York—
The Importance of Living by Lin Yutang.

By special permission of Harcourt, Brace and Company, New York—
The Logical Syntax of Language by R. Carnap,
The Meaning of Meaning by Ogden & Richards.

By special permission of Henry Holt and Company, New York—
Reconstruction in Philosophy by John Dewey,
Logic, the Theory of Inquiry by John Dewey,
The New Rationalism by E. G. Spaulding.

By special permission of the Macmillan Company, New York—
The Logic of Modern Physics by P. W. Bridgman.

The Cambridge University Press by special permission of the Macmillan Company, New York, agent—
The Philosophy of Physical Science by Sir A. Eddington,
An Enquiry Concerning the Principles of Natural Knowledge by A. N. Whitehead,
The Concept of Nature by A. N. Whitehead,
Science and the Modern World by A. N. Whitehead,
Process and Reality by A. N. Whitehead.

By special permission of W. W. Norton and Company, New York—
Philosophy by Bertrand Russell.

By special permission of Charles Scribner's Sons, New York—
Selections from Mediaeval Philosophers by R. McKeon.

INDEX